A Bonfire of Inanities
The Bible Dismantled

VOLUME THREE

Apocalypse Postponed

A Bonfire of Inanities

The Bible Dismantled

VOLUME THREE

Apocalypse Postponed

THE REAL TRUTH ABOUT
THE END OF THE WORLD

Paul McGrane

SINGULAR BOOKS

First published in 2024

Singular Books
www.paulmcgrane.co.uk
All rights reserved

The right of Paul McGrane to be identified as the author of this work has been asserted in accordance with Section 77 of the Copyright, Designs and Patents Act, 1988. No part of this publication may be copied, reproduced, stored in a retrieval system, or transmitted, in any form or by any means without the prior permission of the publisher, nor be otherwise circulated in any form of binding or cover other than that in which it is published and without a similar condition being imposed on the subsequent purchaser.

Text design by Ellipsis, Glasgow

A CIP record for this book is available from the British Library

ISBN 978-1-7393926-4-2 (paperback)
ISBN 978-1-7393926-5-9 (ebook)

1 3 5 7 9 8 6 4 2

For Jonathan Hayden,
who stuck with it.

There exists in human nature a strong propensity to depreciate the advantages, and to magnify the evils, of the present times.
—Edward Gibbon,
Decline and Fall of the Roman Empire

For generation after generation humans have prayed to every god, angel and saint . . . but they continued to die in their millions from starvation, epidemics and violence. Many thinkers and prophets concluded that famine, plague and war must be an integral part of God's cosmic plan . . . and nothing short of the end of time would free us from them . . . but in the last few decades we have managed to rein in famine, plague and war . . . We don't need to pray to any God or saint to rescue us from them.
—Yuval Noah Harari, *Homo Deus*

'We're doomed. We're all doomed!'
—Private James Frazer,
Walmington-on-Sea Home Guard

CONTENTS

Foreword   xi
Preface   xv
Introduction   xxix

PART ONE: BIBLICAL PROPHECY

1 Background   3

2 The First Generation of Jewish Prophets   21

3 The Second Generation of Jewish Prophets   48

4 The Later Jewish Prophets   66

5 The Book of Revelation: First Apocalypse   82

6 The Book of Revelation: Second Apocalypse   88

7 Other New Testament Apocalypses   100

PART TWO: HISTORY

1 Pre-Reformation Eschatology — 115

2 The Reformation — 142

3 Post-Reformation Eschatology — 157

PART THREE: TRUTH

1 Preliminaries — 183

2 The Dozen Jewish Apocalyptic Topics — 191

3 The Dozen Christian Apocalyptic Topics — 276

Afterword — 354
Select Bibliography — 361

FOREWORD

A Bonfire of Inanities: The Bible Dismantled

As a teenager over half a century ago, I had a brief flirtation with evangelical Christianity: the apparent certainties on offer were attractive then to the self-conscious, uncertain youth that I was. The flirtation ended very quickly during my undergraduate years, to be replaced with the atheism that I have held ever since, but the experience left me with a lifelong interest in religious faith. I retired fifteen years ago and have spent much of the time since then in revisiting Christianity from a rationalist point of view. At the heart of my approach has been what is known as 'textual criticism': a critical study of writings emphasizing a close reading and analysis of the text. Specific techniques include: the identification of bias resulting from authorial belief and intent; the identification of possible errors in scribal transcription and mistranslation; and the comparison of different versions of events in different texts. All of these possibilities exist in abundance in the Bible. My own training, experience and qualification is in modern literary texts, but I decided to apply that training in critical analysis to the Bible and other contemporary texts.

I took first class honours in my undergraduate degree at Ulster University, and I subsequently conducted three years' research in an archive of original manuscripts in Duke Humphrey's Reading Room at the Bodleian Library at Oxford University, before attaining my doctorate (DPhil) from the latter. I have subsequently published peer-reviewed articles in respected academic journals. My degrees and my research have been in English literature, specializing in the Victorian period. In the academic world this does not qualify me to write about the early history of Judaism and Christianity, because in that world there are strict and rigid demarcation lines between academic disciplines. There is, however, a growing recognition that those divisions get in the way of real knowledge. In the case of my own research, my stance is that someone like me, trained in textual analysis and practised in working with sometimes chaotic manuscript sources, can have something to bring to the party when studying ancient scriptural texts. Of course, I am dependent on the linguistic, archaeological and historical work of experts in the field – but with my objectivity, borne of a different academic discipline, combined with a lack of supernatural preconceptions – I may be able to offer new insights into the interpretation and meaning of those scriptural texts.

I believe that my researches over the last couple of decades have uncovered a revolutionary new understanding of the roots of Judaism and Christianity. In 2017, I published a book called *The Christian Fallacy* in which I set out my initial findings. This attracted little attention and only a few readers, but undeterred, I continued my research, revised and much enlarged my previous book, and this trilogy is the end result. (That first book now forms the essence of Volume Two, although some of those original arguments, relating to the Book of Revelation and Simon Magus, can now be found in Volume III.) The trilogy offers, for the first time, a complete, rationalistic re-interpretation of the Bible, from Genesis to Revelation, and relates it to other contemporary texts, religious and secular, and to contemporary events and people. Volume I: *Ancestral Tales* analyses the various source texts that make up the so-called Books of Moses in the Old Testament, and in conjunction with the non-Biblical record – notably the Egyptian one – is able to unravel the true roots of Jewish belief. Volume II: *Mistaken Messiahs* traces how Jewish messianic belief finds its way into the New Testament and Christianity, and identifies historical figures behind Jesus and the Apostles. Volume III: *Apocalypse Postponed* then focuses on the Christian belief in imminent apocalypse and traces how thoroughgoing misunderstanding of the relevant texts has led to two millennia of fallacious expectation.

On 7 February 1497 in Florence, the religious extremist Friar Girolamo Savonarola, held the first of his 'bonfires of the vanities' on which thousands of objects, condemned by religious authorities as 'occasions of sin', were consigned to the flames. It is high time we rationalists had our own bonfire on which to consign the sheer inanities of religious belief. This trilogy is a metaphorical bonfire of biblical fallacies. Each volume in the trilogy has been written to stand alone, but there is a natural sequence to the arguments developed, which is facilitated if they are read in order:

Vol I   Ancestral Tales
Vol II   Mistaken Messiahs
Vol III   Apocalypse Postponed[1]

There has never been anything like this – in scope, in

---

[1] This volume in particular is very much a sequel to Volume II, adding to and building on the arguments found there. It begins with a summary of Volume II, but, if at all possible, I would urge that they be read consecutively.

approach and in findings. It may be possible to continue in Jewish or Christian belief in the light of these three volumes, but it would be a very different kind of religious faith from the one normally espoused.

PREFACE

In Volume II of this trilogy, I argued that Jesus Christ is a fictional character. It is a matter of fact, not conjecture or theory, that every event and statement of any significance at all in the gospels can be paralleled in other earlier texts – particularly Jewish religious writings both in and out of the Old Testament. This is a matter of fact because the parallels are clear to see and have been demonstrated exhaustively. The issue at stake here, therefore, is how one interprets this fact. Christians would say that in the case of Old Testament parallels we are dealing with super-natural prophetic texts (and presumably in non-canonical texts, just coincidence). I reject this on the simple ground that extraordinary claims require extraordinary proof. A super-natural explanation by definition is extraordinary, and I see no reason to jump to the extraordinary conclusion if there are ordinary explanations that are satisfactory. Some have argued that Jesus did actually exist but he spent his life consciously or unconsciously conforming to these prior texts. But this explanation does not work. Many of the texts require events that would have been outside his control; for him to be unconscious of the prophecies seems hardly credible either given who He[1] claimed to be; and if Jesus was conforming to prophecy consciously, that would surely be the actions of a charlatan rather than a genuine messiah. In my view the only rational explanation that is psychologically credible is that Jesus was a fictional character concocted from messianic prophecy. The reason we can believe this is that we know for another fact that this was exactly the sort of thing that religious writers were doing at the time. The techniques were known as *Midrash* and *Pesher* and involved convoluted and far-fetched allegorical interpretation of unrelated texts. And if you find that unlikely, listen to a few Christian church sermons and you will find that the technique is alive and well today.

Volume II traced the roots of the Christian religion in the Jewish 'Zealot' movement of the early decades of the first century AD. It showed that there was almost certainly no one living then that equated with the person we now know as 'Jesus Christ', but that the fictional biography of Jesus was created by raiding Old Testament texts, using the Jewish allegorical techniques of Midrash and Pesher. The messiah figure known as Jesus actually lived in the sixth century BC – the first High Priest of the new Jerusalem Temple, built on the Jewish return from Exile in Babylon. The political ideology of the movement was developed by Judas the Galilean, but he took his religious inspiration from the man we now know as John the Baptist. Volume II showed that John's death was followed in the 40s AD by all the founding members of the movement either dying or being one way or another removed from the Judaean scene. It then showed how the chronology of St Paul is also fictional: that he too

---

[1] I give Jesus here the honorary capital 'H', not because I believe in His divinity but because it just looks strange otherwise. In the same way, I shall in this book use initial capitals for other words with divine connotations – such as 'God' – as a convention, not as an admission of any kind of Faith.

Preface

left Judaea never to return in the 40s AD, a decade earlier than previously understood. The book ended with a call to wake up and smell the coffee: since Jesus is a fiction, He is not coming back in an apocalyptic end to history, and beliefs based on that expectation are plain wrong. That is where the present volume takes up the argument.

I ended Volume II with a summary. I reproduce that here for those who have not read the previous book, edited down to focus solely on what is necessary to understand my starting point in the present book. Those familiar with the arguments may wish to skip the next paragraphs – or they may find them a handy recap on the main findings:

1 **The Bible is not the inerrant, inspired word of God; it cannot be because it contains historical errors, and internal inconsistencies.** It has been no part of my purpose to provide a thorough demolition of the principle of 'inerrancy', or the infallibility of scripture, but I do recognize that without an acceptance that scripture is the product of human inspiration rather than divine, then many of my arguments in this trilogy will not convince. To maintain a belief in the inerrancy of scripture in the face of the facts requires some supreme step of faith. It requires a belief that the errors and inconsistencies will turn out to be apparent rather than real – that they are the result of human error in interpretation rather than genuine mistakes. But it also requires a belief that somehow God guides not just the writers of scripture, but all the various copyists, editors and translators over the millennia. Of course, many Christians today accept that the Bible is not inerrant, but maintain, nevertheless, that it contains general truths about God and the moral life. Fair enough – but this is a slippery slope that allows for the kind of radical reappraisal contained in this trilogy.

2 **Prophecies are, therefore, not true; when they appear to be true, it is because they reflect later fictional accounts based on earlier texts.** This, of course, follows on naturally, once one accepts that inerrancy is untrue. But it also fails the test of Occam's Razor – that the more unlikely assumptions you have to make in order to believe something, the less true it is likely to be; or in other words, the simplest explanations are usually the right ones. The simple fact is that each generation of prophets took the prophecies of their predecessors and, by a process of imaginative allegorization, reshaped their perception of contemporary people and events to reflect them. The ancient prophets were deluded about their abilities to see the future, just as some modern-day spiritualists are deluded about their ability to contact the dead. They were sincere but wrong, as were their interpreters in later times.

3 **The prophet Zechariah had visions in the sixth century BC of a decisive intervention by God to establish his Kingdom on Earth.** Given the perspective of points 1 and 2 above, it seems inescapable that Zechariah's visions were the catalyst for the Jesus Movement of the first century AD. Zechariah is the key source for the Christian story – for the coming of the Messiah, the triumphal entry to Jerusalem, the role of the Mount of Olives, the fate of Judas Iscariot, the Crucifixion, the Descent to Hell and the Resurrection. In this context, it seems clear that the Jesus Movement never envisaged the foundation of a religion that would last for two millennia. They believed that they were living in the Last Days and that God's final intervention was at hand. New Testament teachings about how to live one's life were never intended as anything but temporary – the world was about to end so making long-term plans was pointless.

Preface

4 **Zechariah prophesied that there would be two Messiahs in the Last Days.** The Priest-Messiah would be the High Priest of his own time, Jesus ben Yehozedek, who with Zerubbabel commenced the rebuilding of the Jerusalem Temple in the sixth century BC, following the return from Babylonian captivity. He would be raised from the dead, cleansed and act as judge of mankind in the Last Days. Under St Paul, this concept developed into Jesus as the eternal Son of God, member of the Holy Trinity, existent for all time with God. But this was not the original stance of the founders of the Jesus Movement. For them, as for Zechariah, Jesus was a special human being, descended from Zadok, the first High Priest of Israel, and chosen by God to be his judge of mankind. There was no earthly Jesus of the first century and no '*second* coming' – just the belief that the Jesus who had lived 500 years before was returning at any moment. The King-Messiah also prophesied by Zechariah, known as the 'Branch', was to be God's representative on Earth when He established His Kingdom. This seemed entirely logical. Of course, God Himself would not actually rule in person. When He had set the Jews apart to be His people, He had ordained that they should be ruled by kings, and it was that model that would determine the political structure of His new Kingdom on Earth. This King-Messiah had yet to live but, according to Zechariah, he would be a descendant of David and He would lead the forces of good in the final battle against evil on the Mount of Olives. As Christianity developed in the Gentile world, the idea of two Messiahs was merged into one, the Kingdom of God became increasingly spiritualized and the 'return' of Jesus endlessly delayed.

5 **John the Baptist, known as Zadok (or Sadduc), an anti-establishment Pharisee, interpreted the Zechariah**

prophecy as applying to his own time – the first half of the first century AD. John the Baptist is well attested in Josephus[2] and Jewish tradition as well as the Bible. Although the Gospel writers wrote the Baptist out of their narratives as quickly as they decently could, they were nonetheless uncomfortably aware that, nevertheless, someone called John continued to be a major player in the Jesus Movement, so they invented the disciple John, one who had originally followed the Baptist but now switched his allegiance to Jesus. But there was only ever one John: the founder of the Jesus Movement and a key player in it until his death in the 30s AD.

6 **John the Baptist identified Judas the Galilean as the King-Messiah.** A key player in early first Century events in Judæa was Judas the Galilean, who led resistance to Roman rule. The Gospels' account of Jesus' baptism and endorsement by John the Baptist is a garbled memory of John's endorsement of Judas as the King-Messiah. Convinced that they were living in the Last Days and about to witness the coming of Jesus as the Priest-Messiah, they then led the Jesus Movement together. Judas' role in the movement was to build an armed rebellion that itself would finally trigger God's intervention. John's role was to act as the High Priest of the Movement until Jesus did return to Earth as Priest-Messiah. His baptismal rite, foreshadowed in Zechariah, inducted people into the Movement until that day.

7 **Key events in the history of early Christianity took place at least a decade before commonly supposed.** There are significant and suspicious gaps in Josephus' narrative of the early decades of the first century AD. Someone has

---

2 A 1st Century AD Jewish historian, who features in Volumes I and II.

tampered with Josephus' text to make his story fit with the story and chronology of Jesus, as it became established within the church in the early years of the second century AD. When this perception is combined with the realisation that most or all the 'historical' references in the Book of Acts in the New Testament are suspect because they were lifted wholesale from Josephus, a completely new chronology begins to emerge. Standard chronology has Jesus born at the start of the first century AD, and crucified early in the 30s. Paul is then active over the next three decades, arriving in Rome in the early 60s. My revised chronology assumes there was no first-century Jesus but that Judas the Galilean was killed in 19 AD with the connivance of Paul, and that Paul's own activities took place from soon after that date until he arrived in Rome in the mid-40s. It also makes possible the identification of the Christian leaders James the Less and Simon Peter with the two sons of Judas the Galilean, also called James and Simon. This means that by the end of the 40s, all the early leaders of the Jesus Movement were dead, except for Paul who was in Rome. Twenty years then passed, followed by a devastating war that saw Jerusalem utterly destroyed and its inhabitants scattered. Only then – and probably some decades even after this – did Gentile Christians in Rome begin to write down stories about Jesus and his apostles. This alone is capable of explaining why so much of what they wrote now appears to us as fiction – there was no one left who knew what really happened.

8 **After Judas' death, the Jesus Movement split into two branches.** The family of Judas the Galilean, through their claimed descent from King David, regarded themselves as a royal dynasty in waiting. They continued to

believe that Jesus was coming as Priest-Messiah, and that one of their number would be the King-Messiah. They focused their efforts on recruiting Jews in Judæa and the Diaspora to their cause. John the Baptist, however, became leader of a more passivist branch, operating on the east bank of the River Jordan until he was killed sometime around AD 36. His branch also held to the original beliefs of the Movement, and remained an essentially Jewish phenomenon, but following the failure of Judas, ceased to seek to precipitate God's intervention and were content to await his Kingdom in faith. As time went by, and increasingly after John's death, the activists of the movement came to see the passivists as traitors to the cause, and as Josephus testifies, internecine strife broke out sporadically between the two branches until the Jewish War finally united all Jews in what they believed would be the apocalyptic battle at the End of Days.

9 **Understanding the relationship between St Paul and the Jesus Movement requires reconciliation between apparently differing accounts in Acts and Galatians.** Understanding of events in the early church has been obscured by a failure to understand the order of events as described by Paul in Galatians and a confusion in Acts about the prophet Agabus. I have radically reinterpreted the Book of Acts, especially where it seems to be contradicted by Galatians. I have then been able to show that, properly interpreted, Galatians and Acts do in fact tie up together and that, although tensions existed at that time between Paul and the first generation of Judas' family, there was no outright split in the mid-30s. The real split only occurred about a decade later when it became apparent that Paul had taken the final step of asserting that not just Gentiles, but even Jews themselves were now freed by Jesus' sacrifice on the cross

from the requirements of the Jewish religious laws. Judas' family could not countenance a theology that in effect removed the special position of the Jews as God's chosen people with their own special Covenant and their own special role as priests to the world in God's coming Kingdom

10 **Christianity as we know it was developed by St Paul as a Gentile, spiritualized version of the Jesus Movement.** The Apostle Paul participated in the death of Judas and subsequently persecuted the Jerusalem Church, as narrated in Acts and Galatians. He was converted by visions of Jesus, probably around AD 20, to the passivist section of the Jesus Movement, and from the beginning saw his calling as to convert Gentiles to a belief in the imminent coming of Jesus and the Kingdom of God. He had minimal contact with Judas' family in Jerusalem, except to attend the Council of Jerusalem in *c.* AD 34, when it was agreed that Gentile converts were not required to observe Jewish religious Law. Paul developed the essentials of Christian doctrine as we know it today over the ten years following the Council, and eventually taught that even Jews were now freed from the Law. Paul was arrested and eventually deported to Rome in the mid-40s. Meanwhile, persecution of the church in Jerusalem continued and all the leaders of both sections of the Jesus Movement had been killed or exiled from Judæa by the late 40s AD. The family of Judas continued their activities in Judæa and were instrumental in the uprisings that led eventually to the Jewish War of the 60s.[3] The passivist section continued outside Judæa and evolved over

---

[3] In the present book, this will be critical to understanding key personalities and events in Revelation.

time into the Christian church as we know it.

The present book falls into three parts:

PART ONE deals with prophecy in the Bible concerning the Last Days, the End Time and the Last Things. The term 'apocalypse', which is commonly used to describe these future events, actually means merely 'revelation', but it has come to have more cataclysmic overtones. The study of these apocalyptic events is known by theologians as 'eschatology', which means the 'study of the last things'. We shall trace how the original Jewish concept of 'the Day of the Lord' developed down the centuries in Jewish thinking to become a more complex concept of how God would bring time to an end and usher in His eternal kingdom. We shall then trace how this concept transferred into the eschatology of early Christian writers and was augmented and adapted into the sort of apocalyptic scenario we are now familiar with. It is an important finding and theme of this book that the transfer of Jewish eschatology into Christian theology was problematic from the start, because at heart the two religions are diametrically opposed to one another. Judaism is focused on this life – how to lead it in harmony with God's will. Its eschatology, therefore, is bound by those horizons: it envisages a return to an Earthly paradise – a new Eden. Christianity on the other hand is focused on the next life, for which Earthly existence is merely a preparation. Its eschatology concerns spiritual existence in Heaven with God for eternity. We shall see that the transfer of one set of ideas into another has been bedevilled from the start by the Book of Revelation – an essentially Jewish, proto-Christian text which, unlike other New Testament texts, is not content to skim over the problems but can be seen to be grappling with them. Throughout Christian history, Revelation has had its detractors for precisely this reason; its place in the canon has never been secure, and we shall see how it is responsible for endless dispute and schism right down to the present day.

PART TWO will also take a chronological approach, tracing what happened to these ideas as they appear in Christian scriptures, the problems different generations of believers had with them, and the ways in which they sought to accommodate, rationalize and harmonize the various elements of scriptural apocalypse to produce coherent schema for the events that will take place at the end of time. This section covers two millennia of events and theological development so, of necessity, has to be very highly selective. The temptation to delve into detail at points has been overwhelming but resisted in the interests of retaining clarity around the main themes. Another kind of book would have relished some of the detail that has had to be left out – particularly the stories of the countless individuals down the centuries who, in the grip of a convinced eschatological insight, have rivalled for idiosyncrasy and hilarity, the most extreme of the old Biblical prophets. But the purpose of the present book is to stick with the mainstream of ideas, grounded in the canon of Biblical texts accepted by the majority of Christians as 'scripture', and to trace the history of ideas that have been developed to interpret apocalyptic scripture.

PART THREE will then shift to a topical approach. In the course of Part One we shall identify 24 key apocalyptic topics as they arise historically; Part Three will take each of these in turn, analyse the roots of the belief, identify the original author's intention and provide definitive interpretations. Needless to say, the perspective we shall take on all these matters remains that of rationalism: extraordinary claims require extraordinary proof, and in the absence of that, we shall look for mundane explanations rather than supernatural ones. The branch of theology known as eschatology has evolved more than its fair share of obscure and difficult language to cope with the bewildering range of interpretations that can exist given the heterogenous nature of the textual material we are dealing with. In the first two parts, I have avoided getting into any of this in order to provide a plain historical account in plain English. But since anyone with any interest in this subject will, even on casual acquaintance with the literature, be bombarded from the start with this technical language, I have tried in Part Three to introduce the key terms in such a way as to elucidate their meanings and, more important, how and why they have arisen to account for the myriad of conflicts and disharmonies that occur as soon as you try to extract coherent theology from a wide range of texts, written at different times by different people with different axes to grind. I have called Part Three 'Truth'. Arrogant, I know. But in the face of the utter conviction of faith, I feel that nothing less will do. Some of what I shall present as 'the truth' is standard rebuttal of obvious supernatural absurdities from a rational standpoint. But some of it is entirely new and I offer it more tentatively. It arises from the overall stance I have developed and set out in this trilogy so far; as such, it both validates that stance and stands or falls with it. *Pace* the arrogance of the title, I do welcome considered feedback and response – provided it is not of the kind I so often encounter: 'The Bible is the unerring Word of God, so you are wrong.'

The reader need bring nothing to this book other than an open and enquiring mind. All my arguments will be based on the standard, recognized texts of Judaeo-Christianity. There will be no falling back on obscure texts or dubious subjectivity, although I shall argue that some key texts are so garbled that their original meaning has been lost or traduced. The facts I shall present will be those accepted and endorsed by mainstream biblical scholars – it is only the interpretation and conclusions I draw from those facts that are new and almost certainly anathema to scholars with a Christian faith. All quotations from the Bible will be from the King James Authorised Version; you may wish to keep a copy by you, but this will not be strictly necessary as all quotations will be given in full. You will need no other texts. I was tempted to use a more modern translation, but many fundamentalists believe that the Authorised Version is the only one inspired by God Himself and I don't want to leave any room for quibbles on that basis. If you find the archaic language off-putting, please do have a copy of your own favoured translation by you as you read.

INTRODUCTION

Birth and death. Beginnings and endings. For all of us, these are matters of some importance. At the personal level, we all know that things will come to an end. From the moment of birth, the process of dying begins. We do not know when, and actually don't want to know; life would be unbearable if we did. But we all assume we have the biblical 'three score and ten'[1] and we get on and make the most of it; so it is not at all surprising that we are fascinated also about whether the world as a whole had a beginning, and if it will have an end. Over the last hundred years or so, science has answered a lot of these big questions that have puzzled humanity since the first men and women emerged from the African savannah. We now know with amazing precision just how old the universe is; it began with the Big Bang some 13.8 billion years ago. The Earth itself was formed some 4.5 billion years ago. These are not just guesstimates, nor even just theoretical, mathematical calculations – they are based on real experimental evidence and detailed observation, and they are accepted by an overwhelming percentage of scientists. Clearly, the *future* of the Earth and the universe is harder to

---

[1] As we shall see, this is itself a significant number in Jewish apocalypse.

predict with any degree of certainty. But even here, science has made some astonishing progress. We know, for example, based on firm observational evidence, that the universe is expanding. We also know the variables that will determine whether this will continue forever, or the universe will eventually contract, or whether it will run out of steam and reach stasis. The fate of the Earth itself will depend on another range of natural variables, such as comet or asteroid strikes or a star going supernova in our region of space, or the effects of climate change. But we can say with some assurance that the Earth will exist in some form for about 10^{20} years into the future and barring accidents, or the intervention of a deity into the natural order of things, we probably have about seven and a half billion years before life of any kind becomes finally extinct on our planet.

These are some of the most impressive, awe-inspiring revelations of modern science. Yet fundamentalists believe that by careful study of the Bible alone, they can do better. They say that the Earth was created by God, as described in the Book of Genesis, about 6,000 years ago. This idea is usually attributed to the calculations of James Ussher, the Archbishop of Armagh in the 17th century. Based on a literal interpretation of the Bible, Ussher deduced that the first day of creation was October 23, 4004 BC, but others over the centuries, including scientists like Kepler and Newton, reached similar conclusions in a similar manner. Modern believers in this nonsense regard any evidence to the contrary as either the work of Satan to deceive us from the truth, or even by God himself as a test of faith. Muslim fundamentalists take a similar view. And of course, these people believe not just that the Bible has the answer to the age of the world, they also believe that a careful study of scripture will tell us when to expect the end of the world as well. Such is the blind faith of those to whom sacred scriptures are

Introduction

inerrant messages from an omniscient deity. For those of us who are genuinely concerned about where this kind of lunacy will lead us all, in a world where the very same science has made possible weapons of awesome destruction, it is a challenge to find how we can get these people to open their eyes and minds.

It would not be so bad if this irrational blindness affected only the issue of the origin of the Earth. Teaching creationism to schoolchildren is an abuse of their naivety, but deeply regrettable though this certainly is, it does not directly affect the rest of us. What is past is past. But, unfortunately, scriptures also have a lot to say about the future as well, and insofar as believers in such texts are likely to form future actions on such beliefs, we are all endangered by their delusions. In particular, fundamentalists search their Bibles for the detail of future events that they believe will bring about the end of the Earth, the end of time, and the future Kingdom of God. And given the obscurity, confusion and mystification of such texts, they can produce 'evidence' from them for any and all crazy theories about how current events prove we are living in the Last Days before God calls a halt to history. Of course, I cannot prove that a god will not intervene at some point in that future. Unlike purely natural events, where we can make estimates of the odds, a supernatural intervention is not a matter amenable to statistical analysis. The only evidence we have are the scriptural texts that make such claims. But although, by definition, we cannot with any certainty rule any or all of those claims in or out as far as the future goes, we *can* carry out such an analysis of the past. Apocalypse – prophecy of future End Time events – has been a feature of most cultures and civilizations for which we have records, and probably all, since time began.

There does seem to be something inherently attractive for many people – now and over the last few thousand years –

in the idea that the current state of the planet will be halted and replaced with something better. This is particularly true at times of manmade or natural crisis, and as the epigraph from Gibbon at the front of this book says:

> There exists in human nature a strong propensity ... to magnify the evils of the present times.[2]

The birth of the world appears not just in Genesis of course; every culture has its own mythical version of how everything was created out of nothing, from Greek tales of primordial Titans to Australian Aboriginal tales of giant frogs and floods. And most cultures similarly have an account of how it will all end. There are two broad types of such apocalyptic prediction: the linear and the cyclical. The former sees time as going forward in a straight line, and history as a non-recurring unfolding of God's plan. God creates the world, saves it from itself, and eventually transforms its imperfections into a perfect new order that will last for eternity (if, indeed, time itself has any meaning at all in the new order of things). The prime example of linear apocalypse is that envisioned originally by the Jewish faith and then picked up and modified by the Christian and Islamic faiths, which both stem ultimately from Judaism. Over half the world's population adheres to one of these three major religions, and the linear model of apocalypse they espouse will be the main subject of this book. But it is interesting to note that outside of this family of religions the linear model is almost unknown; it is the cyclical model that predominates. From this perspective, the world goes through an endless cycle of recurring events, each cycle ending with catastrophic destruction of

---

2 Edward Gibbon, *The History of the Decline and Fall of the Roman Empire*, Ch. 31.

Introduction

some kind, followed by a fresh start. There are then two versions of this basic scenario. In the first, the cycles are simple repetitions of each other. Any progress made within each cycle is lost when that cycle ends. But in the more complex version, the cycles create an endless upward spiral in which each builds upon progress made in past cycles, towards eternal improvement. The two main world religions that espouse such views are Hinduism and Buddhism.

In Hindu belief, there is a series of cycles nested within each other. The greatest cycle is an eternal succession of universes, the length of each determined by the lifespan of the creator God. The current creator God is Brahma, whose lifespan is over 300 trillion years. For Brahma, a single day and night is measured in several billion years and this cyclic period is known as a 'kalpa'. At the end of each kalpa, all will be brought to nought before a new kalpa begins. Clearly, these immense cycles dwarf the existence of humanity and can have nothing to say about its future. But there are cycles within a single kalpa – periods of creation, continuity and decline – that are on a timescale small enough to encompass human history. These cycles go through a process of gradual decline, from created purity into utter corruption. We currently live at the end of such a cycle, as evidenced (in the Hindu view[3]) by the corruption and impiety of the world. The cycle will end when Brahma, in his final manifestation ('avatar') as Kalki will appear on a white horse and establish a period of righteousness on the Earth. If this sounds reminiscent of the Four Horsemen of the Apocalypse and the Messiah in the Book of Revelation, who also appears on a white horse, it is probably no coincidence: from at least the time of Alexander the Great, ideas were exchanged between India and the Hellenic world via Asia Minor. But in a cyclical model, the outcome is

---
3 But remember Gibbon's remark above.

different. The Four Horsemen bring destruction as a preliminary to the end of history and the establishment of the Kingdom of God. Kalki brings an age of righteousness, creating the necessary purity at the start of the next kalpa. The timing of Kalki's coming is unknowable and solely at Brahma's discretion, unaffected by human desire or action.

Buddhism, on the other hand, does make some predictions of timescale for the end of the world, although these vary with the different forms that Buddhism takes. One Buddhist tradition has it that the Buddha said that his teachings would last just 5,000 years, which would imply an apocalyptic date of around AD 2300 – comfortably still a few hundred years into our own future. As in Hinduism, this event will be preceded by a period of corruption leading to the appearance of a righteous figure – not Kalki, but Buddha Maitreya – who will usher in a new paradise on Earth. Some Buddhists believe he is already here, but most are not holding their breath. For all Buddhists, the ultimate fate of the world comes later, with the appearance of seven suns in the sky – each bringing its own form of destruction. At this point, the whole Earth will be destroyed in a giant inferno. As with Hinduism, this is presumably well into the future so no cause for great concern right now. Neither Hindus nor Buddhists live under any great apocalyptic shadow. They envisage end times, but not tomorrow, and in any case, destruction will be preceded by Earthly paradise, established by a supernatural figure and, crucially, available for all humanity. There is recognition of corruption as well as righteousness, but no trace of the idea that some will be saved and others consigned to torment. Whatever the future, we are all in it together.

However, in addition to the major (and minor) religions now followed by humanity, there have been countless religions in the past that currently have no, or very few, adherents. These are particularly interesting from our point of view,

Introduction

because any predictions they may have made about apocalypse have clearly been demonstrated by history to be false, or you would not be sitting there reading this book (presumably). The coming of Jesus, Kalki or Maitreya may be just around the corner for all anyone can prove or disprove, but the same cannot be said of some of these other, older apocalypses. Ragnarök, for example: the 'twilight of the gods' of Norse mythology, given an accompanying score by Wagner, and providing the Nazis with convenient racist symbolism. Hitler may have been much enthralled by it, but I doubt if, even in his craziest dreams, he actually believed in it. But ancient Scandinavians did – strongly and sincerely. They believed that this world would end in darkness and despair and the resurrection of the dead. Odin and the gods would fight a huge battle with Loki and the forces of evil, resulting in the deaths of virtually all of them. Then the Earth would be destroyed in cataclysmic fire. This, however, would be the beginning of a new cycle. The surviving gods and humans would start again on a new Earth. Odin, Thor and Loki all have a new lease of life in Marvel comics and films, but they are now just 'superheroes' alongside modern fictions like Captain America and Iron Man. No one believes in them as gods anymore, let alone worships them. And no one believes in Ragnarök. Or do they?

Modern believers in the Norse apocalypse are presumably few and far between, but then, I would have said the same about the ancient Mayan religion – before 2012 came along and caused genuine panic across the globe among what would appear to have been ordinary, rational people. The Maya was a South American Indian civilization that was wiped out by the arrival of Europeans on the continent in historic times. Descendants survive, but the civilization itself is long dead. In our western civilization, we base our calendar on the supposed birth date of Jesus Christ. The Maya had a calendar that took its start date from their mythical world creation event, which corresponds to August 11, 3114 BC. They believed that apocalypse would take place 5,126 years after that date. In our calendars, that equates to AD 2012. And for some strange reason, in the years leading up to it, many people around the globe took it into their heads that the Mayans had somehow got hold of 'The Truth' and that the world would end in that year. The internet was largely to blame; there were literally hundreds of thousands of websites inciting wonder if not fear on the subject. And the fear was real. In May 2012, an Ipsos poll conducted for Reuters of over 16,000 adults in twenty one countries found that eight percent had experienced fear or anxiety over the possibility of the world ending in December 2012, while an average of ten percent agreed with the statement 'the Mayan calendar, which some say "ends" in 2012, marks the end of the world', with responses as high as twenty percent in China, thirteen percent in Russia, Turkey, Japan and South Korea, and twelve percent in the United States.[4] There were countless gatherings, religious ceremonies and rituals across the world. Some took to shelters of one kind or another and some followed the example of American reality TV stars Heidi Montag and Spencer Pratt who revealed that they had spent most of their ten million dollars of accumulated earnings by 2010 because they believed the world would end in 2012.[5] And the fear turned into terrible reality for some. Many contemplated suicide and at least one did so. In the US, the 2011 Tucson shooting followed 2012-related predictions. In China, a man attacked and wounded twenty-

---

[4] https://www.ipsos.com/en-us/one-seven-14-global-citizens-believe-end-world-coming-their-lifetime

[5] Heidi Montag and Spencer Pratt starred in The Hills, an American reality television series.

Introduction

three children with a knife: he had been 'influenced' by the prediction of the upcoming apocalypse. In Brazil, police interrupted what was believed to have been an attempted mass suicide by up to one hundred members of a cult headed by self-proclaimed prophet Luis Pereira dos Santos, who predicted the end of the world.

The real irony of all this was that people, influenced by Christian apocalyptic belief, interpreted the Mayan prophecy as a linear apocalypse. In fact, the Mayans seem to have had a cyclical view of history. Scholars are divided on the precise details because our knowledge of Mayan beliefs is based on little real evidence. But it does seem that although the Mayans saw 2012 as the end of a cycle, it also marked the beginning of a new one. The world would not end in 2012 – or, indeed, ever – and some scholars think that 2012 would actually have been a year of celebration, rather like welcoming in the New Year, had the Mayan civilization survived until then. Be all this as it may, the world, of course, did not end; there has not been a major resurgence in Mayan religious belief, and we all go about our lives as normal. The 2012 panic was not a new phenomenon. As we shall see, even without the internet spreading the meme, similar events happened around the end of the first and the second millennia: widespread panic, a resurgence of religious fervour, and apocalyptic dreams and visions swept through Christendom. And we have had false prophets leading people up mountains to await the coming wrath for centuries. But modern media has meant that such prophets can attract adherents more easily these days. In 1978 in Guyana, 918 people including children died by drinking Kool-Aid laced with cyanide in the Jonestown massacre. They believed they were embracing a better life after death. At about the same time, the Heaven's Gate religious millenarian group was founded in San Diego, California. Members believed the planet Earth was about to be 'recycled' and the only chance to survive was to leave it immediately. Twenty years later they saw their chance. They believed an alien spacecraft was following in the wake of the Hale-Bopp comet, and thirty-nine members of the group participated in a mass suicide in order to be mystically transported up.

The question must be asked: why do Christians believe that their own version of apocalypse is any different from these? One can see the attractions, of course. If the end of the world somehow brings with it an antidote to our personal end, how compelling is that? The boast of Christianity is that Christ has triumphed over death – admittedly, not right now, but when Jesus returns in glory we shall be resurrected and live forever. The problem is that, as with the rest of the Christian narrative, we are so used to it from Sunday School and compulsory religious education in schools, we have become immune to its own idiocies. We are told that Jesus will suddenly appear in the sky; that the dead will rise with living believers to meet him; that there will be a major war between the forces of good and evil; that death and destruction will ravage the Earth; but that a new Earth will dawn in its stead. How does this differ in any essential way from the twilight of the gods in Norse myth, from the Mayan end of the world, or from Heaven's Gate adherents expecting to rise to their alien spaceship? On what grounds do we accept one as genuine prophecy of real events to come, and the others as lunacy on the one hand or primitive superstition on the other. Surely, any rational judgement would be that all are cut from the same unlikely cloth. Those who disagree do so on the basis that their version of these supernatural events is unique and true because it comes from unique and true scripture. As with all Christian belief, that is what it finally comes down to. And, apparently, it is not enough just to point out that belief in Maitreya or in Kalki

Introduction

is justified by adherents to Hinduism and Buddhism in exactly the same way. Their scriptures are false; the Bible is true.

At the root of all this is a deluded belief that the world in general and mankind in particular has some sort of historical destiny. This delusion is not restricted to fundamentalists. The twentieth century witnessed the most appalling levels of mass destruction in the entire history of the world, driven not by religious belief in human destiny, but secular ideas of historical determinism. Inspired by pseudo-scientific theories of racial distinctions and of social evolution, the Nazis attempted to give human destiny a helping hand by murdering anyone that did not fit their theories, thus removing them from the gene pool. Nowadays we know that Darwin's theory of evolution is value free – genes propagate through survival of the 'fittest' – but fitness for survival is nothing more than that: a crocodile or shark is as perfectly adapted to survive as it is possible to imagine but does not represent the fulfilment of any manifest destiny. Like Hitler, Stalin also murdered millions of people in the name of historical destiny, driven in his case by the deterministic theories of Marx, who prophesied the coming victory of the working class over their bourgeois capitalist oppressors, as the manifest destiny of mankind. But evolution does not have an end goal; history is a random, chaotic process with no moral compass, and if there is a creator God, whatever he has planned for us remains as obscure today as ever.

In Volume II, I demonstrated the falsity of scriptural 'truth' in relation to the very existence of Jesus and the real roots of Christianity. In this book, I shall use the same techniques to examine the key apocalyptic scriptures of Christianity to demonstrate that they are equally false. If you weren't convinced by my previous book that Jesus never existed in the first place, perhaps I can nevertheless convince you that even if He once lived, the prophecies of His return, and the apocalyptic events surrounding that return, are also a fallacy that is on a par with Heaven's Gate. It is too late to save the lives of those poor deluded 39 people, or the 918 that died in Jonestown, but hopefully this book might be the means by which some at least are relieved from irrational fear of a fictional idea of apocalypse.

PART ONE

BIBLICAL PROPHECY

I

Background

Apocalypse Postponed is about a perennial conviction – one that has plagued humanity for thousands of years – that the arrival out of the sky of some supernatural 'saviour' of mankind is imminent, and that the world is about to end at the hand of God. It is therefore essentially about prophecy and about the individuals who make it. The word 'prophecy' means 'the foretelling of future events'.[1] Seeing into the future has been a human desire from the beginning of time. We survive as a species because we have learnt to avoid dangers, and we do this by reading our environment in a very sophisticated way. We hear a twig snap in the jungle, predict that a tiger is stalking us and run for our lives. We see a log in the water, correctly divine that it is a crocodile and drink elsewhere. By picking up on clues we predict future dangers and avoid them. It is a small step from this to the desire to predict at a longer range – what is going to happen tomorrow, or next season or next year. Unfortunately, of course, that small step in human desire is one giant leap in terms of our perceptive faculties. There may be a few environmental clues, but on the whole nature does not render up its secrets

---

[1] The Shorter Oxford English Dictionary.

easily: the future is a book closed to mere mortals. However, shamans, priests and prophets are not mere mortals – they claim to have access to knowledge denied to the rest of us. That access may be granted by the accident of birth or through years of initiation and training in arcane rites and rituals – often, in a combination of both. But throughout time, cultures have been willing to recognize certain individuals as talented in seeing the future, and to accord them the sort of elevated social status that such useful abilities deserve.

Originally, in primitive cultures, it was only natural to look to the environment for long-term clues as we do for nearer term prediction. If the snap of a twig alerts us to imminent danger, then logically, other natural signs may alert us to less immediate futures. But only if the gods have so ordered the universe – there is no point looking for predictive patterns if the universe has not been constructed with that purpose in mind. That is why seeing into the future has always been bound up with religious belief. If the gods have been properly propitiated, then they might vouchsafe such knowledge to mere mortals. If the natural world is coherent in its organization, then it can be read like a book by those with the necessary skill. This is known as *divination*. Here the ancient concept of 'as above, so below' comes into play. By charting the movements and positions of the heavenly bodies one might be able to see what the gods have in store. Some form of astrology has been practised since ancient times. A bit lower down in the heavens, the flight of birds (*augury*) or the movement of clouds (*nephelomancy*) have often been regarded as reliable indicators. And further below still, there are signs to be read too – reading entrails of various kinds and from various beasts (*extispicy*), particularly the liver if appropriately sacrificed to the gods (*haruspicy*), is known in many cultures, but there are dozens more, from the way a rooster pecks at grain (*alectryomancy*) to patterns in dripping wax (*ceromancy*).

Background

If all this sounds a bit of a lottery,[2] there are other less indirect ways in which the gods can open the portals of the future for those so inclined. Prophetic dreaming (*oneiromancy*) is one such way, and quite popular with biblical prophets. The dreams may be had by the prophet himself, or by another (usually a ruler of some sort), and interpreted by the prophet. Or, if natural dreams are short on the ground, they can be artificially stimulated as waking visions using psychogenic drugs, or trance-inducing techniques involving repetition of simple acts like dance or whirling around, or sounds like mantras and chants. Or, best of all, the deity can communicate directly to the prophet, either personally or via angelic messengers. Such communication may be via visions with greater or lesser opacity of metaphor, or through words, which may then be written down. This last method was popular in classical times, when people would make considerable journeys to visit the oracles scattered throughout the Mediterranean, and it is most favoured by the biblical prophets and by latter-day prophets in the Judaeo-Christian tradition, from the Prophet Mohammed to the founder of Mormonism, Joseph Smith. The recipient of such divine messages may be a willing mouthpiece for his deity, but sometimes in the Bible the prophets resist their calling because it usually entails telling truth to power, which then as now can be a dangerous activity. Often, as with shamans in other cultures, the resulting communication was confused and garbled, even to the point of madness, the prophet being seized with some sort of fit. The optimistic interpretation of such equivocal utterances was that the god spoke in veiled terms that only the devout could interpret. In reality, of course, it allowed for sufficiently divergent and irreconcilable interpretation that any subsequent event might be claimed to accord

---

[2] Prophecy by the drawing of lots is *cleromancy*.

with it. The Greek oracles were famous for this; they deliberately spoke in riddles that could sustain multiple readings. One common factor unites all these methods, however – there are no witnesses to the conversation. Mohammed heard God's dictation alone in his cave and Joseph Smith was given magic spectacles and inscribed tablets which were then conveniently removed when he had finished his transcription.[3]

One of the disagreements among the old prophets of Israel was the degree to which the future is fixed. If we know the future, can we avert or change it? Imagine yourself a hunter-gatherer or early pastoralist. The winter is hard and seems never-ending. Looking into the future for signs of spring is all well and good – but wouldn't it be better if, by some action of your own, you could ensure its return? Again, religion and the future become bound together. Perhaps ritual and sacrifice can be efficacious in securing the end of winter by persuading the all-powerful gods to bring it about. The winter solstice would seem the perfect time for such rituals – perhaps a sacrifice as the sun rises, or again, perhaps the ritual death and burial of a god to be resurrected as the year turns. These possibilities and more have all been explored by societies throughout the ages, seeking to arm twist the deity into future beneficence. And if that sounds primitive to modern ears, is it so different to the modern offering of prayer? What is prayer but a petition to the deity to secure some desire for the future? *Give us good harvests. Bring an end to this cruel winter. Don't let my son die. Let me get this job.* All are about changing the future to accord with our wishes – and the reliance on a deity is no different whether through prayer or sacrifice. And, indeed, are

---

[3] Actually, Mormons will point to the testimony of a few early converts who conveniently swore they too had actually seen the magic tablets. Decide for yourself.

the two that far apart in practice? *Dear God, if you let me pass this exam, I will give up chocolate for a month. Dear Lord, don't let my father die and I will never miss communion again.*

This kind of bargaining with the deity is central to Christianity. When Jacob physically wrestled with God in Genesis,[4] he provided the core metaphor for the process. Wrestling with God in prayer, it seems, is necessary and expected. God only comes across with the goods if we fight him for it. For the atheist, of course, all this is simply to misunderstand the deterministic nature of the universe. The future is already out there, determined and invariable, whether by human or divine agency. The future unfolds as the inexorable arrow of time moves forward, and the wrestling match is fixed. Many Christians themselves are also uncomfortable with the idea of changing God's mind. It does not fit with the concept of an omnipotent, omniscient being whose Will determines all and has been fixed since time began. For them, wrestling with God in prayer is not about changing God's mind – it is about changing our own mind to bring it into accord with God's Will. The devout prays that God's Will be done, on Earth as it is in Heaven, not because there is any chance of God's Will being thwarted, but in order to align the believer's Will with God's. The role of divination thus becomes another means by which the alignment can be achieved. When the Jewish High Priest used the mysterious *Urim and Thummim* to cast lots,[5] or when Jesus' disciples cast lots for a successor to Judas Iscariot,[6] they were inviting God to make His Will manifest.

Predicting the future however is, perhaps surprisingly, not the defining characteristic of prophets, in either the Old

---

[4] Genesis 32:22-32.

[5] Exodus 28.

[6] Acts 1:23-6.

or the New Testament. The early Jewish prophets were not fortune tellers; they were primarily divine messengers who represented a separate religious class with a distinct role in Jewish society – to act as intermediaries between God and His creation. Their messages were often about the future – but always in the context of the present. The future they revealed was a consequence of the present and, depending on present actions, the future could be good or bad. Their role was multi-faceted at different times and in different places. They received waking or sleeping visions and heard voices either directly from God or from Angels. The messages were to be passed on to a variety of audiences – kings both domestic and foreign, individuals, parties and nations. Sometimes the recipients would specifically request the information and sometimes it was thrust upon them by prophets, who themselves varied in willingness to be vehicles of God's intent. There seem to have been communities of prophets – in effect, a religious class distinct from the priesthood – and there were other groups of prophets who were part of the royal court and presumably maintained from court funds to perform their function for the king and his advisers. Their guidance might be sought in military matters, or about future harvests, for example. But they might also not only condemn an administration for ungodly behaviour but play a leading role in deposing such an administration and anointing a successor. In addition, each local community seems to have had its own parochial prophet, concerned with local matters. The priesthood was based around the temple in Jerusalem, so these local prophets also performed rituals associated with worship of Yahweh.[7]

---

7 Ancient Hebrew was written only with consonants. God's name was YHWH, known as the Tetragrammaton. But without vowels, the correct pronunciation is problematical. Traditionally, Jehovah was favoured but modern scholarship inclines to Yahweh so I shall use that.

However, virtually all the prophets whose names and words have come down to us in the Bible did not come from this professional class. Their collective reputation seems over time to have suffered from a cynical belief that the prophets that prospered did so because they told their hearers what they wanted to hear. Prophets like Isaiah, Jeremiah and Ezekiel were non-professionals – solitary amateurs whose messages seemed to succeeding generations to be of sufficient importance, and clear divine imprimatur, that they were preserved in Jewish scripture. As we shall see, they arose at times of crisis, and their prophetic mode was a response to crisis. All prophets, of course, were judged in accordance with the effectiveness or otherwise of their advice, guidance and direction:

> When a prophet speaketh in the name of the Lord, if the thing follow not, nor come to pass, that is the thing which the Lord hath not spoken.[8]

So much, so obvious, one would have thought. One way they all seemed to enhance their chances of positive evaluation was through the performance of 'miracles' – simple magic tricks often, but bringing the 'dead' back to life seems to have been a favourite. Even in the world of modern medicine, we know how difficult it is to define point of death; right up to the 19th century, premature declaration of death and subsequent proof to the contrary (like corpses waking on mortuary slabs) was not uncommon. It was easy, therefore, for a prophet, shaman-like, to claim miraculous responsibility for mistaken diagnosis.

Some prophets went to extraordinary lengths to get their message across, sometimes using outlandish symbolic actions to capture the attention of their target audience. On God's

---
8 Deuteronomy 18:22.

instruction, Isaiah set the trend when he stripped off all his clothes and wandered around naked to symbolize the future humiliation of Egypt and Ethiopia at the hands of Assyrian conquerors.[9] A century or so later, Jeremiah provided an interesting if not puzzling riff on the theme – he hid his underwear under a rock and didn't retrieve it for a 'long time'.[10] Jeremiah's real sartorial innovation was to fasten a cattle yoke to his shoulders as a symbol of Israel's Babylonian Exile – until, that is, another prophet broke it off.[11] One of the most extraordinary prophets was Hosea, who around the time of Isaiah was apparently instructed by God to actually marry a prostitute to symbolize the spiritual harlotry of the Jewish people. But the craziest of all was perhaps Ezekiel who, rendered mute by God for some reason, used drawing on clay tablets to get his message across, after which he lay down on his side with an iron pan separating him from his clay art. After 390 days had passed, he rolled over and repeated the exercise.[12] Other stunts he performed were to eat barley cakes baked with cow manure, again symbolizing the Babylonian Exile, where the Jews would be forced to eat unclean food;[13] and to use a sword to shave off his beard and then, dividing his hairs into thirds, set one third on fire, scatter another third around the city, stabbing it with his sword, and scatter the remaining third in the wind. Other hairs he sewed into his clothing and burned those too.[14] In an age when literacy was low and modern communications undreamed of, these symbolic enactments were no doubt a

---

9 Isaiah 20.
10 Jeremiah 13.
11 Jeremiah 27 and 28.
12 Ezekiel 4.
13 Ezekiel 4.
14 Ezekiel 5.

legitimate tool for getting across spiritual messages. But God is supposed to have inspired these crazy antics; is it likely that any deity worthy of respect should resort to such desperate measures? And is there not at least a hint of mentally certifiable behaviour?

I hope the rest of this book will be an enjoyable read. Part of the fascination of the Book of Revelation and its related apocalyptic texts has been the sleuthing required to solve their mysteries and puzzles. In the pages that follow I often mock the 'trainspotting' mentality of many Christians fascinated by eschatology: here I willingly admit to having at times a similar mentality. The difference is that I am interested in rational explanations of historical and literary conundrums, not in seeking *post hoc* justifications for *a priori* religious beliefs. Finally identifying, as I do in pages to come, the Beast of Revelation and his magic number 666; solving the mystery of the seven kings and 'the eighth who is of the seven'; pinning down the Mother and Child, the Harlot, and the other Beasts; all these things have occupied believers for centuries. I have the temerity to believe I have solved the riddle. People were looking in the wrong place – by which I mean, the wrong timeframe. I have shown thus far how all the key events in the foundation of Christianity took place a decade or so before commonly believed. The same is true of Revelation – it was written in the midst of the Jewish-Roman War, not long after it, and its 'prophecies' relate to that period, not to later times as Church history teaches. I hope you enjoy solving the puzzles with me. Other enjoyment I hope will come from some of the background to all this – the crazy antics of the old Jewish prophets, the contortions of their Christian successors to make sense of it all and the lunacies of more recent interpreters, continuing right down to modern times.

By way of example, as I am writing these very words,

someone who describes himself as a 'Christian numerologist' and goes by the name of David Meade has predicted that the world will end by divine intervention in two days' time from now – on 23 September 2017. He bases this on interpretation of a passage in the Book of Revelation (Chapter 12) in which a mysterious woman gives birth to an equally mysterious child; I shall deal with this prophecy in the course of this book, but his laughable interpretation involves the kind of convoluted mangling of text, perverse symbolism and extraordinary credulity that characterizes all such apocalyptic doomsday predictions. My own prediction is that by the time you are reading these words, this interpretation of prophecy like all the others will have been shown by events (or, more precisely, non-events) to have been false.[15] But many people are drawn in by this sort of puerile speculation, and it causes distress and anxiety to the gullible across the world.

These ideas are, without exception or excuse, some of the most ludicrous, infantile and downright injurious and dangerous ever to be foisted by religion on humanity. From them stems the kind of deranged, vicious and criminal obsessions exhibited by Muslim and Christian fundamentalists alike that will lead us all down a path of death and destruction if we do not stand up and call them what they are. They derive from an illiterate naivety combined with a psychopathic failure of empathy that lifts them into another league altogether from the sort of simple faith that most believers exhibit. What is fundamentally under attack here is not faith

---

15 Doomsday having failed to materialize on schedule, Meade recalculated and fixed on 21 October as the date. This too, of course, came and went without incident. The publication of this book has been delayed for several years, so it could be argued that I wrote about Meade with the benefit of hindsight. I didn't – but I have left these paragraphs unaltered because they illustrate so well the difficulty of proving or disproving prophecy. In the final analysis, trust Occam's Razor!

itself but apocalyptic ideas that are 'exegetically witless and religiously worthless'.[16]

Tradition, both Jewish and Christian, divides the biblical prophets into two groups – the major Prophets and the minor Prophets, and the organization of the Bible reflects this. One important difference worth noting between the major and minor Prophets is that the books named after the former contain a degree of biographical information (that may or may not be founded in fact) while the latter are much more obscure in terms of who wrote them and when: what survives is their prophecies, and biographical detail has in most cases to be deduced from passing references to historical people and events. Clearly in these minor texts, it is the message that is of paramount importance rather than the messenger: the major Prophets were regarded as founding fathers of the Jewish nation and faith, so their deeds were as important as their words, while the later prophets all had pretty much the same message to give concerning the nation's apostasy and punishment. However, for our purposes at least, the major/minor distinction is irrelevant at best and misleading at worst. The twelve *minor* prophets of Jewish and Christian scripture include the Book of Zechariah, which is of *major* importance in understanding the truth about Messianic prophecy and is equally crucial to understanding the origins of Christian apocalypse. Its consignation to the little-read minor league perhaps explains why its explosive implications have lain unrecognized for so long. Another example is the Book of Daniel, which is not regarded by Jews as belonging with the Prophets at all yet is also a fertile source for much of what later emerges in the Book of Revelation. I shall ignore the

---

16 Not my words. They come from p.303 of the Anchor Bible Book of Daniel (see Bibliography), relating specifically to fundamentalist interpretations of Ch. 11:36-39, but equally applicable to all these daft apocalyptic scenarios.

division into major and minor for the purposes of the present book in favour of a chronological approach better suited to teasing out the development of apocalyptic ideas down the centuries. Chronology, however, is bedevilled by the fact that the period when a prophet lived and prophesied may not at all be the same period that the Book named after him was first written down, and still less is it necessarily the same period when it was finally edited or redacted.

More important, however, than any differences between all these prophets, or between the earlier ones and the later ones, is the fact that they were not the only individuals carrying out this kind of religious activity in Israel throughout the first millennium BC. We know this for the ironic reason that they themselves frequently mention other 'false' (from their perspective) prophets. Monotheistic Judaism as we know it emerged gradually over those centuries, and for most of that time vied with acceptance of the existence of other gods, all of whom had their own prophets of one kind or another. And even within the prophets of Yahweh there were many who had entirely different messages to bring from those of the prophets that we read in our Bibles today. As always, it is the victors of any struggle that get to write the history books, and their historical view is tainted by triumphant vindication and handy hindsight. The general message of the biblical prophets is that Israel has sinned, and God has or will punish the nation, but if the people turn back to God, He will redeem and restore. But since the nature of the sin seems to have been, at least in part, a predilection to worship gods other than Yahweh, this was a particularly biased interpretation of events. Other prophets naturally took a different view.

At the time of the Babylonian Exile, for example, there seem to have been prophets who foretold that the nation's sin had been so grievous that God could never forgive it, and the nation was doomed to continued destruction. And others seem to have offered a much more comforting message – that the situation called for no great act of national repentance; God would not desert His people whatever their sins, and all would be all right in the end. As things turned out, of course, by an accident of history the Jewish people were returned from Exile to their land, where they rebuilt their temple and rediscovered their national religious heritage. So, the prophets that foresaw such an outcome are those that survive in scripture. One can well imagine that for many if not most of the people, the message of hope would have been more palatable by far than the sort of gloom peddled by the biblical prophets. But there in a nutshell is the problem with prophets: if they all claim to be messengers of God but they all say different things and cannot even agree which god is the real God, how does a layman choose, and just how seriously should he take their injunctions to this or that code of conduct?

The problem, of course, was recognized from the start. We saw earlier that the obvious way to judge good prophet from bad prophet was from results. But those could be a long time coming. If how one behaves now affects whether national Exile will end or not, it is not much help to be told to wait and see. The issue struck to the very fundamentals of religious belief: elsewhere in the Old Testament we are offered this advice:

> If there arise among you a prophet, or a dreamer of dreams, and giveth thee a sign or a wonder, And the sign or the wonder come to pass, whereof he spake unto thee, saying, Let us go after other gods, which thou hast not known, and let us serve them; Thou shalt not hearken unto the words of that prophet, or that dreamer of dreams: for the Lord your God proveth you, to know whether ye love the Lord your

God with all your heart and with all your soul. Ye shall walk after the Lord your God, and fear him, and keep his commandments, and obey his voice, and ye shall serve him, and cleave unto him.[17]

This really is an extraordinary passage. It acknowledges, in effect, that there are other gods, and their prophets may even get it right. This may come as a surprise to those who cling to the idea that the Jews always regarded their God as the only true God. But this is a fallacy. For most of the Old Testament, Yahweh was a chief God, a tribal God, a pre-eminent God, but not the only God. Yahweh's prophets constantly rail against other gods and their prophets, not because they do not exist, but because they are inferior to Yahweh and because Yahweh has chosen the Jews to be 'His' people. So, even if other gods seem alluring because their prophets correctly foretell the future, they should still be rejected in favour of Yahweh. As always, it comes in the end down to faith: you make your choice of gods, not prophets, and you stick with it – whether his prophets get it right or wrong.

But what are we to make of these old biblical prophets? Fundamentalists may believe in prophecy, but the rest of us are surely entitled to look for more prosaic answers – as ever, extraordinary claims require extraordinary evidence. First, a great deal of prophecy in the Old Testament can be explained very simply by the nature of the texts themselves. All these Old Testament Books are composite texts – ancient stories and writings get combined to create new narratives by editors who cannot resist a bit of updating here and a little creative fictionalizing there. Hundreds of years can separate different sections of single texts, enabling even long-range

---

17 Deuteronomy 13:1-4.

prophecy with the benefit of 20/20 hindsight. And second, the nature of the Hebrew language itself makes it possible for editors to see prophecy where none was intended: ancient Hebrew does not have a simple future tense, so pronouncements about God generally – that he loves, condemns, punishes or saves – become prophecies that he *will* love, condemn, punish or save at some unspecified time in the future, and all the editor need do is slip in a phrase like 'in the latter days' to nail the text as prophetic. But this is not the whole story. It remains true that prophets did make prophecies and sometimes they came true: as we have seen, the prophets we read today are just the ones that have survived the judgements and vicissitudes of history; we do not have the prophecies of prophets that simply got it wrong. Who were these people and what compelled them to prophesy?

The Jewish scriptures are divided into three parts: *Torah* (teaching), *Nevi'im* (prophets) and *Ketuvim* (writings). Christian Bibles do not maintain this distinction, but the Old Testament contains all the *Nevi'im* as twenty-one Books. Six of these are what Jews call the Former Prophets (*Nevi'im Rishonim*) – Joshua, Judges, 1 and 2 Samuel, 1 and 2 Kings. The Former Prophets are really prophets in name only, designated thus to reflect their importance in Jewish myth. Certainly, they contain prophecies – about the specialness of the Jewish nation in God's eyes and, therefore, the special future that awaits them as history unfolds. But they are not Books of prophecy, they are Books of 'history' that record prophecies only as a small part of the myths they recount. They pick up the 'historical' narrative set out in the Torah and cover the conquest of Canaan, its division between the Israelite tribes and the death of Joshua (Book of Joshua); the struggle to possess Canaan, under the leadership of tribal heroes known as Judges (Book of Judges); the people's desire for a monarchical form of government, and the anointing of Saul as the first

King, succeeded by King David (Books of 1 & 2 Samuel); the possession of the land under the kings of the House of David, ending in the Babylonian conquest and subsequent Exile (1 and 2 Kings). All this is different in kind, in genre, from the rest of the prophetic Books, each of which is named after the prophet concerned, contains primarily an account of his words and actions only insofar as they are symbolic gestures to illustrate those words, and provides biographical and historical information only in passing. As a result, they are notoriously difficult to date: scholars have to pick up on the clues and hints from these passing references, and despite their best efforts, considerable uncertainty remains.

These remaining fifteen prophetic Books are for Jews the Latter Prophets (*Nevi'im Aharonim*). There is one other Book of the Old Testament containing eschatological prophecy: the Book of Daniel; Jews assign this to *Ketuvim* (writings) but it will be important to this account. And another important figure in eschatology, Enoch, appears in a few surviving documents; the Book of Enoch is excluded from the canon of most (though not quite all) Jewish and Christian denominations and groups. The prophetic Books are written in both prose and poetry, usually interwoven together; this is immediately apparent in the original Hebrew, of course, making the composite nature of the texts obvious, but the distinction unfortunately gets lost in English prose translation. When one looks at the poetry sections closely, a similar fragmentation becomes apparent, betrayed by rapid changes of subject and/or metre, and an overall incoherence. Apart from a very few exceptions, the poetry passages comprise collections of short fragments, often beginning or ending '(Thus) saith the Lord', that originally had nothing to do with one another. They may well have originated with the prophet concerned, but they have been strung together at some later date by a collector. And very often it is apparent that the collector is also a redactor who cannot resist the temptation to add bits – either attributable in some way to the original prophet or, on occasion, words of his own that he believes would be consonant with the prophet's original viewpoint. This was an entirely valid literary and religious practice at the time. As a rule, therefore, earlier passages in a text indicate earlier date of authorship and later passages are most suspect. A particular example of this is the tendency of most prophets to have happy endings: after all the doom and gloom of apocalyptic prophecy, they will suddenly turn about 180 degrees and prophesy that all will turn out right in the end. It is very doubtful that this *volte face* originates with the prophet: it is a later redactor avoiding a gloomy ending. Thus, as one eminent scholar has put it:

> We thus reach certain general conclusions, subject to slight modifications in individual instances, as to the way in which the poetical sections of the prophetic Books reached the form in which we now find them. We have the original utterances of the prophet, given in short, telling, often passionate, lyrics, remembered and written down separately. Small collections of these were made, and the collectors continued to add from time-to-time passages that came into their hands from one source or another. They were not particular as to the completeness of what they found, nor were they greatly concerned as to authorship, especially in the later stages of the process. The growth of the collections continued over a long period, perhaps over some centuries.[18]

The prose sections of the texts also betray the work of hands other than the prophet himself. Many are written in the third

---

18 *An Introduction to the Books of the Old Testament,* by W.O.E. Oesterley and T.H. Robinson (SPCK, 1934).

person so by definition are reports of the poet's words and actions by the collector – probably collections of popular stories told about the prophet, which may or may not adhere to strict historical truth. Others are written in first person – descriptions by the prophet himself of his experiences. The prophet's call from God or his visions vouchsafed by God are typical of this. In these cases, it is most likely that the prophet's original poetry has been recorded by a collector in prose.

With this general background in mind, let us now turn to a chronological account of these prophets, and trace the development of apocalyptic ideas and imagery over the centuries.

2

The First Generation of Jewish Prophets

The first prophet that has come down to us is confusingly the one that appears third in the Bible's list of the minor prophets – Amos. We need to place him in the chronology of Jewish history as it is told in the Old Testament. The stories of Moses, the Exodus from Egypt and the establishment of the Twelve Tribes in the Promised Land – are Old Testament tales well known to western Christians; readers of Volume I will know that I argue for a date of around 1190 BC for the Exodus (whatever that event was in actuality). For a couple of hundred years after that, Jewish society remained tribal. There seem to have been continual frictions and enmities between the tribes, although from early on it was recognized that there was a northern grouping centred on Samaria, known as Israel, and a southern grouping centred on Jerusalem, known as Judah. Sometime in the eleventh century, King Saul is said to have united them all together for the first time so that the first great Jewish kings that we read of in the Bible – Saul, David and Solomon – all reigned over what is known as the United Monarchy of Israel and Judah. Israel to the north comprised ten of the original twelve Jewish tribes and was both the largest and the richest; Judah to the south comprised (with Benjamin) the other two tribes. According to the Bible, under King Solomon the United Monarchy reached its pinnacle of wealth and prestige and, in particular, Jerusalem became the national capital and was developed into a major city in the region. No small part of this was the centring of all sacrificial ritual and worship in the magnificent temple that Solomon built in the capital city. But grandiloquent public works do not come cheap, then as now, and the centring on Jerusalem placed a heavy financial burden on the richer tribes of the north which, not surprisingly, greatly resented the tax imposition. Following Solomon's death in c. 930 BC, it was hoped that this situation would change, but his successor not only refused to ameliorate the economic burden, he announced his intention of intensifying the enrichment of Jerusalem and the south, with the inevitable result that tensions reached boiling point and the United Kingdom of Israel and Judah split back into two kingdoms. The Northern Kingdom of Israel existed after this as an independent state for another couple of centuries, but by the end of the eighth century it had disappeared from history. The circumstances of the downfall of Israel at the hands of the Assyrians, and the disappearance of its tribes, are the essential background to the earliest of the biblical prophets and resonate in Christian apocalyptic myth down to the present day – 3,000 years later.

Over the early centuries of the first millennium, Assyria was the ascendant power in the region, culminating in the reign of King Adad-nirari III (806–783 BC), when the Assyrians invaded the Levant and variously conquered the Arameans, Phoenicians, Philistines, Hittites and Edomites. But then, for half a century, the Assyrians were on the back foot. A series of weak kings, domestic revolt and plague meant that the Assyrians halted for a while their otherwise inexorable expansion. And this period of Assyrian stagnation in the first half of the eighth century BC broadly coincided with the reign in Israel of King Jeroboam II, who, as a result, presided over a period of unprecedented prosperity in the Northern Kingdom, built on trade in olive oil and wine, greater even than under the United Monarchy. The wealth was, of course, concentrated in the hands of the ruling classes, who lived luxurious lifestyles while the poor, as ever, suffered oppression, exploitation and poverty. However, this period of riches was threatened with the accession to the Assyrian throne of Tiglath-Pileser III, who set about foreign conquest once more. In around 732 BC, he sacked Damascus and the entire Northern Kingdom of Israel and began the resettlement of some of the inhabitants elsewhere in his empire. Then, a decade later in 722 BC, his successors, Shalmaneser V and then Sargon II completed the process: the whole country of Israel was simply wiped from the map and the population exiled and scattered. Little is known in detail about the region during the next half a millennium, but over that period the remaining Semitic population, together with immigrants from elsewhere in the Assyrian Empire, gradually evolved their own version of Judaism, with their own temple in Samaria, their own rituals associated with it, and their own religious myths and sacred sites. At some point they became known as Samaritans, and as we know from the parable of the Good Samaritan, they were despised and scorned by their southern neighbours for their bastardized religion. The Romans eventually subsumed the region into their province of Judæa. But what became of the 'Lost Ten Tribes' has exercised imaginations ever since, as we shall presently see.

 The prophet Amos seems to have flourished in the years leading up to the destruction of the Northern Kingdom of Israel in the eighth century BC. The Book of Amos, like many if not most of the prophetic Books that followed, is evidently comprised of a variety of different elements – some that predate Amos' time and some that postdate it – someone living later having brought all the elements together to make a reasonably coherent whole. The Book as we have it now, predicts the fall of Israel:

> I will cause you to go into captivity beyond Damascus, saith the Lord . . .[1]

Fundamentalists regard this as prophecy made decades before the event. Clearly if this were true, the relative dating of Amos' life, his prophesying, and the final redaction of the Book that takes his name would all be vital if we are to make judgements about the validity of this claim to prophetic insight. According to the writer of the Book, Amos lived at the time when Jeroboam II ruled Israel: 788–747 BC. And Assyria destroyed Israel in 732 and 722 BC, so on the face of it, if he did prophesy that event, either he had inside knowledge from God, or he was an inspired reader of historical trends, or he just got lucky. But which? Unfortunately, the manuscript evidence does not help. Until the twentieth century, the earliest Hebrew text we had for the Book of Amos – and indeed for the whole Old Testament – was what is known as the Masoretic Text, which was copied, edited and distributed by a group of Jews known as the Masoretes between the seventh and tenth centuries AD – a millennium or so after the texts claim to have originated. With the discovery of the Dead Sea Scrolls, most texts could be pushed back a little more, to the first century AD or thereabouts. But in the case of Amos, the surviving Scrolls include just a few fragments, and there is nothing there to indicate how or when the Book was put together.

---

[1] Amos 5:27.

There are, however, some potential clues in the text itself. For example, there is reference to what seems to be a solar eclipse:

> And it shall come to pass in that day, saith the Lord God that I will cause the sun to go down at noon, and I will darken the Earth in the clear day.[2]

Assyrian records show there was just such an eclipse in the region on 5 June 763 BC, bang in the middle of Jeroboam II's reign. Many commentators regard this as dating evidence for Amos. But note that Amos says the earthquake will happen 'in that day'. We shall return to this 'day' later, but the day in question here is explicitly referring to a future intervention by God to punish sin – a 'bitter day' of judgement.[3] This is an apocalyptic prophecy, not a passing reference to a contemporary event. And thus, it cannot be a reference to the 763 BC event because, whatever the scale of destruction then, it clearly did not herald the End Time events that Amos describes. If you want to regard this as evidence of supernatural precognition, you must also accept that Amos got everything else about the event wrong. In my view the relevance of the 763 BC eclipse is that its contemporary reality provided whoever wrote these words with an image of future apocalyptic doom. This then found its way into subsequent apocalyptic imagery and, via the description of the eclipse at Christ's crucifixion, into the Christian apocalyptic lexicon.

Another way to date Amos is his reference to 'the earthquake' in the very first verse of the Book:

---

2 Amos 8:9.

3 Amos 8:10.

> The words of Amos, who was among the shepherds of Tekoa, which he saw concerning Israel in the days of King Uzziah of Judah and in the days of King Jeroboam son of Joash of Israel, two years before the Earthquake.[4]

This earthquake was also remembered by the Jewish historian, Josephus. In his description of King Uzziah, he tells a story of how Uzziah, out of pride, usurped the role of a priest and burned incense in the temple:

> And when they cried out that he must go out of the temple, and not transgress against God, he was wroth at them, and threatened to kill them, unless they would hold their peace. In the meantime, a great earthquake shook the ground, and a rent was made in the temple, and the bright rays of the sun shone through it, and fell upon the king's face, insomuch that the leprosy seized upon him immediately . . . [5]

The same story is also told in the Bible in 2 Chronicles;[6] this version includes the leprosy but confusingly makes no mention of the earthquake. So, we do not know if Josephus was conflating Amos and 2 Chronicles, or he was working from a now lost manuscript of 2 Chronicles, or if he just invented the earthquake to make the story more dramatic. Scholars have argued for all these explanations.

The earthquake reference has received considerable attention in recent years because archaeology in the area can be interpreted to suggest that there was indeed an earthquake in the mid-eighth century, affecting the area of the Northern

---

[4] Amos 1:1.
[5] *Antiquities of the Jews*, 9:224-5.
[6] Ch. 26.

Kingdom. This is hailed as proof of the Bible's historicity.[7] In fact, a review of the archaeological literature reveals that the issue is far from cut and dried; the evidence is capable of many interpretations as to size, extent and date of the earthquake and a scientific consensus is a long way off. Indeed, there is not even scientific agreement about whether an earthquake in this region would have been a rare and significant event, as the text here would suggest, or a commonplace occurrence – tragic but hardly noteworthy. Interestingly, the reference to 'Amos' Earthquake' is picked up 300 years later by the prophet Zechariah:

> And ye shall flee to the valley of the mountains; for the valley of the mountains shall reach unto Azal: yea, ye shall flee, like as ye fled from before the Earthquake in the days of Uzziah king of Judah . . .[8]

This however can be argued in two ways. One view would be that it was such a major event, there was a memory of it even 300 years later. But the other view would be that Zechariah was simply quoting from Amos: after Amos, the idea that the Last Days would be heralded by natural upheavals like earthquakes became a commonplace of Jewish apocalypse all the way down to the Book of Revelation.

Putting earthquakes and eclipses to one side, let us take a close look at the text itself. In Chapter 1, verse 1 quoted above, the first thing to notice is that Amos was not a professional prophet, but a shepherd, and he clearly regarded this as an important element of his prophetic legitimacy: his calling was direct from God, not from membership of the prophetic

---

[7] It is of course 'proof' of nothing except the historicity of this specific reference.
[8] Zechariah 14:5.

community.⁹ In this, he established a precedent for the prophets that came after him who would make similar claims.¹⁰ Second, he came from Tekoa, which was in the Southern Kingdom of Judah. He chose to prophesy in the Northern Kingdom because that was where the wealth was: the sybaritic lifestyles of the ruling classes and the downtrodden misery of the working classes were the sins that he denounced. Third, he lived during the parallel reigns of Uzziah and Jeroboam II. Both had long reigns – the former for about 50 years and the latter about 40 years. Precise dates are difficult, but we can say with confidence that they flourished in the middle of the eighth century and Amos must have been active at that time. And fourth, it is written in the third person. It is not saying *I, Amos, did and said this or that*, it is saying that 'these are the words of Amos'. Amos is not the author of the Book of Amos – it is not an autobiography. Someone unknown to us is asserting, at some point in time also unknown to us, that Amos said and did these things. So, our interpretation of the text is hampered by the intervention of one or possibly more editors or redactors who may for all we know be liars, or writers of historical fiction, or well-meaning but ultimately ignorant recorders of hearsay or myth, or any combination of these.

Given all this, there is nothing remotely approaching proof here that Amos could see into the future. Unless we want to leap to supernatural explanations where none are needed, does it not seem more likely that Amos' 'prophecies' are based on knowledge after the fact – either of an eclipse, an earthquake or an Assyrian invasion? And yet, having said this, it is entirely within the bounds of reason that Amos did

---

9 Shepherding is a solitary occupation. The human mind, left to itself for hours on end, can perform the most extraordinary tricks.

10 Including the Apostle Paul, who relied solely on his personal visions.

indeed accurately forecast an earthquake, an eclipse and an invasion and it still would not be proof of the reality of prophecy generally, or of Amos' foresight specifically. There are two reasons for this. The first reason is a simple matter of logic. As we have seen, the Jewish culture was full of prophets of one kind or another. Some would have been prophesying death and destruction, others would have been prophesying the exact opposite. What we know for certain is that it is not the losers of a battle that get to write the history. Amos survives not because he was special; he survives because he guessed right. The second reason emerges from close attention to the text itself. Amos certainly predicts death and destruction in considerable detail; indeed, all the paraphernalia of subsequent apocalypse are present in abundance in this very first prophet – earthquake, fire, war, pestilence, plague, flood – they are all there. What he does *not* predict is the specific historical fact that Israel was destroyed by Assyrian invasion. And when Amos is explicit, as when he says:

> Jeroboam shall die by the sword, and Israel shall surely be led away captive out of their own land.[11]

he gets it plain wrong. Fundamentalists seize on the reference to Exile as miraculous prophesy but ignore the inconvenient fact that the captivity took place two decades after Jeroboam's reign and Jeroboam himself, as far as we can ascertain, died naturally in his bed after forty years of successful and prosperous rule. They tend just to dismiss this fact as if it were trivial; isn't it enough that Amos knew that the destruction of Israel was imminent without him having to spell out the precise agent of destruction? Well sorry, but no, it is not enough. I can

---

[11] Amos 7:11.

make similar prophesies about the current world situation: I predict right now that over the next decade or two that there will be death and destruction in the Middle East, involving earthquake, fire, war, pestilence, plague and flood. Does anyone doubt that I will be proved right? And would anyone ascribe supernatural powers of prophecy to me unless I was a bit more specific about places and times? The Assyrians do not even get a mention by Amos, which is not at all surprising since, as noted above, at the time Amos lived in the middle of the eighth century BC, Assyria was going through a period of weakness and no one would have predicted its resurgence a few decades later.[12]

Amos was not interested in history – past or future. His only concern was the future abrogation of history by his God; his prophecy was about the Last Days when God would bring time and history to an end. He establishes this from the beginning of 'his' Book. After the opening verse, the next section of the Book probably represents the original message of Amos.[13] He begins:

> The Lord will roar from Zion, and utter his voice from Jerusalem.

What then follows is Amos' report of God's 'roar' of condemnation. He has individual messages for each of the major Gentile nations around Israel – the Syrians, Philistines, Phoenicians, Edomites and Ammonites – cataloguing their sins and describing their divine punishment. And in each case, Amos, or more likely, the later collector of these sayings,

---

12 We know that the Arameans were a threat at that time, filling the vacuum created by the Assyrian pause – perhaps that was where Amos expected the destruction to come from?

13 Chapters 1:2–2:15.

commences his discourse with the same phrase: 'I will not turn away the punishment thereof'. The reason for this is that all the punishments described had already begun when Amos spoke. They are the results of the Assyrian ascendancy. Amos is not saying these things will happen; he is saying they have already happened. His concern is not about timings, but to emphasize that these events are to be understood as the result, not just of blind historical chance, but the out-workings of God's Will. These nations are being punished for their sins by the Jewish God, who is not just a tribal deity but the creator, sustainer and judge of all creation. And all this is just a preamble to Amos' real message:

> The lion hath roared, who will not fear? The Lord God hath spoken, who can but prophesy?[14]

The destruction of the Gentile nations is a warning to Israel that they too will suffer the same fate for the same sins: the lion will roar again. Apparently, Israelites had been smugly believing that because of their special relationship with God, they would be spared the general destruction. Indeed, they (like fundamentalists of today) seem to have been looking forward to these evidences of God's power and wrath:

> Woe unto you that desire the day of the Lord! To what end is it for you? The day of the Lord is darkness, and not light.[15]

This is the first appearance in these prophets of the phrase 'the Day of the Lord' – a phrase to be repeated endlessly down the centuries denoting the Apocalypse. Whatever it means here, it seems it was already current in Israel and/or

---

14 Amos 3:8.
15 Amos 5:18.

Judah as a description of some kind of decisive intervention by God in the affairs of man. Since the Israelites seem to have assumed that they would be exempt from God's judgement on that day – an assumption that Amos is concerned to dispel – we can probably assume that at this time, 'the Day of the Lord' meant the expectation of a time when God would finally make good on his Covenant with the Jews: to establish them as the dominant nation on Earth, a holy people acting as a national priesthood to all creation, centred on the Holy of Holies in Jerusalem.

It is the subject of this book to trace how this term evolves over the centuries into the fully developed apocalyptic scenario envisaged by Christianity. But the roots of it are right here, in the words of the very first of the prophets, at a time when both Northern and Southern Kingdoms of the Jews were still in existence – and seemingly thriving. This then is:

APOCALYPTIC TOPIC NO. 1: THE DAY OF THE LORD

The Book then describes several divine visions attributed – with what accuracy we cannot say – to Amos. These visions reinforce and illustrate the general message that Israel has been condemned to destruction for its sinfulness. There seems no suggestion here that repentance or a change of behaviour will avail Israel at all: God, it seems, has relented in the past but this time he really means it and there is no averting the inevitable. Inserted in Chapter 7 is a short piece of prose describing how Amos' message was rejected by Israel and he was sent packing back home to the Southern Kingdom of Judah, so it seems that any possibility of such reversal of doom has in any case already been ruled out by Israel itself. The Book ends, however, with a final vision of hope – not of averting doom, but of a glorious restoration afterwards:

The First Generation of Jewish Prophets

> And I will bring again the captivity of my people of Israel, and they shall build the waste cities, and inhabit them; and they shall plant vineyards, and drink the wine thereof; they shall also make gardens, and eat the fruit of them. And I will plant them upon their land, and they shall no more be pulled up out of their land which I have given them, saith the Lord thy God.[16]

This promise of return from Exile underlies the later importance of this in Christian apocalypse: from the Middle Ages onwards, many of those looking for the apocalyptic Day of the Lord would regard the return of the exiled Lost Tribes as a sign of the Last Days.

What then can we conclude about the Book of Amos? The core of it was almost certainly written, as it claims, in the reign of Jeroboam II in the mid-eighth century BC. This records the messages and visions that Amos believed he had received from God relating to the sybaritic sins of the wealthy Northern Kingdom of Israel. Amos prophesied that Israel was not immune from God's judgement; just as He had chastised the Gentile nations, so He would also chastise Israel. The precise nature of this future chastisement is never made explicit. The references to the destruction that will be wrought on the Day of the Lord seem at times to involve natural phenomena like fire, flood, earthquake and eclipse, but at other times it involves war and exile. But none of this can be tied down unequivocally to later historical or natural events. What Amos did do was establish the extraordinary idea that a Day of the Lord could be expected anytime soon. I have no doubt Amos believed himself to be living in the Last Days. Unlike us today, who benefit from centuries of historical and archaeological scholarship, he had little

---

16 Amos 9:14-15.

written, historical knowledge that would enable him to contextualize contemporary events – to see them as just relatively minor traumas in a long human history of misery and oppression, rather than major apocalypse. All around him he saw awful natural and human events and wrongly interpreted them as evidence that God was showing His hand in history. His message to Israel was not one of repentance, it was that a new era was about to begin, and whatever the final outcome for the Jews, they too would have to go through a period of wrath before the hoped-for Kingdom of God would be established on Earth. As that modern believer in historical determinism Marx would have observed, you cannot make an omelette without breaking eggs. And Christian thinking two millennia later would tie itself in knots trying to find reason to believe that believers would in some way be allowed to escape the 'bitter' aspects of the Day of the Lord and shoot straight through to the good times.

I have dwelt in some detail on the prophet Amos, partly because he provides an early stake in the ground for the idea of a coming Day of the Lord, and partly because he set the prophetic trend, and the Book of Amos provides the model for most of the prophetic Books that were to follow. Amos was the godfather of them all, setting the prophetic agenda for 1,000 years, creating a prophetic pattern of thought and introducing a prophetic vocabulary that was to be repeated time and again over that period. Not bad for a 'minor' prophet.

Three other prophets that have survived in the Bible were active at around the time of the Assyrian invasion and destruction of Israel. One of these we have met already – Hosea.[17] He has the distinction of being the first listed of the minor proph-

---

17 The name Hosea means 'salvation', or 'He saves', and it comes from the same Hebrew root as Joshua and Jesus – the clue to identifying the model for Jesus Christ in the Book of Zechariah (see Volume II).

ets, but probably came a little later than Amos. As noted earlier, his distinction was that his dreadful marriage was ordained by God as a symbolic enactment of God's own marriage with the Jewish people. Hosea, like Amos, seems to have prophesied in the Northern Kingdom of Israel. According to the Book that bears his name, God commanded him to marry a prostitute, Gomer, who then ran away and slept with another man; we are told that this is an allegory for the unfaithfulness of God's 'bride', the Jewish people, who go whoring after other gods and idols. Hosea divorced her but then, like God and at His command, forgave his wife's sins and took her back. Similarly, his three children's names made them allegories of God's final rejection of his people and the consequent fall of Israel: Jezreel – the name of a valley famous for its military bloodshed,[18] Lo-ruhamah, which means 'unpitied' or 'unloved'; and Lo-ammi, which means 'not my people'. The story, however, has the usual happy ending: Gomer and Hosea are reconciled as a symbol of God's eventual reconciliation with Israel. The idea of Israel being God's 'bride' is first developed in this way by Hosea and comes down the centuries into the Christian era as the Christian Church being the bride of Christ and Catholic nuns wearing wedding rings as a symbol of their mystical marriage to Jesus.

Hosea's focus on religious unfaithfulness as the chief sin of Israel is thus different from Amos, who focuses on sybaritic lifestyles and social exploitation. Also, unlike Amos, he tells Israel that a turning from sin and repentance *will* avert the disaster; Amos, by contrast, is ultimately deterministic in his visions of destruction. In these respects, Hosea adds to the standard prophetic lexicon some pieces that were missing from Amos. As with Amos, scholars are divided about the

---

[18] This valley will be important when we come to examine the topic of Armageddon.

authenticity and dating of the Book of Hosea. Some, unwilling to accept that God would have required Hosea to live out such a miserable marriage just to make a point, see it as entirely fictional, like the Books of Job and Jonah. But most of them regard it as containing a core of biographical information and a record of actual prophecies made by someone called Hosea, probably around the time of Assyria's first predations against Israel under Tiglath Pileser in *c.*730 BC, but before the final scattering of the Ten Tribes in *c.* 720 BC. The Book that has come down to us is the usual mix of fragments, prose and poetry, collected and redacted in later times by unknown hands. From the point of view of this book, Hosea is not well known in apocalyptic circles since, beyond the usual descriptions of doom and disaster around the corner, he makes no specific prophecies about the Day of the Lord or the End of Days. But this has not stopped fundamentalists finding such indications lurking in his text.

Right now, as I write, in the latter half of 2017, websites are proclaiming, and the tabloid press picking up on, the idea that the world will end soon because of what Hosea said or wrote in the eighth century BC:

> Therefore shall the land mourn, and every one that dwelleth therein shall languish, with the Beasts of the field, and with the fowls of Heaven; yea, the fishes of the sea also shall be taken away.[19]

This passage comes from a section of Hosea in which the prophet is describing the way God will punish Israel for its sins. There is no mention here of the Day of the Lord or any other indication that this can be interpreted as apocalyptic. Yet it is interpreted today as a prophecy of twenty-first

---

19 Hosea 4:3.

century species extinction and therefore a sure sign that the world is about to end:

> End Time Sign – MASS ANIMAL DEATHS ... During the last few years we have seen fish, birds and other animals die in huge numbers ... the Book of Hosea not only applied to the nation of Israel. It also applies to our day and contains prophecies concerning the state of the world we live in today. So is this text from Hosea fulfilled in our day? Is it a sign of the end times? Yes![20]

Where does one start with this? The prophecy was certainly not fulfilled in the eighth century BC, to which period it quite explicitly applies itself. And the web commentator clearly has no interest at all in the historical context, only in promoting any text that can remotely be used to illustrate modern developments. To argue that an ancient prophecy is being fulfilled now, nearly 3,000 years later, is beyond belief.

The next minor prophet who seems to have lived around this period is Micah: specifically, he flourished in Judah in the last few decades of the eighth century and into the early years of the seventh century BC. In this period, Sargon II and his successor, Sennacherib, continued the military expansion of the Assyrian Empire. When Israel was destroyed, the Southern Kingdom of Judah was spared the same fate but became a vassal state within the Assyrian Empire. However, when the King of Judah, Hezekiah, rebelled against Assyrian rule at the turn of the century, Sennacherib invaded Judah and lay siege to Jerusalem. The city withstood the siege and eventually Judah came to terms with Assyria and continued

---

20 From www.signs-of-end-times.com (Accessed on 30 November 2017). Assuming it still exists when you read this, it is a fun site for anyone who wants a taste of the sheer lunacy these people embrace.

as a vassal state. Micah therefore actually witnessed both the destruction of the Northern Kingdom and the near destruction of the Southern Kingdom. Unfortunately, he prophesied that Jerusalem would fall and Judah would be exiled, as had happened with Israel. Of course, we now know he was wrong. Unless, as many scholars believe, only part of the Book of Micah was written concerning eighth-century events and the references to the fall of Judah and Jerusalem and subsequent Exile were written later and relate to those events 150 years later when the aggressor was Babylon not Assyria (of which, more later). Personally, I have no idea what the truth is: the Book of Micah is so convoluted and confused, anything is possible.

Micah seems to be a southern version of Amos – more concerned with social evils like Amos, rather than religious sins like Hosea. And like Amos, he speaks *inter alia* of a time when God will intervene and both defeat the great earthly powers, and set the Jewish nation above all others:

> But in the last days it shall come to pass, that the mountain of the house of the Lord shall be established in the top of the mountains, and it shall be exalted above the hills; and people shall flow unto it. And many nations shall come, and say, Come, and let us go up to the mountain of the LORD, and to the house of the God of Jacob; and he will teach us of his ways, and we will walk in his paths: for the law shall go forth of Zion, and the word of the LORD from Jerusalem. And he shall judge among many people, and rebuke strong nations afar off; and they shall beat their swords into plowshares, and their spears into pruning hooks: nation shall not lift up a sword against nation, neither shall they learn war any more.[21]

---

[21] Micah 4:1-3.

The First Generation of Jewish Prophets

This famous and moving passage is followed by more in a similar vein, describing a future age of peace and prosperity. Here, Amos' Day of the Lord has become the Last Days, but the message is the same: this is not the Christian apocalypse, it is a description of the Jewish hope of return from Exile and the redemption of the Jewish nation. Israel has fallen and Judah is a vassal state (to Assyria and/or possibly Babylon, depending on what view you take about dates), but God's punishment for Jewish sin will eventually pass and then God will fulfil his Covenant with the Jewish people and elevate them above all other nations. Of course, these passages have provided modern believers in Christian Apocalypse with some magnificent language to describe the age that will follow Christ's second coming – but that is to misappropriate a Jewish text that has much more parochial concerns and that envisages a timescale considerably shorter than three millennia.

The return of the lost Ten Tribes of Israel and the re-establishment of a United Kingdom of Israel merge in modern apocalyptic thinking to become our second key apocalyptic topic:

APOCALYPTIC TOPIC NO. 2: THE RETURN AND EXALTATION OF THE 12 TRIBES

But modern-day searchers for Old Testament clues to the Last Days tend to focus on the next chapter of Micah:

> But thou, Bethlehem Ephratah, though thou be little among the thousands of Judah, yet out of thee shall he come forth unto me that is to be ruler in Israel; whose goings forth have been from of old, from everlasting. . . . And this man shall be the peace, when the Assyrian shall come into our land: and

when he shall tread in our palaces, then shall we raise against him seven shepherds, and eight principal men. And they shall waste the land of Assyria with the sword, and the land of Nimrod in the entrances thereof: thus shall he deliver us from the Assyrian, when he cometh into our land, and when he treadeth within our borders.[22]

Christians find their way to this obscure passage of course because of the reference to Bethlehem and the ruler that is to come from there,[23] ignoring of course that the ruler, whoever he was, was destined to 'waste the land of Assyria with the sword'; this didn't happen in the eighth century and by the first century AD, when Christians believe the Messiah came, the Assyrian Empire was a distant memory. Neither are these modern pursuers of arcane truth put off trying to identify the 'seven shepherds, and eight principal men' in modern twenty-first century politics in Palestine and Israel. In fact, they did not exist in the seventh century either – or at any other time. The phrase 'seven . . . and eight' should be translated 'seven . . . even eight'. This construction is found in other places in the Old Testament and is a figure of speech,[24] a colloquialism meaning something like 'more than enough', in this case, more than enough leadership and strength to withstand the Assyrian advance.

Finally, the first of the Latter Prophets to appear in the Bible, and almost certainly the oldest in time, is Isaiah who also probably lived in the eighth century BC. But, like most of these texts, the Book ascribed to him comprises elements

---

22 Micah 5:2-6.

23 I showed in Volume II that according to the Old Testament, the Messiah was to come variously from Bethlehem, Nazareth and Egypt – hence the convoluted Gospel nativity story of the census, the stable and the flight to Egypt.

24 Ecclesiastes 11:2 ('seven even eight'), Job 5:19 and Proverbs 6:16 ('six even seven'), and Amos 1:3 ('three even four').

written centuries apart. The core of the Book, the first thirty-nine chapters or so (about two-thirds of the Book), date to the eighth century: probably around 740–690 BC, so contemporary with Micah. This is calculated by internal references to rulers of that time. We might as well say they were written by Isaiah since we have no external knowledge of this prophet outside the Book, and, therefore, no way of knowing whether he was a historical figure or a fictional character created at that time: either way, Isaiah is as good a name as any. These chapters are interspersed with commentaries of various kinds, probably composed a century or so later. And the remaining third of the Book, Chapters 40 to 66, has a familiarity with the Babylonian Exile, a hundred years later still in the sixth century, and so can be dated to that time. Inevitably, the complex history of authorship and redaction means that scholars still hotly debate the precise details of this, but since even the latest elements are still half a millennium before the time of Christ, we can examine the eschatological themes as they relate to Christianity without worrying too much about precise issues of dating and authorship.

Eschatology is far from central to Isaiah's concerns. The main theme of the author(s) follows the traditional pattern outlined above: national sin, punishment, repentance and salvation. But an eschatological element is introduced right at the beginning in Chapter 2; verses 2–4 are in fact almost word for word the same as Micah 4:1-3 quoted above. So, who said these words – Micah or Isaiah? Perhaps one is quoting the other without the courtesy of an acknowledgement? Perhaps God likes to repeat himself? Or, most likely, the texts are, as usual, very garbled and trying to establish authorship or dates is virtually impossible. There is no indication in Micah or Isaiah of when the Last Days will arrive, but the meaning is clear: at some point in human history,

God will intervene and introduce a new dispensation of peace between nations, and a leading role for the Jewish people. The nature of this new dispensation is elaborated upon in another passage written 200 years later, right at the end of the Book:

> For, behold, I create new Heavens and a new Earth: and the former shall not be remembered, nor come into mind. But be ye glad and rejoice for ever in that which I create: for, behold, I create Jerusalem a rejoicing, and her people a joy. And I will rejoice in Jerusalem, and joy in my people: and the voice of weeping shall be no more heard in her, nor the voice of crying. There shall be no more thence an infant of days, nor an old man that hath not filled his days: for the child shall die an hundred years old; but the sinner being an hundred years old shall be accursed. And they shall build houses, and inhabit them; and they shall plant vineyards, and eat the fruit of them. They shall not build, and another inhabit; they shall not plant, and another eat: for as the days of a tree are the days of my people, and mine elect shall long enjoy the work of their hands. They shall not labour in vain, nor bring forth for trouble; for they are the seed of the blessed of the Lord, and their offspring with them. And it shall come to pass, that before they call, I will answer; and while they are yet speaking, I will hear. The wolf and the lamb shall feed together, and the lion shall eat straw like the bullock: and dust shall be the serpent's meat. They shall not hurt nor destroy in all my holy mountain, saith the Lord.[25]

At first glance, this too is a restatement of Micah's millennial vision, but it introduces another element that is new and echoes down the years until it finds its way into Christian

---

25 Isaiah 65:17-25.

theology. The passage is full of deliberate references to, and echoes of, the original creation stories in the Book of Genesis, where Adam and Eve sinned in the Garden of Eden and lost for humanity the possibility of Earthly Paradise. Isaiah here offers the belief that God will at some point relent and reverse the Fall: he will create Heaven and Earth anew, and humanity shall return to the sort of Paradise enjoyed by the first man. Both passages have become important to Christianity and, via that route, phrase after phrase above has entered the common language. This becomes our third apocalyptic topic:

APOCALYPTIC TOPIC NO. 3: THE NEW HEAVEN AND EARTH

Later prophets would address the question of exactly how long this new creation would last – presumably, like the old one, it too would come to an *end* sometime? But the more pressing question all this raises and that preoccupied the prophets of the time is not when it will *end* but when will the new age *begin*, and through whose human agency?

The issue of timing is never directly addressed in Isaiah, any more than in the other prophets of the time. The implication seems to be that it is imminent, but it is clearly not an issue that concerns the writers overmuch: it is the expression of hope in salvation that is pre-eminent. The question of agency is, however, comprehensively addressed, in two different ways. First, there are passages that are without any doubt Messianic in nature; as with Micah, they look to a future king who will be anointed by God to rule humanity in the new creation. Again, these passages are familiar to those of us raised in 'Christian' households because they have been co-opted by Christianity as descriptive of Jesus Christ:

> For unto us a child is born, unto us a son is given: and the government shall be upon his shoulder: and his name shall be called Wonderful, Counsellor, The mighty God, The everlasting Father, The Prince of Peace ... And there shall come forth a rod out of the stem of Jesse, and a Branch shall grow out of his roots: And the spirit of the Lord shall rest upon him, the spirit of wisdom and understanding, the spirit of counsel and might, the spirit of knowledge and of the fear of the Lord. And shall make him of quick understanding in the fear of the Lord: and he shall not judge after the sight of his eyes, neither reprove after the hearing of his ears: But with righteousness shall he judge the poor, and reprove with equity for the meek of the Earth: and he shall smite the Earth: with the rod of his mouth, and with the breath of his lips shall he slay the wicked. And righteousness shall be the girdle of his loins, and faithfulness the girdle of his reins. The wolf also shall dwell with the lamb, and the leopard shall lie down with the kid; and the calf and the young lion and the fatling together; and a little child shall lead them. And the cow and the bear shall feed; their young ones shall lie down together: and the lion shall eat straw like the ox. And the sucking child shall play on the hole of the asp, and the weaned child shall put his hand on the cockatrice' den. They shall not hurt nor destroy in all my holy mountain: for the Earth shall be full of the knowledge of the Lord, as the waters cover the sea.[26]

Depicted here is the Jewish and later Christian Messiah who rules over the Kingdom of God: a new Earthly creation to replace the one lost in Eden, in which disease and war shall be no more and people will live long and happy lives. It is not, however, the Kingdom of God envisaged by Christians – an eternal Heaven occupied solely by the saved and

---

26 Isaiah 9: 6; 11:1-9.

opposed to an eternal hell to which are consigned all those, Jew and Gentile alike, who do not accept the saving grace of the Lord Jesus Christ. Much of the language sounds similar, which is why it can be so easily co-opted into the Christian understanding. But it is a different vision entirely.

The same reservations apply to the other agent of God's Will identified by Isaiah – the 'suffering servant' of Isaiah 52 and 53. I discussed this fully in Volume II so shall not repeat myself here. These passages were the foundation for the fictions that are the four Gospels. They contain all the key elements of the story of Jesus and were used by the Gospel writers as a biographical framework for their narratives. Christians see them as miraculous prophecies of their Jesus Christ. Jews today, however, see them for what they are: metaphors for the Jewish nation itself and its suffering through the ages in the service of its God. Comparison with the genuinely Messianic passages above is instructive. The Messiah is depicted in these as an active agent of God, endowed by Him with the attributes necessary to rule the new Kingdom of God in justice and peace. The 'suffering servant' is an agent of nothing; like the nation of Israel for which he stands, he is a passive figure – the victim of history, consigned to undergo punishment in fulfilment of God's great plan. That plan envisages a return to Eden under a Messianic king and a redemption of Jewish suffering, but we do not know when or how. Isaiah provides all the key elements of both Jewish and Christian Messianic hope. The Jews are still waiting. Christians believe their Messiah did come in the person of Jesus, but since he seems not to have reversed the effects of the Fall, they of necessity must look to a 'second' coming when that reversal will be made manifest.

These then – Amos, Hosea, Micah and Isaiah – are the four prophets of the eighth century BC, who flourished at a time when Assyria was ascendant and both Israel and Judah, the Northern and Southern Kingdoms, were beset by the threat of invasion and Exile. They provide us with our first three apocalyptic topics: the ideas that there will be a Day of the Lord in which God will intervene decisively in human affairs; that on that day the scattered tribes of the Jews will be reunited around the holy city of Jerusalem and exalted by God above all other nations; and that these events will herald a return to Paradise for all humanity – a new Heaven and Earth in which sin and suffering would be no more. These prophecies were a response to the Assyrian threat and it seems possible that they heralded a new kind of prophecy that developed precisely because of that threat. Up to that point, prophets had been a professional class within Jewish society, earning a living from routine interpretation of God's Will. The threat of that society being completely exterminated at worst, and at best, subsumed in a greater empire with consequent loss of sovereignty, was a game changer for the Jewish world view. How could this be happening, they asked themselves? Assyria could conquer all the Gentile nations surrounding them, and Jews could understand that in terms of God's judgement on the sins of other nations. But the Jewish Kingdoms were different. God had brought them out of Egypt into the Promised Land and had established a Covenant with Moses that promised them a special place in history if they obeyed His requirements. The only explanation for their current plight had to be that they had reneged on their end of the bargain and God was punishing them for it. Amos made it clear they could not be exempt from the general punishment; Hosea showed it was like a divorce; Micah, however, promised that all would be right in the end; and Isaiah promised that the Jewish nation – the 'suffering servant' of God – would in the Last Days be raised up again and God would establish His Kingdom – a new Heaven and Edenic Earth on which mankind would live in peace and plenty.

The First Generation of Jewish Prophets

None of these prophets put their money on when exactly the Day of the Lord or the Last Days would arrive; but all their prophecies related to the Assyrian threat, and it is quite clear from that context that they expected the Last Days to take place soon by means of an overthrowing of the Assyrian Empire. But it did not transpire that way. The threat to Israel in the north became horribly real and by the end of the eighth century the nation no longer existed, and the Ten Tribes disappeared from history. Judah in the south came within an inch of the same fate, but somehow survived at the cost of its independence. For a hundred years, the Jews in the Southern Kingdom clung to their belief that God would intervene, but Assyria did not fall until the end of the seventh century and was then, in effect, replaced by Babylon, who proceeded to do to the Southern Kingdom what Assyria had done to the North. Once again, the Jewish nation faced extinction. And once again, prophets arose to deal with the crisis. They inherited the allegories, symbols, language and apocalyptic expectations of their predecessors, but they had to deal with the uncomfortable fact that history was repeating itself.[27] Had the Jews really been that neglectful of their covenant with God? Had their sins really been so great as to deserve all this a second time? And that meant that the prophets of that time had to invent some new angles on the basic apocalyptic plot to account for God's great delay in coming to their aid. Perhaps they had misunderstood His game plan all along? Perhaps there was a dimension or two of the divine purpose that they had overlooked? We shall turn now to this second generation of prophets to see what new topics they introduced to the Apocalypse meme.

---

27 In the immortal words of John McClean/Bruce Willis in *Die Hard* 2: 'How can the same shit happen to the same guy twice?'

3

The Second Generation of Jewish Prophets

The Southern Kingdom of Judah existed as an independent state for longer than its northern counterpart. But in the end, a century or so later, it too suffered a similar fate, this time at the hands of the Babylonians, who had by the sixth century become the dominant force in the region. In 597 BC, the Babylonian King Nebuchadnezzar deported thousands from Judah to Babylon, and then in 587/6, thousands more. But unlike the Northern Kingdom, Judah was not wiped off the map. Jerusalem, including Solomon's temple, was destroyed, but the Babylonian practice was to leave populations in place, removing only their ruling elites to prevent future uprising, and foster integration across the empire.[1] The Exile lasted about fifty years before Babylon in turn fell to the Persians and the Persian King Cyrus permitted the Jewish return to Judah, whereupon the Temple was rebuilt in Jerusalem and a new Jewish state grew around it. Prophets arose to forecast these events, and to forecast how they would end

---

[1] It is this Exile, not the northern one, that is famously commemorated in Psalm 137 (and in *By the Rivers of Babylon* by Boney M).

– as ever, the ones that survive are the ones whose words most closely accord with the way things turned out. But the usual interpretation of what they were about puts the cart before the horse.

The way the story is usually told is as follows:

Condemnation – despite the warnings of the prophets, the people sin against God's commandments and God condemns them to destruction. The specific sins differ from period to period and from prophet to prophet. Usually, the worship of other gods is involved to some degree, but transgression against all the Ten Commandments feature prominently.

Retaliation – God's condemnation is followed by his retaliation, either directly through famine and pestilence, or most often, through war: other nations become the instruments of God's wrath by persecuting the Jewish state in some way.

Salvation – however, even during His condemning and retaliating, God offers out hope to His people – hope that *in the end* He will relent and restore them to nationhood and prosperity. The key phrase here is the one in italics. When exactly that might happen was a moot point; rarely particularized by the prophets themselves and left open, it offered unlimited scope for eschatological speculation down the ages.

But this is, of course, to confuse cause and effect. Whatever view one takes about 'sin', and the behaviours that the Jewish God seems to have included in that category, there is no evidence at all that sinfulness in the eighth or the sixth century BC was any worse, or indeed, different at all, from all the other centuries before, during and after. Fornication, adultery, homosexuality, dishonesty, violence, greed – these have all been found in human societies from the beginning of time. What constitutes 'crime' changes from culture to culture, but human nature does not change. *It was not sinfulness that brought the crises on: sinfulness was used to explain the crises after the event.* The prophets did not see sinfulness abounding and warn people that God would punish them for it; they saw the political realities and drew not unreasonable conclusions about likely futures. Theological interpretation of events followed on after – either by the prophets themselves, or very often by their editors years later, seeking supernatural explanations for the natural workings of an indifferent historical process. And as we concluded in the previous section, those theological explanations needed to get more sophisticated in the face of the apparently indefinitely delayed third stage – where and when was salvation coming?

The first of the new generation is a disappointment in this respect; he was a prophet almost no one has heard of today – Nahum, the seventh of the minor prophets, who seems to have flourished around the time of the fall of the Assyrian Empire at the end of the seventh century BC. In only three chapters, he celebrates the fall of the empire and its capital, Nineveh. The reason Nahum is disappointing, and little read these days, is that beyond asserting that Assyria's fall is the work of God, and an underlying assumption that with Assyria gone Judah can prosper again, he has nothing to say about the future fate of the Jewish nation in general, and the End Times in particular. Depending on the view you take about these things, Nahum either wrote a prophecy of the fall of Assyria, or he wrote an epitaph to its fate; there is nothing in the text that would substantiate the former and rational common sense would suggest the latter. In any case, let us swiftly pass on.

Zephaniah, the ninth minor prophet was chronologically probably the next to live, a decade later than Nahum perhaps, but the Book attributed to him, like all the others, contains sections written over the following couple of centuries. It follows the usual pattern of condemnation, retaliation and salvation, and like Nahum, forecasts the fall and destruction of Assyria and Nineveh. Unlike Nahum, Zephaniah does contain apocalyptic passages or, to be more precise, passages that lend themselves to apocalyptic interpretation, but these add little or nothing to the apocalyptic paradigm already established, beyond an allegory of the Day of the Lord as a great sacrificial feast prepared by God – 'the day of the Lord's sacrifice' – and an assertion that:

> The great day of the Lord is near, it is near, and hasteth greatly, even the voice of the day of the Lord: the mighty man shall cry there bitterly. That day is a day of wrath, a day of trouble and distress, a day of wasteness and desolation, a day of darkness and gloominess, a day of clouds and thick darkness[2]

– echoing Amos' insistence that the 'great day' will be no picnic. In fact, he asserts that:

> the whole land shall be devoured by the fire of his jealousy: for he shall make even a speedy riddance of all them that dwell in the land.[3]

Clearly what is envisaged here is a repetition of God's previous decision to destroy all life on Earth. He had promised Noah he would not do it again 'while the Earth remains': presumably the use of fire rather than water this time and the promise (elsewhere) of a 'new' Earth neatly gets God out

---

2 Zephaniah 1:14-15.
3 Zephaniah 1:18.

of that particular contradiction. The passage also confirms explicitly what hitherto has been largely implicit: that the Day of the Lord is not far off. Zephaniah would be astounded to hear that 2,500 years later, there are those that think 'near' means millennia rather than months or even years.

Moving on, we come to the wonderfully named Habakkuk.[4] His Book has much to say of condemnation and retaliation, but he knows next to nothing of salvation. We know nothing of the man himself beyond the Book that bears his improbable name; both the name and most of the Book itself is subject to so much textual corruption that it is impossible to say with any certainty exactly when he lived or, indeed, who exactly he is condemning. The innovation he brings, however, is interesting. He is the first prophet to record himself losing patience and arguing with his deity:

> O Lord, how long shall I cry, and thou wilt not hear! Even cry out unto thee of violence, and thou wilt not save! Why dost thou shew me iniquity, and cause me to behold grievance? For spoiling and violence are before me: and there are that raise up strife and contention. Therefore the law is slacked, and judgement doth never go forth . . .[5]

None of the previous prophets did this: they seem to have been compliant mouthpieces. Habakkuk wants to know why God keeps rubbing his nose in mankind's sinfulness but does nothing about it. In other words, he wants to know when the Day of the Lord is coming when everyone gets their comeuppance. Previous prophets have been content to say

---

[4] The name occurs nowhere else and although it sounds probably Egyptian, its etymology is completely obscure.

[5] Habakkuk 1:2-4.

the great day is 'near'. Habakkuk wants to know exactly when that will be. And the answer from God is:

> I will work a work in your days which ye will not believe, though it be told you.[6]

Presumably, this refers to the Day of the Lord. Apparently, it involves 'the Chaldeans' but Habakkuk gets very confused about whether they are the goodies or the baddies. Some passages present them as God's instrument of condemnation of an unnamed tyrant, but others seem to identify them with the tyrant himself. All very confusing, and no one to my knowledge has come up with a satisfying solution. The Chaldeans were a Middle Eastern people who came to rule Babylon in the sixth century BC; the precise historical details remain less than clear but, for the purposes of this argument, I think we can identify them with Babylon and thus date Habakkuk to the period just before the Babylonian invasion – whenever the various elements of the Book itself were written down and finally redacted. The key point though is that Habakkuk provides the first evidence that the old prophetic paradigm is beginning to be questioned: just when exactly does God propose to hold up his end of the bargain? How much longer must the Jews be the 'suffering servant'? When is God going to intervene?

The next prophet can be seen trying to find an answer. The Book of Isaiah is immediately followed in Christian Bibles by that of the second of the major Prophets, Jeremiah. This is another Book that is the result of many hands over a long period of time. It purports to be the words and reported actions of the prophet Jeremiah, who prophesied the Babylonian Exile in the decades leading up to that event in 586 BC. But it is

---

6 Habakkuk 1:5.

an unstructured collage of poetry, prose narrative and biography betraying its composite nature: at the heart of it perhaps are some original words of someone called Jeremiah, who may have been actual or fictional, but whatever prophecies about the period can be discerned within its pages can be discounted as having been added after the fact. The burden of Jeremiah's message was that unless the Jews changed their sinful ways, they were doomed to destruction and Exile, hence the use of 'Jeremiah' today as a description of purveyors of modern doom. Interestingly, the Book recounts the prophecy of another Jewish prophet, also claiming divine inspiration at the time: the prophet Hananiah claimed (wrongly of course) that he had it direct from Yahweh himself that the Exile would end in two years. Jeremiah curses him and Hananiah dies a few months later.[7]

Jeremiah had his own revelation about the length of the Exile: he prophesied it would last seventy years.[8] The problem with this prophecy is that the start and end dates are left so vague that it is possible to fiddle with events miraculously to arrive at the required number of years. The prophecy was supposedly made in the first year of the reign of the Babylonian King, Nebuchadnezzar II. This was 620 BC. It says that Judah will be completely destroyed. Assuming that this refers to the destruction of the capital city, Jerusalem, this took place in 587 BC. Jeremiah then prophesies that after seventy years God would punish Babylon as he had punished the Jews and that they in their turn would be enslaved to another nation – although the Persians are not named. The Babylonian Empire fell to Persia in 539 BC, so we have an eighty-one-year period in which to fit the seventy-year prophecy. The most rational interpretation is the period between the

---

7 Ch. 28.

8 25:11 and 29:10.

fall of Jerusalem and the fall in turn of Babylon (587–539), but this gives just forty-eight years, not the required seventy years. It is this kind of problem that has fundamentalist trainspotters licking their lips. The word of God must be right, so there must be some way in which the maths can be fiddled to fit. And, of course, it can be done. For example, take the start date as the beginning of the Babylonian Empire in 609 and the end date as the fall of Babylon in 539, and lo and behold, you get the magic number seventy. Don't fancy that one? OK – take the date of the destruction of the Temple in Jerusalem (587) and the date of the rebuilt Temple's dedication to God (517) and again, miraculously, you get seventy years. Or perhaps, take Nebuchadnezzar's first invasion of Judah (605) and the foundation of the rebuilt Temple rather than its completion and dedication (536) and you get sixty-nine years. Good enough perhaps? Putting aside the question of whether this is prophecy with hindsight, the simplest 'explanation' is that the seventy figure was never meant to be exact. In Psalm 90 we are told:

The days of our years are threescore years and ten.[9]

Surely all Jeremiah was saying was that a whole generation would be born and pass away before the Exile would end.

But the Book of Jeremiah is not all doom and gloom, for like Isaiah, it offers consolation and hope for better times. We saw in Volume II that Zechariah envisaged a King-Messiah, described as a Branch. Isaiah too had spoken of a Messianic Branch of the House of David who would usher in a new Kingdom of God. Jeremiah also speaks of the Branch,[10] but describes the new dispensation, not in terms of

---

9 Verse 10.

10 23:5-6 and 33:14-15.

a new Eden – a reversal of the Fall – but in terms of a new Covenant to replace the Mosaic Covenant broken by Israel's sinfulness. Habakkuk asked when God would fulfil his side of the Covenant; Jeremiah tries to answer him. This becomes important in Christian theology, which regards Jesus Christ as having introduced this new Covenant through his sacrificial death, sweeping away the requirements of Mosaic Law and replacing them with the sole requirement of faith. However, although Jeremiah put his money where his mouth was (sort of) with the precision of the seventy years prophecy, this related solely to the return from Exile. The best he could do in terms of the new Covenant, like Isaiah before him, was to say that 'the day(s) cometh'. At one point, however, he does refer to 'the latter days' (presumably preceding the new Covenant) and he makes a specific prediction – the destruction of the city of Elam. This passage gets fundamentalists hot under the collar because Elam was situated at the northern end of the Persian Gulf in the modern state of Iran, and (depending on when you read this) its current collapse into civil war is regarded by them as indicating that we are indeed living in the Last Days. This we shall call:

APOCALYPTIC TOPIC NO 4: THE FALL OF ELAM

The third and final major Prophet after Isaiah and Jeremiah was Ezekiel, and he too was active during the period of the Jewish Exile in Babylon but did not begin to prophesy until a few years into the Exile itself. The Book is more coherent than its predecessors, but it shows clear signs of being the work of multiple hands writing at different times. It follows the by now familiar pattern of God's condemnation, then retaliation, and finally, salvation. It is, however, different from the previous two major Prophets in that Ezekiel does not just get *messages* from God, he is vouchsafed some remarkably vivid *visions* of God himself, riding his war chariot. These visions have inspired not just fundamentalists, but also believers in extra-terrestrial visitors: Erich von Daniken famously interpreted the chariot drawn by angels as a description of a spacecraft and many have developed the idea. Just for once, one must side with fundamentalists: this was no spacecraft; Ezekiel was just another in a long line of deluded individuals who mistake hallucination for reality. In the vision, God calls Ezekiel, like Isaiah and Jeremiah, to prophesy and those prophecies, while echoing his predecessors in theme, are different again in that they too are informed by a visual sense largely missing from the others. This may be the reason why Ezekiel is a major influence on the Book of Revelation, also written by a prophet who was subject to vivid hallucination. References to Ezekiel are entirely absent, however, in the rest of the New Testament, which points to an important issue. As we shall see in a later chapter, Revelation is not a Christian text at all. It was written by Jews, not Christians, awaiting the advent of the Jewish Messiah, as prophesied in this and the other Old Testament prophets.

The concept of salvation in Ezekiel is given a striking visual metaphor of dry bones coming to life – well known to Christians through the Black Spiritual song. However, the form of that salvation is strikingly un-Christian. We saw that Isaiah's new Eden and Jeremiah's new Covenant both translate into the Christian concept of Christ's new Kingdom. Twin Jewish concepts are transformed into a vision for a new world – for the whole of humanity. But Ezekiel's version does not lend itself so easily to such universalism. He sees the new dispensation as a New Jerusalem, a peculiarly Jewish vision. And this is no passing reference; the city is described in immense detail over the last eight chapters of the Book. Again, holding considerable appeal for John the Baptist and the Jewish Messianic movement he founded, but harder to fit into the new, Gentile Christian concept. Revelation also sees the New Jerusalem in its own vision of the new Heaven and Earth:

> And I saw a new Heaven and a new Earth: for the first Heaven and the first Earth were passed away; and there was no more sea. And I John saw the holy city, new Jerusalem, coming down from God out of Heaven, prepared as a bride adorned for her husband.[11]

Hosea saw the relationship between God and his chosen people, the Jews, as like a marriage contract; the contract might be broken through infidelity and even divorce, but in the end it would be renewed. Ezekiel builds on this; he sees Jerusalem as God's bride – whether in a new marriage ceremony or as a more modern 'renewal of vows' it is hard to say.

As ever, no indication is given as to when this new dispensation will begin, so it is of little help to fundamentalists. But elsewhere in Ezekiel we find a strange reference that not only finds its way into Revelation, but through that route into the long list of eschatological events and characters that are so cherished by them. This is the description of Gog and Magog in Chapters 38 to 39.[12] This immediately precedes the description of the New Jerusalem, so seems to be a prophecy that can be measured against historical events in the search for clues to the End Time. The prophecy relating to Gog *of* Magog, outlined in Ezekiel, tells how after the return from Exile, in the 'latter days', Gog and his armies will attack the restored Israel but God will ensure their destruction, after

---

11 Revelation 21.

12 In British mythology, Gog and Magog are giants and hills near Cambridge, but this has no bearing at all on the biblical names.

which He will establish His new Temple and new dispensation. This is, therefore:

APOCALYPTIC TOPIC NO. 5: GOG AND MAGOG

So, all three of the major prophets lived and prophesied during the period of the Babylonian Exile, and there are six more of the minor prophets who flourished in this second generation – clearly the great age of Jewish prophecy. The first of these is Obadiah who almost certainly lived at the same time as Jeremiah. The Book attributed to him is the shortest in the Old Testament – just one chapter of twenty-one verses. In it, Obadiah tells of his encounter with God, whose condemnation this time is of the people of Edom. This small area between the Red Sea and the Mediterranean, now straddles modern Israel and Jordan. According to Jewish tradition, while the Jewish people were descended from Jacob, the Edomites, and via them the Arabs, were descended from his brother Esau.[13] But although they were a Semitic people too, they were looked down upon by their Jewish neighbours and had for many years been a vassal state of Judah. When Babylon sacked Jerusalem in 586 BC and sent its upper classes into Exile, the worm turned, and Edom sided with Babylon. Now, God tells Obadiah that on the Day of the Lord, he will destroy Edom in retaliation for its familial betrayal of Judah:

> For the day of the Lord is near upon all the heathen: as thou hast done, it shall be done unto thee: thy reward shall return upon thine own head. For as ye have drunk upon my holy mountain, so shall all the heathen drink continually, yea, they

---

13 See Volume I: *Ancestral Tales*.

shall drink, and they shall swallow down, and they shall be as though they had not been. But upon mount Zion shall be deliverance, and there shall be holiness; and the house of Jacob shall possess their possessions. And the house of Jacob shall be a fire, and the house of Joseph a flame, and the house of Esau for stubble, and they shall kindle in them, and devour them; and there shall not be any remaining of the house of Esau; for the Lord hath spoken it.[14]

In historical fact, this particular Day of the Lord never materialized. The Edomites survived and were one of the surrounding peoples that gradually migrated into Judah during the Jewish Exile. In Roman times, the area was known as Idumea, still reflecting the old name, and a certain Idumaean called Herod (of Christian Nativity fame) ruled the whole of Judæa for decades. Obadiah could not have got it more wrong. But of course, two and a half millennia later, this is another obscure passage that gets fundamentalists in a lather. Because of course, the state of Israel does indeed exist again and, equating Edom with one or other of the modern Arab states surrounding Israel, they regard this as another prophecy of a future Day of the Lord when Israel will emerge triumphant over its Arab enemies. For these dangerous lunatics, every step towards nuclear war in the Middle East is welcomed as a sign of fulfilled prophecy. We shall, of course, return to all this craziness in Part Three.

The prophets that come after Obadiah lived in the period when the Babylonian Exile was over. Judah was conquered and Jerusalem sacked, and the original Temple destroyed in a succession of conflicts over a period of twenty-five years or so, from 605–581 BC. Babylon itself then fell to the Persian King Cyrus the Great in 539 BC, after which exiled Judæans

---

[14] Obadiah 15-18.

The Second Generation of Jewish Prophets

were permitted to return to Judah, but again, the return took place in more than one phase, so all attempts then and now precisely to date the period of 'the Exile' can only be approximate, and almost any prophecy about it can be massaged to fit somehow. The dates of the rebuilding of the Temple in Jerusalem suffer similar problems. The first returners seem to have begun the work a couple of years after the fall of Babylon around 537 BC, but little progress was made (blamed by the Bible on those villains the Samaritans) for another couple of decades. The first surviving prophet of this exilic period is Haggai, and he, along with his contemporary Zechariah, is remembered for having been instrumental in re-energizing the project. His Book is mostly concerned with his pronouncements from God about the importance of rebuilding the Temple, including the usual divine threats of poverty, famine and drought if His Will was not obeyed. In fact, of course God got His way, and the temple was rebuilt in the lifetimes of Haggai and Zechariah.

For Haggai, the issue was not just about a building: it was about the restoration of Jewish culture itself after half a century or more of Exile. He tells us about the two key people in this enterprise. The first is Zerubbabel, who was the grandson of the last king of Judah and the Persian-appointed Governor of the region. Haggai foresees with approval Zerubbabel becoming the first King of the newly restored country, picking up the royal line of King David again. The second key individual is by now familiar, of course – Joshua/Jesus, the son of Yehozedek, the first High Priest in the new temple and the subject of Messianic fallacy.[15] There is little if anything apocalyptic in the Book of Haggai, which is very short – only two chapters long. But the Book of Zechariah, which parallels

---

15 See Volume II: *Mistaken Messiahs*.

Haggai, both in terms of date and in its descriptions of Zerubbabel and Joshua/Jesus, is different: it is 14 chapters long and contains the longest and most important apocalyptic passages in the entire Old Testament. Indeed, in the whole Bible, excepting only the Book of Revelation in the New Testament, which is more heavily influenced by Zechariah than any other Book. Zechariah single-handedly adds no less than four new elements to the apocalyptic mythology:

APOCALYPTIC TOPIC NO. 6: THE FOUR HORSEMEN OF THE APOCALYPSE

Zechariah has two visions of four horsemen from the four corners of the Earth.[16] These, of course, re-occur in Revelation as the Four Horsemen of the Apocalypse, although here in Zechariah they do not bring death and suffering, but simply patrol the Earth for God.

APOCALYPTIC TOPIC NO. 7: THE TWO MEN OF OIL

Zechariah sees a seven-branched golden candlestick fed with oil from two olive trees on either side,[17] and is told that the olive trees 'are the two anointed ones, that stand by the Lord of the whole Earth'.[18] These are clearly the King- and Priest-Messiahs, which we identified in Volume II. Puzzlingly, when they emerge in the Book of Revelation, they seem to have been downgraded to two witnesses who preach repentance to the world in the last days before the final apocalypse.

---

16 1:8-10; 6:1-9.
17 4:2-3.
18 4:14.

The Second Generation of Jewish Prophets

APOCALYPTIC TOPIC NO. 8: THE GREAT TRIBULATION

Zechariah describes a period of great suffering before the final resolution of the Last Days. This emerges in Revelation and elsewhere as a period of worldwide hardships, disasters, famine, war, pain, and suffering known as the Great Tribulation. It is followed by:

APOCALYPTIC TOPIC NO. 9: THE BATTLE OF ARMAGEDDON

Zechariah then envisages a great battle in which the nations of the world will unite against Jerusalem in the Last Days; this emerges in Revelation as what we now call Armageddon.[19]

Anyone who doubts that key New Testament passages, both about the Messiah and about the Last Days, are just imaginative re-workings of the Old Testament in a new Christian paradigm should read the Book of Zechariah. Any translation will do for the purpose. Zechariah takes the prophetic tradition about Messiah and Apocalypse, and through vivid visions, elaborates and extends these ideas in a way that enabled the writers of the New Testament to concoct their fictions with no effort at all. And for those that still doubt me, perhaps the most ironic fiction of all is the earliest doubter of all: Doubting Thomas. In the Gospels, the resurrected Jesus challenges the disciple Thomas to put his fingers in the wounds of His hand. Graphically moving as this may be, Zechariah said it first:

---

19 Chs.12, 13 and 14 describe the time of tribulation and the final battle.

And one shall say unto him, What are these wounds in thine hands? Then he shall answer, Those with which I was wounded in the house of my friends.[20]

Prophecy or fiction?

The next Prophet was Malachi, who seems to have flourished in the period after the new Temple had been built and opened for business in the early fifth century. He is called Malachi but the name means 'My or God's Messenger' so may simply have been the prophetic designation of an unknown prophet. The Book attributed to him, the last of the minor prophetic Books, comes immediately before the New Testament in Christian Bibles. The reason for this is that no other Old Testament Book is quoted as often in the New Testament, and particularly in the Gospels, as this one. Most of the quotations relate to the Messiah so the Book handily acts as a bridge between the two Testaments, despite there being half a millennium between them. There is, however, little if anything of specifically apocalyptic interest here. The same is true of the Book of Jonah (which relates the story of the eponymous hero and the whale)[21] which although appearing fifth in the order of minor Prophets, was probably written after the Babylonian Exile and contains no prophecies at all: it is a fictional tale with a religious purpose and moral, about a reluctant prophet. All of which just leaves Joel. I deal with him here because no one knows when this Book was written; different scholars have argued for every period from the eighth to the fourth centuries BC, and after much thought I must confess, I cannot tell. But in a sense, it hardly matters. Joel is the perfect exemplar of the Old Testament prophets and that is why he could have written at

---

20 13:6.
21 Or big fish.

The Second Generation of Jewish Prophets

almost any time. He talks of God's condemnation of the Jews for their sins; he threatens God's retaliation through plague (of locusts) and drought; and he promises God's final salvation. And all is described in the context of the Day of the Lord' the final crushing of God's (Israel's? Judah's?) enemies, and the exaltation of Jerusalem. And so, we end as we started. Over a period of eight centuries, two invading empires and two exiles, the core of the message remains unchanged. But the detail evolves and matures. By the end of the Old Testament, we know that there will be a final Day of the Lord; it will be preceded by tribulation (war, plague, famine, etc.) but end in the triumph of God at a decisive battle with His enemies, the return of the Jewish tribes to their Promised Land, the vindication and exaltation of the Jewish people and, at last, a return to Eden, in a new Covenant with God, and a renewed Heaven and Earth. But what we still do not know is *when*!

4

The Later Jewish Prophets

The 'golden age' of Jewish prophecy thus began with the eighth-century prophets, flourishing in the period immediately preceding the fall of the Northern Kingdom, and coming to an end with the return from the Babylonian Exile at the end of the sixth century BC. The period of half a millennium that now follows is the period between the Old and the New Testaments: 500 years in which only a couple of new Books are added to the Jewish biblical canon and, crucially, no new prophets arose – or at least, none that have survived in the Bible. This 'New Temple' period as it is known is not without incident – quite the reverse – but the biblical canon silently passes over it and modern (Protestant) Christians are barely aware of the existence of this hiatus in the scriptural record. Over these centuries, Judaism as we know it today gradually emerged out of the competing religious ideas of previous centuries. In a sense the prophets had won their battle. The Jews now settled on their distinctive monotheism, expressed through sacrifice and ritual at the New Temple in Jerusalem. There were several streams of thought within the emerging consensus about normative Judaism – Pharisees, Sadducees, Essenes all emerged in this period – while in the lands about them in the Middle East, Diaspora Jews,

The Later Jewish Prophets

Samaritans and others developed hybrid Judaisms, divorced from the mainstream in Jerusalem, sometimes even establishing their own temples – in Samaria and in Egypt for example. Christianity was one of these, that arose in Galilee in the first century AD and quickly spread to the wider Roman Empire. In the second and third centuries, following the utter destruction of the Jewish state by the Romans, Christianity survived as a Gentile religion with little understanding of its Jewish roots, and Judaism itself became formalized into the religion we know today by the Jewish Rabbis of the time. Both religions were forced to define themselves in ways that could co-exist with Roman authority. Christianity did this most successfully by becoming adopted eventually as the official religion of the Roman Empire; Judaism survived by the Jewish Diaspora closing ranks, discouraging outsiders and surviving as minority racial belief, dispersed among the nations of the world and suffering endless persecutions that have only tended to strengthen them.

From the defeat of Babylon by the Persian Empire at the end of the sixth century BC onwards, power in the region began to shift from the great eastern empires like Assyria and Babylon, towards the newer western civilizations – Greece and then Rome. Throughout this period, Judah retained its nationhood, but always as part of a wider empire. The result was that, even as the Jewish nation evolved the distinctive Jewish religion as we have come to know it, at the same time many Jews emigrated into the wider Hellenistic world and immigrants into Judah brought Hellenistic influences into the Jewish state itself. By the third century BC, Judah was part of the Hellenistic Seleucid Empire, which sought actively to integrate the region into wider Hellenistic society; a move welcomed by some Jews but resisted by others. In 167 BC, Antiochus IV Epiphanes, the Seleucid king, introduced a programme of destruction of the Jewish religion and legal system, culminating in desecration of the Holy of Holies itself in Jerusalem. Eventually this provoked outright rebellion, led by the Maccabee family, which led ultimately to the re-establishment of an independent Jewish state. This major crisis provoked a reawakening of the prophetic spirit and renewed apocalyptic expectation, but with no prophets around, how did this manifest itself?

The Jews had come to believe that the great age of the prophets was over. There would be no more prophets until a final Last Prophet would arise and he would herald the Last Days. But many Jews were not content to accept this – to wait in patience for the Last Prophet without knowing when or how he would arise. God no longer spoke through prophets, but surely He would not leave His people with no guidance for 500 years. He must have chosen another means of revealing Himself to His people. They looked for their answer in existing scripture. But so much of it was simply old history, ancient tales and prophecies about times and events long gone. How could these texts – revered as scripture though they were – speak in a meaningful way to more modern generations? And thus arose the concepts of *Midrash* and *Pesher* – techniques for studying scripture that became increasingly evident and popular as the last years of the millennium approached. The belief underlying these techniques was that God had effectively smuggled hidden meanings and guidance into these scriptural texts for future generations. He had not gone silent: He had just changed the way He communicated. When He had spoken through the prophets of old, He had been speaking for all time, but finding these enduring messages was not available to all. God expected His people to be diligent in searching Him out. The messages were in effect a hidden code, waiting for the spiritually enlightened to discover and reveal to people generally. And so, the role that had previously been undertaken by Prophets was now undertaken by great spiritual leaders and rabbis, who immersed themselves in scripture, and interpreted it.

As one might expect, this development went hand in glove with an increase in mystical belief. The parallel here is with the ancient mystery religions of the Greek and Roman worlds; full understanding of God's arcane truths was only available to those prepared to make the sacrifices of initiation and commitment to what were, in effect, ancient cults. Truth was revealed in deeper and deeper layers – in scripture as in mystery cult rituals. And just as the prophets of old had to contend with false prophets who also claimed to be directly inspired by one God or another, so the practitioners of *Midrash* and *Pesher* had to vie with others who found their own mystical explanations in the texts. So, none of the old problems about which prophecies to believe went away; the battleground just shifted from oracular prophecy to scriptural interpretation. The absence of any central authority to pronounce on authenticity inevitably meant that, as the centuries passed, the interpretations grew wilder and wilder and more and more diverse. New spiritual leaders would arise all the time, and often disappear just as quickly. Each would offer new interpretations and gather adherents around them. When we read in the Bible or in the Jewish historian Josephus of this magician, or that sorcerer, of this troublemaker, or that rebel leader, we are reading the inevitable outcome of uncontrolled scriptural interpretation with a mystical bent. History would repeat itself in this way when, following the Reformation – when the availability of scripture to the masses in vernacular languages occurred for the first time – mystical cults and sects arose out of extraordinary interpretations of isolated scriptural passages, until the new Protestant authorities established themselves and cracked down on dissent, as the Papacy had done before them.

In the New Temple period, these interpreters of scripture produced their own literature, describing their ideas. But since they would not claim to be prophets themselves, they had to find ways of giving their pronouncements authority. And a popular way to do this was to ascribe their words to ancient prophetic sources: to people who lived in prophetic times. Some of this literature survived and has been known about for centuries, but the discovery of the Dead Sea Scrolls has added more texts to the collection and aided scholars in dating and interpretation. Maximum credibility in the scriptural stakes was held by the earliest Books of the Bible, the Torah, so many of these new writings were attributed to characters from those ancient Books: Adam and Eve; Noah's great-grandfather, Enoch; the twelve sons of Jacob; Abraham; Moses; and Solomon. *Midrash* on the Prophets was popular, both in itself and woven into narratives purporting to have ancient holy authorship. And a whole seam of mystical ideas, deriving from stories in Genesis about angels and giants, reveals itself for the first time.

The first Book of Enoch is perhaps the most prominent and influential of all these. Enoch was picked because, uniquely among the figures described in the Book of Genesis, he appears not to have died, but to have been taken up into Heaven alive at the end of his life. The Book was originally five separate texts, the earliest dating to Maccabean times, but some of it at least was known to the writer of the New Testament Epistle of Jude, who quotes it by name, and its popularity continued well into the early period of the Christian Church. As we shall see, its ideas about angels and fallen angels make their way into the Book of Revelation, and its concept of the Son of Man, a divine Messianic figure who has existed from before Creation, emerges notably in the Gospel of St John. But neither the Book of Enoch, nor any of these other texts, made it into the main canons of Judaic or

Christian scripture. The reasons for this are as various as the texts themselves, and not fully explained by scholars, but given the reluctance to accept the Book of Revelation into the Christian canon, it seems likely that similar misgivings were felt about the mystical eschatology of these writings. So, while they are nowadays a fertile field for scholarly endeavour, particularly in trying to tease out all the various strands of Judaism and early Christianity, and their relationships with each other, their non-canonical status rules them outside the scope of this book.

The same can be said of the apocalyptic texts of the sect probably responsible for the Dead Sea Scrolls. Many of the scrolls are manuscripts of the Old Testament Books and *Midrash* and *Pesher* upon them. But some of the texts originate with the sect itself and describe its organization and beliefs. The sect was founded by their Teacher of Righteousness, probably in the Maccabean period, but all attempts to identify him are inconclusive. What we do know is that the sect he formed was warlike in its attitude and its writings look forward to the End of Days, when twin Messiahs would herald a great war between Good and Evil, and God would finally establish His kingdom. I argued in Volume II that the best way to regard all these Jewish sects that arose in the last few centuries BC is to distinguish between the active and the passive. The Dead Sea Sect was one of the former – organizing itself as an army of God, prepared to usher in the End of Days by acts of aggression. Passive sects, like the Essenes, believed that their task was to await God's intervention in His own time, maintaining themselves in righteousness and purity meanwhile. Another sect arising at this time seems to have called themselves the Hasideans, or 'pious ones' (not to be confused with the Hasidic Jews of modern times, although the names come from the same root). These were active: they allied themselves with the

Maccabees and fought alongside them to expel the forces of Antiochus. They too produced a literature of their own, notably a collection of tales about a character called Daniel who received God's grace and favour because he accepted foreign rule and, indeed, lived and worked in the courts of Gentile emperors, but demonstrated through his life a devotion and loyalty to the Jewish God, and a refusal to compromise religious belief despite his political acquiescence.

The Book of Daniel was originally regarded as belonging with the rest of the Prophets in the Jewish scriptures but it is interesting that after the two Jewish Wars with Rome in the first and second centuries AD, the Jewish rabbis, seeking to redefine their religion in the aftermath, downgraded the Book of Daniel from Prophets to just other Writings. As we shall see, Daniel is a central Jewish text in the emergence of Christianity, and it seems probable that the two facts are related. The events in this collection of texts ascribed to Daniel are set at the time of the Babylonian Exile and most, not all, found their way into the Old Testament canon (the latest to do so) as the Book of Daniel. In fact, Daniel was probably a fictional character; no one has identified anyone in history with that name at that time, although fundamentalists regard the Book of Daniel as inerrant scriptural authority for his historical existence. The Book that bears his name is composed from several individual stories about him and there are other surviving stories about Daniel that did not find their way into Jewish and Protestant Bibles but are included in Catholic scripture. He seems by the second century BC to have been regarded as an ancient prophet, famous for wisdom and integrity, and that is the period when the Book of Daniel was put together from these ancient tales. The first six chapters of the Book relate in third person the stories that will be well known to many readers from childhood scripture classes: 'Daniel in the Fiery Furnace' (Chapter

3) and 'Daniel in the Lion's Den' (Chapter 6) being the obvious examples. These are all set explicitly in the time of the Babylonian Exile: Daniel is depicted sequentially in the Babylonian, Median and Persian Courts. Chapters 7 to 12 are quite different; they relate in the first person a series of apocalyptic visions vouchsafed to Daniel and interpreted for him by divine messengers. It is these apocalyptic visions that make Daniel such a happy hunting ground for symbolic interpretation. They had a huge influence on the later Book of Revelation and together these two Books are the twin pillars of most apocalyptic speculation today.

The first of these visions describes four 'Beasts' rising from the sea.[1] The first three – lion, bear and leopard – are recognizable, but the fourth is a mythical monster that prefigures similar monsters in Revelation. This fourfold symbolism parallels an earlier vision, described in Chapter Two, where Nebuchadnezzar, King of Babylon, has a dream of a giant statue made from four different metals. In this earlier case, it is Daniel who interprets the symbols, so it is strange that he has difficulty reaching a similar interpretation of his own vision without divine help. In any case, the meaning of the two sets of symbols is quite explicit in the text: the four Metals/Beasts represent four great successive empires of the ancient world. But which ones? The solution to this hangs on the identity of the fourth and last Beast/Monster, which is clearly different in nature to the previous three. It has ten horns, which we are told represent ten kings. A further small horn arises and uproots the previous three horns – representing an eleventh king who lays low three previous kings. This last king will blaspheme, persecute the 'pious ones' and devastate Jewish religion for two and a half years before God destroys him and ushers in His Kingdom.

---

1 Ch. 7.

The second vision describes a ram with two horns, one longer than the other, that is butting towards the north, the south and the west – so presumably comes from the east.[2] Then a he-goat with one large horn comes from the west and savagely attacks the first ram, knocking off its two horns, and trampling it down. The he-goat grows in size but at the height of its power, its big horn breaks off and four new ones grow in its place – facing to all four points of the compass. Then, from out of one of these, grows yet another small horn, growing in power towards the south and east. The description of this small horn is the same as the small horn of the previous vision – it too is characterized by blasphemy, defilement and persecution. In this vision, the two and a half years of persecution becomes 2,300 days, equivalent to six plus years, before God intervenes and establishes His Kingdom. Another innovation in this version is that 'the Prince of the Host' is mentioned as being subject to the small horn's predations.

The third vision (Chapter 9) occurs because Daniel is contemplating Jeremiah's earlier prediction that the devastation of Jerusalem under the Babylonians will last for seventy years. The angel Gabriel tells him that seventy *weeks* have been decreed by God as the time between the return from Exile in Babylon and the Kingdom of God. The first seven weeks cover the period between the return and the coming of an 'anointed leader' – a Messiah. The new Jerusalem will last a further sixty-two weeks, but in distress. And then, in the final, seventieth week, another 'anointed one' will be cut down and a 'prince' will wreak 'appalling abomination' on the city, until God intervenes.

The fourth vision is by far the longest and most detailed and takes up the final Chapters (10–12) of the Book. In the

---

[2] Ch. 8.

third year of King Cyrus of Persia, Daniel is met by a guardian angel who promises to foretell what is to happen in the 'last days'. Then, over the space of forty-eight verses, he relates the future history of the world in obscure detail. This involves successions of kings, including two key figures – the King of the North and the King of the South – who battle each other endlessly. It becomes clear from the language used, that the King of the North is the same abominable persecutor of the Jews who appears in the three previous visions, and he is prophesied to suffer the same fate when God finally intervenes. The vision ends with some more forecasts of time periods that sound exact but prove hard to pin down.

These four visions of Daniel are packed with apocalyptic themes, all of which recur in Revelation and have fascinated interpreters down the years. We shall simply group them together at this stage as:

APOCALYPTIC TOPIC NO. 10: THE APOCALYPSE OF DANIEL

We shall leave detailed elucidation to Part Three, but a few words of explanation will be helpful here. For fundamentalists, these four visions are very exciting and references in them to 'anointed ones' and 'princes' are interpreted by them in a Christian context. As a result, these passages from Daniel, combined with New Testament references to End Time characters, such as the Antichrist and the Beast from the Sea, can be made to yield up the most extraordinary prophecies concerning modern times. But for anyone with even a nodding acquaintance with Jewish history, the identity of the two small horns, the abominable prince and the King of the North is obvious, unequivocal and certain: they all refer to Antiochus IV Epiphanes who tried to enforce the Hellenization of the Jewish people. Jewish texts from the second century onwards abound with references to 'the Abomination of Desolation', when Antiochus IV Epiphanes sought to eradicate the Jewish religion and, in doing so, desecrated the Holy of Holies in the Temple. As described in Volume II, it is the essential background to the stories of Jesus cleansing the temple in the Gospels; it provoked the Maccabean uprising; and alongside the Babylonian Exile, it is the most traumatic event in Jewish history. No wonder so much of Daniel was written at the time of Antiochus but is set in the time of the Exile, and constantly measures the periods of history between these two climactic events. All the apocalyptic speculation about these prophecies is misguided and plain wrong. Whether supernatural prophecy, or stories told after the event, these visions relate to events that occurred millennia ago, not to geopolitical upheavals in the twenty-first or any other subsequent century. We shall call this concept:

APOCALYPTIC TOPIC NO. 11: THE ABOMINATION OF DESOLATION

And we shall, of course, tease out all the detail in Part Three of this book.

For many scholars, the story of Jewish prophecy and apocalypse ends here, with Daniel; the last Book to be written and to be accepted into the Old Testament canon. But I take the view, along with some recent scholars, that the Book of Revelation, the last Book in the *New* Testament, is also largely a work of *Jewish* prophecy. Revelation has been controversial for two millennia and remains so right up to the present day. The problem lies not with the manuscript evidence: we have well over 230 Greek manuscripts surviving, including quotations and fragments from the second and third centuries and complete versions from the fourth century onwards. The issue is its theology. It just does not read like a Christian document. Its focus is on God's punishment of sin and retribution to a fallen world, rather than the saving grace of Jesus Christ. From that perspective, it reads more like a Jewish apocalyptic text than a Christian one. Although it was regarded in the second century as emanating from the hand of the Apostle John, this was already in doubt by the end of the third century and it was, in fact, the very last Book to be admitted to the New Testament canon (in AD 419). Doubts then subsided during the centuries of church dominance of biblical interpretation, but the leaders of the Reformation, examining scripture for themselves, raised all the old doubts again. Luther regarded it as extremely suspect, and it is the only New Testament Book on which Calvin did not write one of his monumental commentaries. It is, of course, a favourite source document for fundamentalist and apocalyptic sects of the present day, but there remain still some branches of Christianity that regard it with suspicion.

The Book of Revelation claims to be the work of an unspecified 'John' who has visions while on the Greek island of Patmos. The author has traditionally been identified as the disciple John, who is also supposed to have written the Gospel of John and the Epistles of John, all in the New Testament. Yet nowhere in Revelation does the author claim to be that or any other Apostle and I have, of course, argued in Volume II that the disciple John is a fiction that substitutes in the Gospels for John the Baptist. However, I would not claim that the Baptist wrote the Gospel or the Epistles of John and neither would any reputable scholar. Indeed, they were certainly written long after his death. They do not, in fact make any authorship claims within their texts and the attribution to the disciple came much later. They are written in Greek, as is the Book of Revelation, but whereas the Greek of the former is correct – educated and even elegant – the Greek of Revelation is the opposite: scholars are agreed that the author of Revelation must be another John entirely. And since most scholars date the Book to either the seventies or nineties AD, or both, they rule out the disciple and the Baptist and simply refer to the author as 'John of Patmos'[3] which does not get us very far.

In her Yale University 'Anchor' Edition of the Book of Revelation, Professor J. Massyngberde Ford argues persuasively that Chapters 4–11 were written by John the Baptist *before* the Christian era, or at the very least are a record of his ideas if not his actual words; Chapters 12–22 date to the mid-sixties AD and emanate from the Baptist's Movement; and the rest of the book, notably Chapters 1–3 and the last chapter, are unmistakeably Christian additions. Although many, perhaps most, scholars would not go quite so far, there does seem to be a consensus that the Book as we now have it emanates from two or three different writers, and that its theology is as much Jewish as Christian.[4] Ford shows how key Christian terms such as 'Jesus Christ' and 'Lord' only appear in chapters other than 4–11 and that, on the other hand, those chapters read like Books of Jewish prophecy, rather than Christian theology.

---

[3] Because it was supposedly written there – see below.

[4] Ford was a Roman Catholic and Professor of New Testament Studies at the University of Notre Dame in Indiana. I argue in this book that when Professor Ford's ideas are viewed in the context of my new paradigm, the arguments for the Baptist's authorship become almost irresistible. And as a result, we are given a unique insight into the way in which Jewish Apocalypse transformed in the hands of early Christians to a most un-Jewish set of beliefs about someone called 'Jesus Christ'.

Parts of Revelation undoubtedly *are* Christian in origin, but those parts are restricted to the first few chapters and some verses at the end, none of which have any apocalyptic content and are accepted by most scholars as later additions.[5] The rest of the Book simply does not concern itself with Christian themes. It shows no knowledge of, or interest in, the earthly life of Jesus, and even its apocalyptic themes omit those concepts that, as we shall later see, typify Christian apocalypse. It is pure Jewish apocalypse as we have come to understand it over the course of my book so far. It is primarily concerned with a Jewish future: the redemption of the Jewish people and of Jerusalem. Chapters Four to Eleven form what I shall term, 'the First Apocalypse'. Following Ford, I too attribute this apocalypse to John the Baptist. It contains nothing at all that can be called Christian as we currently understand the term; in fact, there is not a single reference in it to Jesus or Jesus Christ. Chapters Twelve to Twenty-One form what I shall term 'the Second Apocalypse'. This contains six references to Jesus or Christ but as Ford argues, correctly in my view, these are clearly later additions. They are superfluous to the narration and removing the words does not alter or impair the sense at all. The word 'Christ' *does* appear in the second Apocalypse, but it is always as '*the* Christ' or '*His* Christ'; the significance of this is that the meaning here is the original Jewish one of 'anointed', rather than the Jesus figure of the Gospels.[6] There are many references to 'Lord', but most of these clearly relate to God or are, again, later Christian additions. For convenience, I shall

---

[5] Although, as we shall see, are nonetheless helpful in pinning down apocalyptic elements in the rest of Revelation.

[6] The references are 20:4, 20:6, 11:15 and 12:10. Translation does matter here. The KJV omits the definite article and possessive pronoun because the translators believed these were Christian references – but they are present in the original Greek.

call the writer of the First Apocalypse 'John A'; of the Second Apocalypse, 'John B'; and of the Christian passages at the beginning and end of the Book, 'John C'.

Messianic references in Revelation centre around the symbol of the Lamb. As already discussed, this symbol goes back to the early prophets, notably Isaiah, and represents the Jewish people as a whole, suffering like the sacrificial lamb, as they await God's intervention and salvation. The Lamb references in the First Apocalypse in Revelation can all be interpreted in that way. But the references in the Second Apocalypse, written decades later, do show a development from this. The Lamb now seems to represent the embodiment of the Jewish people in their anointed Messiah figure. But this is emphatically not the Jesus Christ of the Gospels; that association is a Christian one and entirely absent here. The Lamb of Revelation, when not simply a symbol of the Jewish people, is their apocalyptic representative, who will appear on the Day of the Lord to win victory over Satan and establish God's Kingdom. His victory over sin is simply an overthrow of evil, not a symbol of personal salvation, which is alien to Jewish religious thought and entirely alien to the Book of Revelation. The Lamb opens the seven seals and as is later made clear, represents 'The Lion of the tribe of Juda, the Root of David'.[7] He is therefore the King Messiah – not the Priest Messiah in Heaven awaiting the Day of the Lord, but a human Messiah who will arise at the end of time and lead the Jews into their final destiny.

The content of Revelation is unremittingly apocalyptic. Almost every verse echoes images, symbols, characters and events from the great Jewish prophetic Books, both canonical and outside the accepted canon. The first section of the Book, which quite clearly stands out from the rest, is the first

---

7 5:5.

three chapters. Here, the author introduces himself (as John) and describes how while on the island of Patmos,[8] he was 'in the Spirit on the Lord's Day' and was vouchsafed a series of visions. However, the visions in this section are not apocalyptic in the present sense of the word; they are of letters that John is instructed to write to 'the seven communities in Asia'. These communities are clearly 'churches' of some kind in that they comprise early Christians of some sort, who believe in Jesus Christ and his atonement for sin. The letters concern themselves with admonition and encouragement and seem to reflect some of the concerns and debates that were the subject of the Council of Jerusalem, although since these allusions are imprecise, there is no scholarly consensus about much of this. Ford has also suggested that at least some of the verses that end the Book in Chapter 22 also belong with this section in the sense that they were written to bracket the intervening text when the Book was written down sometime late in the first century. The intervening text dates from earlier; the question is, how much earlier?

---

8 There is some evidence that Patmos was used by the Roman authorities as a prison island for political prisoners.

5

The Book of Revelation: First Apocalypse

Ford has proposed that Chapters 4–11 emanate from John the Baptist himself. Let us examine it in that light. The text begins with a voice 'as it were of a trumpet', calling the Baptist to make a spiritual journey to Heaven where he will be shown 'things which must be hereafter'.[1] This is classic Jewish apocalypse; the Baptist is following in the footsteps of Ezekiel, Daniel and Enoch, who all made similar celestial journeys. The real action though begins in Chapter 5. On the right hand of God is a scroll 'written within and on the backside, sealed with seven seals'.[2] The Baptist looks towards the throne of God and sees 'a Lamb as it had been slain'; it is this Lamb that is to open the seals; those celestial beings around the throne chant:

> Thou art worthy to take the book, and to open the seals thereof: for thou wast slain, and hast redeemed us to God by thy blood out of every kindred, and tongue, and people, and nation;[3]

---

1 4:1.

2 5:1.

3 5:9.

Because we read this in the context of two millennia of Christian belief, we naturally interpret this passage as a reference to Jesus Christ and his atoning blood. But this is not what is going on here. The word translated 'slain' here does not refer to sacrifice. It *can* have that meaning, but it is *never* used in that sense in the New Testament. Its normal meaning is 'violent death' in battle or some other physical strife. Just as the suffering servant of Isaiah 53, imaged there as a slain, sacrificial lamb, was a symbol of the sufferings of the Jewish nation, so too is the symbolic Lamb in this passage. This is made clear by the next lines:

> And hast made us unto our God kings and priests: and we shall reign on the Earth.[4]

By patiently suffering the vicissitudes that God allows them to suffer, the Jewish nation is empowered to exercise its role as a priestly nation for the whole of humanity. This text, written by a Jew some decades before the birth of Christianity, is not some miraculous prophecy of a sacrificed son of God, but a symbolic vision of the Jewish people who, after all their suffering, are now able to release the scroll that will finally bring the 'curse' of God raining down on a sinful world as He brings the old world to an end. This is the Great Tribulation – Apocalyptic Topic No. 8.

Then in Chapter 6, the Lamb starts to open the seals of the scroll, releasing its 'curse'. The first four seals release the famous 'four horsemen of the apocalypse' to the Earth. We have already met them in Zechariah – Apocalyptic Topic No. 6. After the four horsemen of the first four seals, the fifth seal rather strangely does not release a 'curse', but when opened reveals:

---

[4] 5:10.

under the altar the souls of them that were slain for the word of God, and for the testimony which they held.[5]

Note the use of 'slain' again, referring not to a crucified saviour, nor to martyred Christian saints (because this is a pre-Christian document) but to the suffering Jewish nation. They call out for God to bring about the End of Days but are told to wait a little longer until the events of the End Times have played out. The opening of the sixth seal commences those end time events.[6] There is a great earthquake, the sun is darkened, the moon becomes like blood, the stars fall to Earth, and Heaven is wrenched apart 'as a scroll when it is rolled together'.[7] Again, all familiar themes from the Jewish prophets, going right back to the earthquake and eclipse in Amos. As a result, everybody seeks refuge from the day of wrath, except for those who are to be saved from the scroll's curse. Then the twelve Jewish tribes receive the seal of God to protect them – 12,000 from each of the twelve tribes. A symbolic number you might think? Not so for some fundamentalists who believe this to be a precise number, as we shall see in Part Three.

The seventh seal is then opened,[8] but instead of ending things, it merely heralds another round of tribulation. We are told that after half an hour's silence there are to be seven angels blowing seven trumpets. The first four rain even more devastation down on the Earth:

1. Hail and fire mingled with blood is hurled to Earth, destroying all vegetation.

---

[5] 6.9.
[6] 6:12.
[7] 6:14.
[8] 8:1.

2. A great mountain (presumably a volcano) spews fire into the sea, killing one third of all marine life.
3. A great star falls burning from Heaven, poisoning all fresh water with wormwood.
4 All the lights of the sky are diminished by a third.

Again, all paralleled in the Old Testament prophetic Books. As if to emphasize that even all this is not enough slaughter, an eagle cries out 'Woe' to humanity for the last three trumpets will bring destruction to everyone. These three 'woes' are described in the glorious, satanic detail that inspired Hieronymus Bosch:

1. Stinging locusts swarm out of hell with a mandate to torture mankind beyond endurance for five months.
2. A hellish cavalry of 'a myriad of myriads', breathing smoke and sulphur, now set about killing one third of all mankind.

Like the 144,000 souls to be saved these too are regarded by fundamentalists as specific End Time prophecies. At this point the reader, if he is not lost already among all the sevens, fours and threes, is beginning to wonder what possible new variation on the theme will be unveiled by the seventh trumpet as the third and final woe.[9] And then, the text does some very strange things.

The sixth trumpet/second 'woe' concludes Chapter 9. However, where we might have expected the seventh, final trumpet or third 'woe', we are now, in Chapter 10, given another vision entirely. This is heralded by 'another mighty angel'[10] who holds 'a little book open'.[11] He announces that:

---

9 9:21.

10 10:1.

11 10:2.

in the days of the voice of the seventh angel, when he shall begin to sound, the mystery of God should be finished, as he hath declared to his servants the prophets.[12]

But this is not followed by the blowing of the trumpet as we might expect. Instead, the Baptist is instructed to eat the scroll, which tastes sweet in the mouth but bitter in the stomach. He is then told:

> Thou must prophesy again before many peoples, and nations, and tongues, and kings.[13]

Note that unlike the Jewish prophets of old, whose job was to pass God's pronouncements to His people, the Jews, the Baptist's commission is universal – Gentiles as well as Jews, kings as well as their nations. He is then, in Chapter 11, told to take a 'a reed like unto a rod' and to 'measure the temple of God, and the altar, and them that worship therein.'[14] The intent of measurement seems to be to protect the holy city from its enemies. And still the final trumpet remains silent. Instead, we are now told about God's 'two witnesses ... clothed in sackcloth' who will be allowed to prophesy for 'a thousand two hundred and threescore days'[15], i.e. three and a half years. Clearly, these are the Two Men of Oil from Zechariah (Topic No. 7), but they have been reduced from messiahs to witnesses: we shall see why in Part Three.

Following this is yet another earthquake killing another 7,000 people and then we are told:

---

12 10:7.

13 10:11.

14 11:1.

15 11:3.

> The second woe is past; *and*, behold, the third woe cometh quickly.[16]

Then – at last – the seventh trumpet finally sounds and loud voices in Heaven proclaim that the kingdom of the world is now replaced by the kingdom of God and his anointed:[17]

> And the temple of God was opened in Heaven, and there was seen in his temple the ark of his testament: and there were lightnings, and voices, and thunderings, and an Earthquake, and great hail.[18]

And with that final, almost perfunctory list of 'curses', the Baptist's text ends. This then is the First Apocalypse of John A:

APOCALYPTIC TOPIC NO. 12: THE ORIGINAL APOCALYPSE OF JOHN THE BAPTIST

This First Apocalypse seems rooted in Jewish apocalypse, and nothing in it comes as any surprise, except for the strange delay in the 'third woe', which seems to suggest something in the text as we have it has become corrupted or disordered in some way, and the intervening downgrading of the twin messiahs of Zechariah to the twin witnesses. In Part Three I shall show that the text here has indeed become confused; that the third woe did originally follow straight on from the second, and the two witnesses are then restored in status to the twin messiahs of Jewish expectation.

---

16 11:14.

17 11:15.

18 11.19.

6

The Book of Revelation: Second Apocalypse

Most of the characters and events we now associate with Christian apocalypse have their roots in what follows in Chapters 12–22, which are usually taken as being a sequence of events following on from the previous Chapters 4–11, but if Ford and I are right, then of course this second section is another text entirely, by other hands at other times, and tagged on to the former section by a later redactor. And in this case, it represents a coherent apocalyptic account in its own right – a Second Apocalypse. Revelation has rightly been reviled down the centuries for its never-ending, gruesome catalogue of tribulations, but at least part of the explanation for this is that we have two separate accounts here of the same prophesied events. Interpretation of this Second Apocalypse depends crucially on who wrote it and when. Ford argues convincingly that we are still dealing with Jewish apocalypse here rather than something overtly 'Christian' as we would understand it today. She and others would allow that it may be 'Jewish Christian' – that is, deriving from the earliest Christian community, comprising mainly Jews, and still immersed in Jewish apocalyptic concepts. In

The Book of Revelation: Second Apocalypse

my view, this can only be resolved by the chronological issue: the earlier the text, the more likely it will be to be Jewish in origin. I have shown in Volume II how all the key events of Christianity took place at least a decade earlier than previously thought and that all the key players, including the Apostle Paul, were dead or missing in action in some way by the end of the fourth decade AD. I shall argue in Part Three of the present book, that this is also true of this part of Revelation. It is usually ascribed to the seventies, eighties or nineties AD. But all the previous apocalyptic texts were written at times of trauma for the Jewish nation: the destruction of the Northern Kingdom; the Babylonian Exile; the Maccabees Rebellion. Is it not likely that this final Jewish apocalypse should follow suit? If it were written in the seventies or eighties, it would postdate the major trauma of the first century: the Jewish uprising against Rome in the sixties; and that is where we shall eventually locate the author of the Book, John B, and the events and characters he describes more convincingly and precisely than any other dating or interpretation.[1]

Two caveats about methodology need to be made before we plunge into this text. First is a question of translation. I am using the King James Version of the Bible for reasons alluded to earlier. I recognize that for those unused to it, this can be off-putting. However, some of the most extreme fundamentalists regard this version as actually inspired by God and the only one, therefore, that can be relied upon. And since these are the very people for whom apocalyptic texts are to be taken as infallible prophecies of future events, it seems safest to use a text that they have no quarrel with. However, there are points in my argument where choice of

---

[1] Professor Ford also dates it to this period although her identifications with contemporary people and events differ from mine.

translation becomes critical to meaning; on these occasions, I shall be explicit about the issues and, at a few points, offer my own translations that I believe shed new light on old problems of meaning. The second caveat is about interpretation. The text that we shall now deal with is the most heavily scrutinized by fundamentalists for their beliefs. Almost every verse can be, and is, interpreted differently by different sects and individuals. To avoid the danger of prejudging any of those issues at this stage, I shall attempt in the section that follows to relate the text narrative relatively naively and literally – taking what is said in the King James Version simply at face value. To take an example: the section concerning the Millennium has been interpreted from earliest times both literally and symbolically;[2] at this stage I shall simply relate the literal sense of the passages concerned and deal with questions of interpretation in Part Three.

The text begins in Chapter 12 with a 'great wonder' – a vision of a mother and her child. Described in that way, one immediately thinks of the Madonna and Baby Jesus of Christian myth, and that indeed is how many (but not all) fundamentalists interpret this passage. But the interpretation does not fit. The mother is in Heaven and her child 'was caught up unto God, and to his throne':[3] no mention of an earthly Mary, or a crucified Christ. There is much more in this chapter that needs elucidation: a dragon attacks the mother and child, and this event gets mixed up with an account of an angelic war in Heaven, but we shall leave untangling this puzzling text until Part Three:

---

[2] To avoid confusion, I shall henceforward use Millennium (capital 'M') to denote the Christian concept of the 1,000-year period of Earthly paradise; I shall use millennium (lower case 'm') in its everyday sense of 1,000 years.

[3] 12:5.

The Book of Revelation: Second Apocalypse

APOCALYPTIC TOPIC NO. 13: THE MOTHER AND CHILD AND DRAGON

Chapter 13 is not a continuation of this but seems to represent yet another new start and certainly another seemingly unrelated vision, this time of a pair of Beasts. Obviously influenced by the Beasts with horns in Daniel, these two Beasts really start to get to the heart of later Christian apocalypse. The first Beast rises from the sea:

> . . . having seven heads and ten horns, and upon his horns ten crowns, and upon his heads the name of blasphemy . . . and the dragon gave him his power, and his seat, and great authority. And I saw one of his heads as it were wounded to death; and his deadly wound was healed: and all the world wondered after the Beast. And they worshipped the dragon which gave power unto the Beast: and they worshipped the Beast, saying, Who is like unto the Beast? who is able to make war with him? And there was given unto him a mouth speaking great things and blasphemies; and power was given unto him to continue forty and two months. And he opened his mouth in blasphemy against God, to blaspheme his name, and his tabernacle, and them that dwell in Heaven. And it was given unto him to make war with the saints, and to overcome them: and power was given him over all kindreds, and tongues, and nations.[4]

There is much symbolism here needing explication: the identity of the Beast itself, the seven heads, the ten horns, and the wounded head that is healed. This text therefore becomes:

---

4 13:1-7.

APOCALYPTIC TOPIC NO. 14: THE BEAST FROM THE SEA

The second Beast comes from the land:

> ... and he had two horns like a lamb, and he spake as a dragon. And he exerciseth all the power of the first Beast before him, and causeth the Earth and them which dwell therein to worship the first Beast, whose deadly wound was healed. And he doeth great wonders, so that he maketh fire come down from Heaven on the Earth in the sight of men, And deceiveth them that dwell on the Earth by the means of those miracles which he had power to do in the sight of the Beast; saying to them that dwell on the Earth, that they should make an image to the Beast, which had the wound by a sword, and did live. And he had power to give life unto the image of the Beast, that the image of the Beast should both speak, and cause that as many as would not worship the image of the Beast should be killed. And he causeth all, both small and great, rich and poor, free and bond, to receive a mark in their right hand, or in their foreheads: And that no man might buy or sell, save he that had the mark, or the name of the Beast, or the number of his name. Here is wisdom. Let him that hath understanding count the number of the Beast: for it is the number of a man; and his number is Six hundred threescore and six.[5]

There is even more to unravel here: the identity of the Beast itself and its relationship to the first Beast, the two horns, the miracle-working including the power to bring an idol to life, the Beast's 'mark', and the mystical '666'. It may surprise some readers that there are two Beasts – the second has become so overwhelmingly familiar in popular culture and

---

5 13:11-18.

imagination. And of course, fundamentalists have felled innumerable forests (and nowadays, consumed countless megabytes) in fanciful explication of these mysteries. Even rational scholars have failed to nail unanimously agreed answers to these conundrums. I believe I can settle the matter in a new way by applying the New Paradigm[6] in Part Three, under the headings:

APOCALYPTIC TOPIC NO. 15: THE BEAST FROM THE LAND

APOCALYPTIC TOPIC NO. 16: 666

Chapter 14 then describes how before the Tribulation that is to come, the righteous will be 'redeemed'. The number 144,000 (12 x 12,000) appears again as the number of the 'first fruits' of those redeemed in Heaven. Then angels preach the Gospel to the rest of mankind; announce that 'Babylon' has fallen; pronounce damnation for followers of the Beast from The Land:

> If any man worship the Beast and his image, and receive his mark in his forehead, or in his hand. The same shall drink of the wine of the wrath of God . . .[7]

and finally, announce the 'harvest' of souls. Chapter 15 then begins with another new vision – of the 'seven last plagues', carried by seven angels in 'seven golden vials' or bowls. These bowls are poured out in turn in Chapter 17:

---

6 See Volume II.

7 14:9.

1. First Bowl: A 'foul and malignant sore' afflicts the followers of the Beast. (16:1–2)
2. Second Bowl: The sea turns to blood and everything within it dies. (16:3)
3. Third Bowl: All fresh water turns to blood. (16:4–7)
4. Fourth Bowl: The sun scorches the Earth with intense heat and even burns some people with fire. (16:8–9)
5. Fifth Bowl: There is total darkness and great pain in the Beast's kingdom. (16:10–11)
6. Sixth Bowl: The River Euphrates is dried up and preparations are made for the kings of the East and the final battle at Armageddon between the forces of good and evil. (16:12–16)
7. Seventh Bowl: A great earthquake and heavy hailstorm: 'every island fled away and the mountains were not found.' (16:17–21)

These seven bowls of the Great Tribulation do not precisely match the seven seals or the seven trumpets in the earlier text, but it is a mistake to interpret them as following on from the previous two in a never-ending torment. The number seven has mystical qualities (e.g. God created the world in seven days = 1 week) and the seven plagues of Egypt form the obvious model for these seven tribulations: this is an alternate account of the *same* symbolic series of seven tribulations.

In the aftermath of the Great Tribulation comes another vision of a Beast with seven heads and ten horns; so identical with the first Beast above that comes from the sea. In this vision, we learn that the Beast from the Sea 'was, and is not, and yet is' – a satanic pun on Yahweh's 'I am that I am' and a clue to its identity. We are also told the mystical meaning of the seven heads and the ten horns of the Beast:

> And here is the mind which hath wisdom. The seven heads are seven mountains, on which the woman sitteth. And there are seven kings: five are fallen, and one is, and the other is not yet come; and when he cometh, he must continue a short space. And the Beast that was, and is not, even he is the eighth, and is of the seven, and goeth into perdition. And the ten horns which thou sawest are ten kings, which have received no kingdom as yet; but receive power as kings one hour with the Beast.[8]

This has had scholars and fundamentalists alike puzzled for centuries, so becomes:

APOCALYPTIC TOPIC NO. 17: THE SEVEN, EIGHT AND TEN KINGS

The Beast from the Sea in this vision has a rider:

> I will shew unto thee the judgment of the great whore that sitteth upon many waters: With whom the kings of the Earth have committed fornication, and the inhabitants of the Earth have been made drunk with the wine of her fornication. So he carried me away in the spirit into the wilderness: and I saw a woman sit upon a scarlet coloured Beast, full of names of blasphemy, having seven heads and ten horns. And the woman was arrayed in purple and scarlet colour, and decked with gold and precious stones and pearls, having a golden cup in her hand full of abominations and filthiness of her fornication: And upon her forehead was a name written, Mystery, Babylon The Great, The Mother Of Harlots And Abominations Of The Earth.[9]

---

8 17:9-12.

9 17:1-5.

We are told that she is 'that great city, which reigneth over the kings of the Earth'. She is:

APOCALYPTIC TOPIC NO. 18: THE GREAT HARLOT

Following the judgement and destruction of the Harlot, the Messiah makes his appearance, riding a white horse and leading the armies of Heaven, also on white horses. Ranged against him in war is 'the Beast, and the kings of the Earth and their armies'. This is Armageddon and the Messiah is triumphant, casting the Beast and his followers into 'a lake of fire burning with brimstone'. The Beast in question here is the Beast from the Land because he is accompanied by those who have received his 'Mark'.

The passage that then follows has been (and is) the source of more controversy and dissension among fundamentalists than all the other apocalyptic topics put together:

> And I saw an angel come down from Heaven, having the key of the bottomless pit and a great chain in his hand. And he laid hold on the dragon, that old serpent, which is the Devil, and Satan, and bound him a thousand years, And cast him into the bottomless pit, and shut him up, and set a seal upon him, that he should deceive the nations no more, till the thousand years should be fulfilled: and after that he must be loosed a little season. And I saw thrones, and they sat upon them, and judgment was given unto them: and I saw the souls of them that were beheaded for the witness of Jesus, and for the word of God, and which had not worshipped the Beast, neither his image, neither had received his mark upon their foreheads, or in their hands; and they lived and reigned with Christ a thousand years. But the rest of the dead lived not again until the thousand years were finished. This is the

The Book of Revelation: Second Apocalypse

first resurrection. Blessed and holy is he that hath part in the first resurrection: on such the second death hath no power, but they shall be priests of God and of Christ, and shall reign with him a thousand years. And when the thousand years are expired, Satan shall be loosed out of his prison, And shall go out to deceive the nations which are in the four quarters of the Earth, Gog, and Magog, to gather them together to battle: the number of whom is as the sand of the sea. And they went up on the breadth of the Earth, and compassed the camp of the saints about, and the beloved city: and fire came down from God out of Heaven, and devoured them. And the devil that deceived them was cast into the lake of fire and brimstone, where the Beast and the false prophet are, and shall be tormented day and night for ever and ever. And I saw a great white throne, and him that sat on it, from whose face the Earth and the Heaven fled away; and there was found no place for them. And I saw the dead, small and great, stand before God; and the books were opened: and another book was opened, which is the book of life: and the dead were judged out of those things which were written in the books, according to their works. And the sea gave up the dead which were in it; and death and hell delivered up the dead which were in them: and they were judged every man according to their works. And death and hell were cast into the lake of fire. This is the second death. And whosoever was not found written in the book of life was cast into the lake of fire.[10]

There is clearly a great deal to unpack here. The key elements of this passage are:

– Satan is bound and thrown in 'the bottomless pit' for a 'thousand years';

---

[10] Revelation 20.

- Christ the Messiah reigns in Jerusalem for that period;
- Martyrs for the faith will be resurrected to reign with Christ;
- This is a limited 'first' resurrection;
- After the thousand years, Satan will be set free again for a short period;
- Satan will gather his forces ('Gog and Magog: Topic No. 5) for a final battle;
- They will surround the martyrs in the 'beloved city' (presumably Jerusalem?);
- Satan's horde are utterly destroyed by fire from Heaven;
- The rest of the dead are resurrected in the 'second' resurrection;
- The final judgement takes place;
- Those not saved are cast into the 'lake of fire';
- The old Heaven and Earth are swept away and replaced with a new creation (Topic No. 3);
- This will include a new holy city of Jerusalem, symbolized as 'a bride adorned for her husband'; and
- Pain and death are abolished.

These are the elements, unpacked in simple terms as they appear in the text, but I have tried to omit any reference to the timings, the order and the interpretation of these events. We shall trace all these in Part Three. The most significant element is:

APOCALYPTIC TOPIC NO. 19: THE MILLENNIUM

And so ends the Second Apocalypse of Revelation, written by John B: reasonably consistent with the standard Jewish apocalypse that we have traced over the preceding 2,000 years, but introducing some important new elements of detail. The various symbols regarding beasts and horns are by now familiar territory from the Jewish prophets: whatever else they are, they have 'crowns', authority and power, so presumably they represent kings, emperors or other influential people who will arise in history as the Day of the Lord approaches. The text then describes the Great Tribulation, Armageddon, the Final Judgement and the New Heaven and Earth – all aspects of the Day of the Lord as we have come to understand it. Christianity took over this apocalyptic model in its entirety, reinterpreted some of its symbols and added some new elements of its own that we shall discover in the next chapter. The difficulty Christianity had in appropriating Jewish apocalypse was that the Messiah had already come, and he was not a conquering Jewish hero, but a man of peace; according to the Gospels, he was not interested in apocalyptic themes about the future of Jerusalem and the Jews, he was solely interested in bringing personal salvation. It is a miracle that the Book of Revelation made it into the Bible, and it has been an embarrassment to Christians ever since. But Christianity, like Judaism and every other religion in the world, had to confront the issue of whether this sinful world would continue for ever or be transformed eventually into something better, and with its roots so deep in Judaism, it somehow had to integrate the Jewish answers to those eternal questions within a Christian framework. In Part Three, we shall trace how this was done.

7

Other New Testament Apocalypses

So far, we have discovered that most of the elements that we have come to associate with Christian apocalypse are in fact Jewish – they were all in place centuries before the Christian era. They reach their apotheosis in the Book of Revelation which, although it is placed in the New Testament so that it can end the Bible with its revelation of the future, is in fact a Jewish text with a few additions and augmentations to make it fit in a Christian context. I have argued that Professor Ford was absolutely right to ascribe the core of Revelation – the two apocalyptic sections – to John the Baptist (John A) and his later followers (John B), in the first century AD. I have also shown in Volume II how the original ideas of John the Baptist and Judas the Galilean provide the ultimate roots of Christianity, but that it was already splitting in different directions in the first half of the first century AD. Paul was the real founder of Christianity as we know it today: he took the original Jewish beliefs and, in effect, removed their apocalyptic elements. The military Messiah of Jewish apocalypse became an agent of personal salvation, and although he and his followers lived in expectation of an imminent 'coming' of their Saviour, they were less interested in the details of events leading to that, and more in getting themselves personally and individually ready. This then led to a wide range of Gnostic sects, who took Paul's concept of freedom from Jewish Law to extreme lengths; Gnostics were less concerned with future judgement and more with getting in touch with the spark of inner divinity today. If all this is right, and I believe it is, then we would expect the earliest Christian texts — that is, texts originating either with Paul himself or his followers — to show little concern with Jewish apocalypse. And that is precisely what we do find, which may come as a surprise to many fundamentalists, for whom the expectation of an imminent Day of the Lord seems to have become the dominant element of their faith.

The earliest unquestionably 'Christian' texts that we have are the Epistles of the Apostle Paul, written in the generation after the supposed life of Jesus. However, not all of these are genuine; many were written decades later and falsely ascribed to Paul. The problem is that there are so few clues within the texts to authorship and dating, unless you are a fundamentalist and naively believe that everything in the Bible is exactly what it claims to be, it is hard to be certain of anything. In this respect, we are no better off trying to trace the development of early Christian apocalypse than we were in dealing with the old Jewish prophets. Nevertheless, as we saw in Volume II, it is probably safe to say that with very few reputable exceptions there is nearly universal consensus in modern New Testament scholarship on a core group of authentic Pauline Epistles whose authorship is rarely contested: Romans, 1 and 2 Corinthians, Galatians, Philippians, 1 Thessalonians, and Philemon. Yet the only ones to contain anything that can be called apocalyptic are the two Epistles to the Corinthians and the first Epistle to the Thessalonians. And although these do contain passages of apocalypse, they are short, few and far between, and contain absolutely nothing of the vicious retribution and punishment of Jewish apocalypse. When one reads these texts, the first thing that strikes one is how little apparent interest Paul has in apocalypse. I showed in Volume II how Paul also had little or no interest in the earthly life of Jesus; his faith was based on visions of a Messiah called Jesus who was in Heaven. His interest is in individual personal salvation made possible by faith in that Jesus figure. However, that salvation was urgent because Paul did certainly believe that Jesus, as Messiah, was imminently to inaugurate the Day of the Lord. But for Paul, that Day was less about Armageddon and a new Jerusalem and all about the fulfilment of individual relationship with Jesus. Apocalypse is about retribution, judgement and condemnation; Paul is about reconciliation, forgiveness and love; no wonder then that in his Epistles, Jewish apocalyptic themes are few and far between.

According to the Book of Acts, Paul personally founded the Christian Church at Corinth and his letters to it deal with doctrinal and behavioural issues that have arisen there since his departure. The first Epistle is a hefty sixteen chapters long, dealing with a wide range of issues, from immorality and sexual purity to marriage and Christian worship. The apocalyptic text is towards the end and represents less than 2 percent of the whole;[1] powerful evidence of how little importance Paul placed on eschatological detail. It appears that some in the Church were questioning the doctrine of resurrection of the dead. Paul states that at the coming of Christ, 'they that are Christ's' shall be resurrected, after which will come 'the end' when Christ will 'subdue' all things. And that is it. No other detail and no mention of timing. It is quite evident that Paul is not setting out some

---

[1] 1 Corinthians 15:20-28.

Christian apocalypse, he is simply re-affirming the belief in the face of Corinthian scepticism that when Christ comes, the dead will be revived. The same is true of the only apocalyptic passage in 2 Corinthians[2] – just a few verses out of 13 chapters, concerned with the nature of the resurrection and nothing else. Turning to 1 Thessalonians, the apocalyptic passage is only four verses long, but it does add a wholly new concept; the context is the same as Corinthians – the 'comfort' of the assurance of the resurrection of the dead – but the order of events is particularized:

> For this we say unto you by the word of the Lord, that we which are alive and remain unto the coming of the Lord shall not prevent them which are asleep. For the Lord himself shall descend from Heaven with a shout, with the voice of the archangel, and with the trump of God: and the dead in Christ shall rise first: Then we which are alive and remain shall be caught up together with them in the clouds, to meet the Lord in the air: and so shall we ever be with the Lord. Wherefore comfort one another with these words.[3]

This concept we shall call (following Christian custom):

APOCALYPTIC TOPIC NO. 20: THE RAPTURE

Christians have great fun trying to shoehorn this concept into the standard Jewish apocalypse, the problem being that it describes the 'how' of the resurrection, but the 'when' in the chronology of eschatological events it fits is uncertain. And this will turn out to be the case with all these new

---

[2] 5:1-3.

[3] 4:15-18.

'Christian' topics: Paul had no interest in Jewish apocalyptic events, only in the promise of the resurrection. It was only later that Christians, having decided to accept Jewish apocalyptic texts (like Revelation) into Christian scripture, had to find some way of reconciling the two.

All the remaining apocalyptic texts in the New Testament are of completely uncertain date. Depending which scholar you choose, they plausibly could have been written at any time between about AD 70 and the middle of the second century – a period of nearly 100 years. However, I would argue that if, as we shall now see, these texts show signs of combining Christian apocalypse as it appears in the early texts above with elements of Jewish apocalypse, this in itself argues for a later dating. This stands the traditional mode of working on its head. In the absence of better evidence scholars normally argue issues of dating in terms of Greek style and by seeking correspondences with the few texts that can be dated with reasonable assurance. I argue that Christian doctrine started with a complete lack of interest in apocalypse. Early Christians assumed that they were already living at the end of time and that the Messiah's coming was imminent; their only concern was that they would be 'saved' and that the believing dead would be resurrected and also saved. It was only as the decades passed and, despite tribulations, Messiah still did not come, that they felt the need to insert texts borrowed from Jewish apocalypse into their scriptures, fleshing out the signs to look for and the order of events on the Day of the Lord.

One such text is 2 Thessalonians, thought by a minority to be the work of Paul, but by the majority of scholars to be a later forgery presented as a sequel to Paul's first letter. According to Acts, the Church at Thessalonica was founded by Paul among Gentiles there (Jews of the city rejected his message) so we can perhaps assume that decades later the Church was still a Gentile foundation. It is not surprising, therefore, that this Greek Church was becoming confused by different messages coming out of the Holy Land, and particularly by the fact that the Messiah had still not come. And this again points to a later date for the Epistle: they had been led to expect the Day of the Lord imminently, but years and even decades had passed with no sign. The Epistle is written with the express intention of explaining this postponement and reassuring the Church that, nevertheless, the Messiah would come. The unknown writer first assures them that the 'Lord Jesus Christ' is indeed 'at hand', and that he will come in 'vengeance' and 'destruction'. But they are not to hold their collective breaths. Certain events have to take place first: a great 'falling away' followed by the coming of a 'man of sin'. And the reason why the latter has not yet appeared is that he is being restrained by someone or something:

> Let no man deceive you by any means: for that day shall not come, except there come a falling away first, and that man of sin be revealed, the son of perdition; Who opposeth and exalteth himself above all that is called God, or that is worshipped; so that he as God sitteth in the temple of God, shewing himself that he is God. Remember ye not, that, when I was yet with you, I told you these things? And now ye know what withholdeth that he might be revealed in his time. For the mystery of iniquity doth already work: only he who now letteth will let, until he be taken out of the way. And then shall that Wicked be revealed, whom the Lord shall consume with the spirit of his mouth, and shall destroy with the brightness of his coming . . . [4]

In these few short verses, three important new topics of Christian apocalypse are introduced:

---

4 2:3-8.

APOCALYPTIC TOPIC NO. 21: THE GREAT APOSTASY
APOCALYPTIC TOPIC NO. 22: THE MAN OF SIN
APOCALYPTIC TOPIC NO. 23: THE RESTRAINER

None of these come from Jewish apocalypse. They are introduced here (and nowhere else), not because the Jewish apocalypse was in any way deficient. It was simply irrelevant to the writer's purposes. He needs to reassure the Church that although the Day of the Lord has not arrived as promised, and no one knows exactly when that will be, nevertheless, it is still imminent but has been held back by issues surrounding this Man of Sin, whoever he might turn out to be. He then explains God's purpose behind this delay:

> And for this cause God shall send them strong delusion, that they should believe a lie: That they all might be damned who believed not the truth, but had pleasure in unrighteousness.[5]

If more proof were needed that this is not Paul writing, this rationale provides it. Paul (had he been alive) might have argued that God, in his infinite patience and love, had delayed His Day to give more time for the wicked to repent and be saved. This writer is saying the opposite. God has deliberately sent the Man of Sin to delude people – in effect, to winkle out even more unbelievers for eternal damnation. But, he reassures his readers again, you are going to be all right: God has chosen you to be saved. Smug Calvinism at its earliest and worst!

Before turning to the Gospels, we have just a couple more texts to consider: the Epistles of John, which appear in the Bible immediately before Revelation but were written later – probably at the turn of the century. These are not generally

---

[5] 2:11.

considered to be apocalyptic in content, but they do contain reference to a figure that is lodged in the popular apocalyptic imagination:

APOCALYPTIC TOPIC NO. 24: THE ANTICHRIST

It will perhaps surprise many readers that the term 'Antichrist' does not appear at all in the Book of Revelation, just in a few passages in the first and second Epistles of John. And even there, it never has a definite article or a capital letter – so, 'antichrist' not 'The Antichrist'. The term is found once in plural form and four times in the singular. The reason why it is often assumed that the Antichrist features in Revelation is that he/it is often associated with one or all of the Beasts described there. There is no evidence for this, and, in fact, this mistaken identity obscures much of what is going on in these passages, as we shall see.

Turning now from the Epistles to the Gospels, the three synoptic Gospels all contain a text that has become known as the Little Apocalypse or the Olivet Discourse because (we are told) it contains words spoken by Jesus on the Mount of Olives. As we saw in Volume II, the relevance of the location is of course that, according to Zechariah, the great battle between Good and Evil will take place in the Last Days there. The close similarity between the three versions in the synoptic Gospels indicates that there was almost certainly a single source document that all three drew upon. Traditionally it has been assumed that this document was some sort of record of the actual words that Jesus spoke. Let us look at it to see. We shall follow the Mark version because most scholars agree this is the earliest,[6] although the differences

---

6 Ch. 13.

between the three versions are so slight as to make no difference to the argument. One of the disciples asks Jesus about the Temple and Jesus foretells that the Temple will be destroyed. This provokes the question that has never been answered by any of the prophets: when will this happen and/or what will be the signs to look out for? Jesus warns that there will be many false Messiahs and Tribulations – 'wars and rumours of wars' including civil war, earthquakes, famine, troubles and sorrows – and the disciples will be persecuted. And he says that the Gospel must first be published to all nations. But the final sign will be 'the abomination of desolation, spoken of by Daniel the prophet'; at that time, he advises them all to head for the hills (literally) because that is when the real Tribulation will begin: 'affliction such as was not from the beginning of creation'. However, for the sake of His Elect, God will shorten this period. Then the sun and moon will go dark and the stars will fall from the Heavens, and then at last 'they shall see the Son of Man coming in the clouds', the Elect will be gathered from the four corners of the globe, and there will be a new Heaven and Earth.

The Olivet Discourse must have been put together some time after the Jewish uprising and war with Rome in the sixties AD because the rational interpretation of the references to the destruction of the Temple must mean that they were written after the Romans destroyed the Temple at the end of the war. And this in turn means that much of, if not all, the references to Tribulation are also references to that war. The source for the references is Jewish apocalypse, but the interpretation of the writer of the Discourse must have been that they were miraculously coming true in the historical events of the sixties. So, the coming of Messiah and the Day of the Lord were still imminent. The reference to Daniel and the 'abomination of desolation' is puzzling because, as we have seen, the original reference to it in Daniel seems unequivocally to refer to Antiochus IV Epiphanes in the second century BC. As we shall see in Part Three, this reference by Jesus to it as a future event provides modern fundamentalists with the ammunition they need to search for it as a contemporary sign of the Second Coming. But, otherwise, there is nothing remarkable in any of this. It is lifted straight from Jewish apocalypse: if there was a source document for the Olivet Discourse, I suspect, therefore, that it was based on Zechariah and Daniel. But in the midst of all this there is an unequivocal statement by Jesus that must rank as the most embarrassing in the entire Bible for those that want to believe either in the Second Coming of the Messiah, or in any of the apocalyptic events that are supposed to surround that. Jesus says:

> Verily I say unto you, that this generation shall not pass, till all these things be done.[7]

Certainly, he qualifies this by stressing that no one knows the *precise* timing but there is nothing equivocal, uncertain or imprecise about this statement. Jesus says that his disciples will still be alive when he returns in glory. Christians have weaselled their way around this for centuries; some have even interpreted it to mean that the disciples are still alive today, wandering around incognito, unable to die until Jesus returns. One interpretation says this does not refer to the Day of the Lord at all, but to some other event, such as the advent of the Holy Spirit at Pentecost. Another view is that the translation is wrong: generation should read 'race' – so Jesus is saying that the *Jews* will survive until the Second Coming. And for some, Jesus *did* come back at the time of the destruction of Jerusalem in AD 70; it is just that he did it

---

7 Mark 13: 30.

invisibly. But we know that Paul and the early Christians were expecting the Day of the Lord imminently; the Epistle to the Thessalonians was written precisely to confirm that expectation in the face of inexplicable delay. And it is hard to see how any of these excuses can stand in the face of other passages in the Gospels that say pretty much the same:

> Matthew 16:28 'Verily I say unto you, There be some standing here, which shall not taste of death, till they see the Son of man coming in his kingdom.'

> Mark 9:1 'And he said unto them, Verily I say unto you, That there be some of them that stand here, which shall not taste of death, till they have seen the kingdom of God come with power.'

> Luke 9:27 'But I tell you of a truth, there be some standing here, which shall not taste of death, till they see the kingdom of God.'

These quotations are not from other versions of the Olivet Discourse. They are independent passages, all attributing the same thought to Jesus. The coming of the Son of Man and the Kingdom of God are quite clear in reference: this is the Jewish Day of the Lord that we are talking about here, and no amount of special pleading can get round the fact that Jesus says it will happen in the lifetime of his hearers. Of course, since Jesus is a fictional construct, we do not need special pleading here: the words placed in his mouth reflect only what all the Jewish apocalypses say from the very beginning – that the Day of the Lord is just around the corner. They were wrong in the eighth century BC, and in the sixth century BC, and in the second century BC and in the first century AD. Why on Earth do modern fundamentalists think that 2,000 years later they have got it right? The endless postponements of Apocalypse must surely suggest that perhaps the whole concept is a fallacy.

To conclude this chapter therefore: the earliest Pauline Christians, as opposed to John the Baptist's Jewish followers, were blithely unconcerned about apocalyptic signs. They expected Jesus at any moment and lived their lives accordingly. But as time passed and Jesus did not come, they had to rationalize the postponement. The first Christian apocalypses focused on this issue alone. And then, as even more time elapsed, they began to ransack Jewish apocalypse – particularly Zechariah and Daniel. Crucially, there is no evidence that they were even aware of Revelation because the extra topics introduced in that Book are without exception, missing from all these early Christian apocalypses. The Olivet Discourse draws on Jewish apocalypse, and particularly Zechariah and Daniel, for its signs of the end times, and adds Christian elements in the way that the other New Testament apocalypses do. Revelation only begins to enter mainstream Christian apocalyptic thought as the Book itself slowly and painfully makes its hesitant way into the biblical canon.

Part Three will trace this process. But first, we shall now, in Part Two, trace how all these topics have been interpreted by Christians over the two millennia that have elapsed, waiting for the Day of the Lord to materialize.

PART TWO

HISTORY

I

Pre-Reformation Eschatology

Christianity emerged over the first few centuries AD, out of a wide range of competing sects. The history of the Church Fathers is littered with accusations of heresy, defences and counter accusations, and resulting schisms large and small. At the time, no one could have predicted winners and losers; it is only with the perspective of history that we look back and trace the religion that we know today to this or that early Christian writer. This maze of ideas and speculation is still in the process of being unravelled by scholars, given added impetus by new manuscript discoveries in the twentieth century, notably the Nag Hammadi library of texts and the Dead Sea Scrolls. The former has given us a better understanding of the whole range of beliefs that we now call Gnostic; and the latter help interpret how Christianity emerged from Judaism. One way to understand all these different sects is to view them, in their different ways, as coming to terms with the huge discrepancy between the stern, judgemental, Judaic idea of God and the forgiving, fatherly, Christian one. For the Gnostics, the discrepancy could only be explained by proposing a complete discontinuity between the two. For them, the God of the Old Testament is the jealous, vengeful, tribal deity of the Jewish people – a

Demiurge whose powers are limited and restricted to Earth. The God of the New Testament is the all-powerful divine Father, creator of the entire heavens and cosmos, who has revealed himself to his creation through his Son, Jesus. Within the mainstream of the early Christian Church (if there can be said to have been such a thing), the tension was between those who regarded Jesus as the Jewish Messiah and sought to accommodate belief in His existence to Jewish belief, and those (mainly Gentiles) who saw Christianity as a new religion with roots in Judaism but a distinct and separate future. Attitudes towards the Old Testament, the nation of Israel, and the Jewish people all shifted during this period as Christian thinkers wrestled with these problems, and eschatology was strongly influenced by the outcome.

In fact however, and broadly speaking, the focus throughout the first 500 years of the Christian era was not on eschatology at all but on christology: Was Christ human or divine? Was he co-existent with God or created by God? – at the beginning of time or later? How exactly did God the Father, God the Son and God the Holy Spirit relate to each other? And in what sense was one to understand Mary as, effectively, the Mother of God? These seemed far more pressing matters than apocalyptic ideas that seemed, on the whole, pretty well laid out in Daniel and Revelation. Indeed, there were seven formal ecumenical councils convened in the first century after Christ to provide the faithful with settled pronouncements on all these major issues of contention, and not a single one set out to resolve eschatological matters: hard to believe given the near obsession that some Christians today exhibit with the subject. Unlike now, the identification of people, symbols and events in those Books with historical equivalents was not a game that people chose to play much at this time. The attitude was pretty much to wait and see – no doubt all would be clear in due time.

Pre-Reformation Eschatology

The first 500 years or so after the apostolic era when the Gospels and Epistles were written is usually referred to as the era of the early Church Fathers. In their writings, some of which survive (although not always with known authors), they debated with one another (variously in Greek, Latin and Syriac) the doctrines that became established for the Church. The watershed during this period is, of course, the adoption of Christianity as the official religion of the Roman Empire in the fourth century. The emperor Constantine was largely responsible for the proclamation of the Edict of Milan in AD 313, which declared religious tolerance for Christianity in the Roman Empire, and he convened the first Council of Nicaea in AD 325, at which the Nicene Creed was adopted by Christians – effectively setting in stone the doctrinal consensus that had been reached by that time. Prior to the Edict of Milan, the young Church was subject to continual persecution and sporadic pogroms; after Milan, Church and State gradually aligned themselves. This background is responsible for different attitudes to eschatology either side of the watershed. Before Milan, the expectation of Christ's imminent return was what sustained the Church through the worst times. As with the Jewish nation at times of invasion, the belief that the Day of the Lord was at hand provided comfort and hope; God intended very soon to bring history to an end, put wrongs right, and usher in a Millennial Kingdom in which suffering, sorrow and pain would be unknown. After Milan, as the pressure eased, Christians became unconcerned about the Second Coming. It now looked as if God's purpose were gradually to redeem the world through the Gospel; the Church saw its new approved, and then official, status as clear evidence of God's working through history. God had triumphed already and His Church could look forward to a long and prosperous future, rather than a short and nasty one. The need for Eternal comfort receded as Earthly comfort hove into view, particularly for the evolving church hierarchy, who now enjoyed growing status and wealth to parallel their secular ruling counterparts.

The earliest writings of the Church Fathers date back to the end of the first and first half of the second centuries, so although non-canonical they are roughly coincident with the New Testament texts and were broadly regarded at the time as authoritative. The writers that we know of are remembered as early bishops: Clement (Rome), Ignatius (Antioch), Polycarp (Smyrna) and Papias (Hierapolis). Two anonymous texts also date from this early period: Didache and Shepherd of Hermas. The former claims to be the 'teaching of the Lord to the Gentiles' by the twelve Apostles. The latter describes visions, commandments and parables vouchsafed to Hermas, a former slave; an 'Angel of Repentance' appears to Hermas in the guise of a shepherd, hence the title. The preoccupations of all these works are broadly twofold. On the one hand, the writers debate major issues of Christian theology, notably the human and/or divine nature of Christ and the nature of the Trinity; these linked issues were a key bone of contention right up until they were settled (more or less) at the Council of Nicea. On the other hand, as one might expect from bishops in particular, a lot of attention is given to ecclesiology: church structure, administration, and rituals. What is glaringly missing, as it was with the canonical works of the time, is any preoccupation with eschatology or apocalypse. This could be an accident of history; much of these texts is lost to us and we know of their contents only through later reports. But then, it is interesting that the aspect of their teaching that was remembered was mainly christology and ecclesiology. Whatever eschatology there may or may not have been in these texts, no one thought it important enough to preserve.

Pre-Reformation Eschatology

We know next to nothing about the beliefs of the laity in this period, except we must assume that they reflected those of their priests. But I think we can also assume that as the ascendancy of the Church grew, hand in glove with the secular powers of the time, the eyes of everyone were on earthly matters of today rather than seeking eternal comforts. Like the Thessalonians, the laity needed reassurance of the resurrection and eternal life; and they needed to believe that, through the sacraments of the Church, they would be spending eternity in Heaven rather than Hell. But beasts and horns, tribulations and millenniums, would not exactly be top of mind in a world where, although the Church was now triumphant, the economic lot of the common man was still dependant on long hours of toil, leaving little room for eschatological reflection. And we must remember that access to the scriptures was mediated solely by the Church, partly because most people were illiterate and partly because, in any case, the only approved version of scripture was in Latin. So, any understanding among the laity of eschatological matters was limited to what was preached from the pulpit and depicted in sacred art.

As we move further into the second century, however, the next generation of writers do begin to show more of an interest in apocalypse, particularly in their interpretations of Daniel and Revelation. It was now getting on for a hundred years since the supposed death of Jesus. Throughout that time Christians had believed themselves to be living in the last times, surrounded by antichrists and expecting the true Christ to return at any moment. But a hundred years is a long time. Clearly that expectation was wrong. The Church was becoming more established; bishops were now in place, and approved rituals and doctrines were starting to be formalized. Now bishops and theologians began to search scripture (and remember, the canon was not fixed by this time, so scripture could include non-canonical texts) for indications of signs of the last days. If not now, then when? Interpretations in the first century that identified people and events from that time must be wrong, so the belief arose that these texts are prophecies of an unspecified future time. Justin Martyr and Irenaeus, Bishop of Lugdunumin (now Lyon) were the prominent Christian thinkers of the first half of the second century AD. Both were well versed in Daniel and Revelation and both took a literal approach to both Books, following the outline of John B's Second Apocalypse. In particular, both (like Papias) believed that after Christ's Second Coming there would be a thousand-year period in which Christ and his resurrected saints would physically rule the Earth from Jerusalem. This literalism was to dominate the entire period before the Constantine watershed.

In the debate about the old Jewish religion, the predominant view that arose over the first and second centuries was that when God sent Jesus to Earth, he signalled that he was washing his hands of the Jews. The testimony of the Old Testament seemed to be that, time and again, the prophets had warned the Jewish people that unless they mended their ways, they would forfeit their special relationship with their deity. The time of the prophets was ended and there were to be no more warnings. Now, in final punishment for the Jews' infidelity, God was cutting them off from their ancient Covenant. In effect, divorcing them and remarrying the new Christian church. The Jews had only themselves to blame: by rejecting Jesus as Messiah, they had been responsible for their own demise. And the evidence of history seemed to reinforce this view; the Jewish nation had been decimated in the first of the two main Jewish wars with Rome, and scattered to the four winds in the second – the strongest possible evidence which side God was backing. During those wars, the Christian church had refused to help the Jews,[1] which had done nothing to reconcile the two religions to one another and, as a result, Christian churches that had begun as predominantly Jewish institutions – Christian synagogues in effect – with a handful of Gentile god-fearers, were now solidly Hellenistic, Gentile institutions, looking to Rome rather than Jerusalem for leadership and excluding Jews from fellowship unless they effectively renounced their Jewish heritage. By the fourth century, John Chrysostom, Archbishop of Constantinople, took the anti-Jewish trend to its logical conclusion and denounced from the pulpit Jews and 'Judaizing' Christians who were taking part in Jewish festivals and other Jewish observances. The long history of Christian anti-Semitism really begins at this point; veneration for Jewish scripture becomes replaced by Christianity's own scriptures, and an attitude towards Jews that moves from respect for the roots of the faith to antipathy towards the race that had rejected Jesus and still resists his claim to be the Messiah.[2]

One of the 'proofs' of this transfer of divine allegiance from Jews to Christians was the matter of ongoing prophecy. We have seen that for Jews, the age of prophecy ended with the second generation of prophets 500 years before the Christian era. Uncertainty about the status of the Book of Revelation seems to some degree to have stemmed from this: if God no longer communicated in that way, what was the source of John's visions? How could they be regarded as authentic? It was believed that at the End Time a final prophet would arise to usher in God's Kingdom, but for

---

[1] The legend had it that the nascent Christian church fled the destruction of Jerusalem to Pella, across the Jordan.

[2] Indeed, John Chrysostom was cited by the Nazis in their ideological campaign against the Jews.

Jews that still lay in the future; John the Baptist was regarded as that prophet by early Christians but has never been part of the Jewish scriptural canon. From the very beginning, Christianity seems to have had its own prophets. For several centuries after Christ, there seems to have been a view that while God may have stopped communicating with the Jews in this way, he continued to speak through prophecy to Christians. As Christianity developed, there seems to have been a recognition that some members of a church congregation were granted special gifts from the Holy Spirit and among these was the gift of prophecy. Indeed, it was regarded as more important than other gifts, such as 'speaking in tongues', and unlike that 'charismatic' phenomenon, was required to be conducted soberly, without the frenzied fits of the shaman. But the problem of sorting good from bad remained. Prophetic utterance was to be tested and evaluated by the community of Christian prophets;[3] and the criterion for evaluation was to be whether the content of the prophetic message was in accordance with the generally accepted beliefs and customs of the Church.[4] In which case, one might well ask what was the point of it if nothing new could be accepted?

Around the middle of the second century, a Christian from Phrygia called Montanus began to have frenzied, ecstatic experiences in which the Holy Spirit seemed to possess him and speak through him rather like, as it was described at the time, a plectrum plucking a lyre. He founded a movement called the New Prophecy. What was its status regarding old prophecy? And Revelation? Montanus himself regarded his prophecies as *superseding* those of the Jews – their function was to explicate all the ambiguities left by previous prophecy.

---

[3] 1 Cor 14:29.
[4] Rom. 12:6; 1 Cor. 12:3.

Accompanied by two prophetesses, Priscilla and Maximilla, who made similar claims for themselves, he travelled about, pulling huge crowds and building an army of support. 'The Three', as they were known, split Christendom down the middle. Many regarded this as evidence of God's favour, but others were disturbed by the way these new prophets spoke in the first person as God Himself. The Church hierarchy solved the problem by neither recognizing the phenomenon nor denouncing it. They presumably just hoped it would go away, which indeed, over time it did, although there seem to have been Montanists still around in the sixth century. However, the idea that the Holy Spirit speaks the word of God through individual Christian prophets, undoubtedly sanctioned in the New Testament, never completely went away. As we shall see, it was to reappear time and again over the next 1,500 years. Sometimes it would lead to new religions, such as Islam or Mormonism; sometimes it created schism and sectarianism within the mainstream church; and sometimes it emerged as a strong force for reinvigorating the mainstream with a new impetus and belief.

Central to Montanism was the Book of Revelation. It provided both a model for Christian prophecy and a sourcebook for Montanist themes. But among most Christians, the book was as suspect as its Montanist champions. The Eastern Churches had the greatest difficulty with it, and this attitude was absorbed by the Byzantine Church as the first millennium progressed. It was still not regarded as canonical even by the seventh century in the East, and to this day it is still rejected by some Eastern sects. Eastern theologians and divines tended to just ignore the Book, and in their eschatological deliberations relied solely on Daniel and the other Old Testament prophets, and other New Testament texts. In particular, they fixated upon the idea of the Antichrist: if he could be identified with a living historical figure, then this would confirm that the Last Days were indeed at hand. Eschatological theories and calculations were initially attempts to identify the Antichrist with this or that king or emperor, but as history failed to coincide with prophecy in this respect, the Antichrist figure evolved into a more mystical concept. In the West, views about Revelation were more varied and muddled. Eusebius, for example, writing in the fourth century referred to the Book as both 'accepted' and 'rejected'.[5] It was not authoritatively accepted as canonical until the Synod of Hippo in AD 393. Prior to that, and even afterwards, Christians were as likely to consult Daniel, the Epistles of John and Thessalonians as Revelation for eschatological guidance.

The Book of Revelation, straddling the Old and New Testaments, was a touchstone for the issue of the relationship between Christianity and the Jews. A related touchstone theological issue arising from this Jewish question was the topic of the Millennium: it sat badly with Christian theology, but was unavoidably prominent in Jewish apocalyptic scriptures, so somehow had to be accommodated. It also turned out to be a useful concept for calculating the likely date for the Day of the Lord. Theophilus of Antioch seems to have been the first to do so in the second century. The technique he used was similar to that employed centuries later by the likes of Bishop Ussher: using the chronologies and histories in the Old Testament to calculate the date of Creation; in this case, Theophilus arrived at a span of 5,515 years between Creation and the birth of Jesus. This calculation suggested to him that God's own timetable was mystically revealed by the Bible. In Psalm 90, we are told that 'One day with the Lord is as a thousand years' and the same equation was repeated in 2 Peter 3:8 in the New Testament. Using the kind of illogical, creative thinking that characterizes

---

[5] Eusebius. *Church History*, Book III Chapter 25.

Pre-Reformation Eschatology

fundamentalists then and now, he argued that just as God created Heaven and Earth in six days and then rested on the seventh, taking each day as 1,000 years, the day of the Lord would come after 6,000 years – so sometime around the year AD 500. Others by a similar method fixed on 5,325 BC or thereabouts as the date of Creation, so expected the day of the Lord a little later in around AD 675. Arguments like these served a twofold purpose: they explained why Christ's return was postponed beyond the expectation of previous generations; and they provided a rationale to justify the belief that arose at times of trouble, that this was the prophesied End Time. In this respect, for the last 2,000 years Christians have simply mirrored the Jews of the previous 2,000 years, assuaging their despair with apocalyptic hope.

But the concept of the Millennium itself remained problematical for Christianity. The original Jewish concept was for the Messiah to rule a new Earthly Kingdom of God from the Jewish religious centre of Jerusalem. The Book of Revelation was incorporated into Christian eschatology by the simple expedient of replacing the coming of Messiah with the Second Coming of Jesus Christ. But if the Jews were no longer God's chosen people, then this central role for Jerusalem had to go. Neither the Jews, nor their capital, had any logical role to play. Salvation was through Jesus, not through Jewish religious laws or Jerusalem Temple sacrifices. It ran counter to the whole thrust of Christianity as it was moving further and further away from its Jewish roots; Jewish religious thought was concerned with earthly existence, racial superiority, and divine intervention in human history. Christianity was now focused on the individual soul, universality, and individual salvation. How then to explain away the unwelcome idea of Jewish Millennium? The initial answer was that the Millennium should be understood literally as a limited earthly kingdom, between Christ's Second Coming and the creation of a new eternal Heaven and Earth. But for many, the whole idea of a *literal* Millennium just did not feel right. What was the point of it? Surely something was being missed or misunderstood. Ironically, the solution adopted by early Christian writers, like Clement and Origen, was made possible by Christian adoption of the old Jewish technique of scriptural interpretation – *Midrash*. They did not call it that, but in essence that is what it was, and I have no doubt they inherited it through lingering Jewish tradition in the Church.

Midrash reflected the belief that beneath the literal sense of scripture there often lurked a deeper allegorical or symbolic meaning, intelligible only to the spiritually advanced believer who made the effort to uncover it. It is precisely that belief that the Church Fathers appropriated from Jewish practice. They gradually came to regard the entire Jewish scripture as pointing to Jesus; not just the odd prophecy here and there, but the entirety of the Old Testament could be read allegorically or symbolically in the light of Christian belief. They outdid Jewish *Midrash* in their creative determination to find the hidden meanings in every passage. The surface, literal import of scripture was to relate what *Jewish* people said and did in history; the deeper allegorical meanings were there as guidance for latter day *Christian* belief. Applied to the touchstone topic of the Millennium, it is then easy to see how the literal meaning obscures the symbolic meaning. A thousand-year period when Christ would again be physically present on Earth simply seemed to delay the looked-for time when physical forms would pass away and be replaced by the spiritual. If Jesus was coming back in human form, what was the point of his first appearance? Better, it was thought, to explain away the Millennium as a *symbolic* time period (like those in Daniel) – an allegory of Christ's return rather than an *actual*, physical 1,000 years.

Pre-Reformation Eschatology

The focus of debate was then around the few verses in Revelation 20 describing the periods before and after the putative 'Millennium'. Theologians at the time referred to literal belief in the Millennium as Chiliasm after the Greek word for millennium. But others were already taking an allegorical approach to the issue at the time. We know because Irenaeus fulminates against this as rank heresy. The opposite view was expressed most forcibly by Origen later in the second century/early third century who, although well versed in scripture, took an idealist Platonic view and argued vehemently against literal interpretation.[6] In the next couple of centuries, people like Victorinus of Pettau and Jerome had the perspicacity to see that Revelation repeated itself endlessly and argued importantly that all the series of 'seven' tribulations should be regarded as concurrent, not sequential. And they began to argue against the prevailing Chiliasm. But it was not until after the Constantine watershed that a new interpretation began to prevail. The new era moved from persecution to recognition; from tribulation to peace and security; and from passive self-defence to active evangelism and the expansion of the Gospel throughout the world. At such a time of hope and triumphal expectation, it was inevitable that a new, more optimistic interpretation of Revelation should emerge.

The architect of this was St Augustine of Hippo, who wrote on almost every Christian topic and therefore made some forays into eschatology. He took the Millennium debate to its logical conclusion. He started out in life as a

---

6 Ironically, given that Origen was widely believed to have castrated himself, as many did in these early centuries, following the words of Jesus in Matthew 19:12. Nowadays, the Church teaches that Jesus' approbation of castration is symbolism for celibacy, although personally I see no grounds for anything but a literal interpretation and live in constant hope that Christian clergy everywhere will obey the dictates of their Lord.

literalist, but he moved over time to a symbolist position that was to become Christian orthodoxy throughout the subsequent medieval period. The literal view, as outlined earlier, was that there will be the Great Tribulation; then Christ returns; the 'saved' are resurrected and rise up to join Jesus in the sky; Satan is 'bound; 'Jesus and the saints then rule the Earth from Jerusalem for 1,000 years; at the end of that time, Satan is released for a few years before finally being defeated; then the rest of humanity is resurrected and judged; followed by the creation of a new Heaven and Earth. Augustine developed a different, allegorical interpretation. He argued that the Great Tribulation was the Roman occupation of Judæa; when Jesus died on the cross, that was the point when Satan was bound; the 'first resurrection' was the rite of Christian baptism; the Millennium is the period of the Church Fathers, when the consequences of the Edict of Milan meant that the Gospel would spread inexorably across the world, bringing peace and righteousness to all; the Millennium would not necessarily last precisely 1,000 years because this is a symbolic number, but after a long period of time, Satan would be loosed again for a short period (again, the three-and-a-half years is to be taken symbolically) before Christ's Second Coming, the Resurrection and Judgement, and the new Creation. From that day to this, these are the issues that fundamentalists debate endlessly. In Part Three we will dissect each topic in turn in an attempt to put these matters to a final rest.

The next 500 years were a turbulent time in Christendom. From the third century onwards, the Roman Empire was engulfed by continual crisis: invasions, civil strife, economic disorder and plague all wrought havoc with the idea that Christianity and the Empire together would lead the world into not just a Pax Romana, but an era of Christian beneficence. Augustine at the turn of the fourth century could still

Pre-Reformation Eschatology

argue that he was living in the prophesied millennial kingdom, but the writing was on the wall. Even by the reign of Constantine, the Empire was breaking up. He imposed order on the chaos that lasted for a few decades, using Christianity as a tool for unification. But the Empire inexorably split into two along an east–west axis, with dual power centres in Constantinople and Rome. Theodosius I was the last emperor to rule over both East and West, and following his death in AD 395 the Western Empire fell apart. Increasing incursions of pagan Germanic tribes, culminating in the sack of Rome itself by Alaric and his Goth hordes in AD 410 marked the effective ending of the classical Roman Empire. The Byzantine Empire in the East, on the other hand, survived until the middle of the second millennium after the fall of its Western counterpart and became the most stable Christian realm during the Middle Ages.

Augustine's interpretation of the key Christian themes was to dominate the Western Roman Catholic Church throughout the Middle Ages and right down to the Reformation. But there were challenges to his orthodoxy almost as soon as he died. Augustine was Bishop of Hippo in North Africa (in modern day Algeria). Contemporary with Augustine, but the Bishop in Constantinople, was Nestorius, who took a different view on matters such as Christ's divinity and the role of Mary. The teachings of Nestorius were proclaimed heretical at the Council of Ephesus in 431, the year after Augustine's death, but over time the Byzantine Church in the East took its lead from Nestorius and, on matters like these, developed its own version of Christianity that remains to this day. And while the two versions of Christianity argued over sectarian issues, a threat greater than any internal schism was looming from Arabia following the birth in around AD 570 of the man who was to become the Prophet Mohammed. By the time of his death in AD 632, Mohammed had united many of the Arabian tribes, and in the decades that followed his successors rapidly spread the new Islamic faith east and west.

From the outset, Islam was clearly a huge threat to Christianity. The relationship between the Christian Church and the Roman State was clear – the former had the sanction of the latter, but the two were separate and the State exercised power as it saw fit. The key distinction of Islam was that it countenanced no such separation: the Islamic State was (and is) a theocracy; Islamic law determines all State actions, and the conquest of the world is its united political and religious aim. Islam did not spread through the Word; its rapid expansion was driven by the sword. And it saw easy pickings in the Middle East, where Roman and Persian wars had left a vacuum. In little more than a decade following the death of Mohammed, three out of the five patriarchates of Roman Christendom were under Arab Muslim rule. Most crucially, the occupation of the holy city of Jerusalem by Islamic fighters in AD 634 was a shock that rippled throughout Christendom. It was interpreted by many as 'the abomination of desolation'. Constantinople itself managed to repel invasion, but by the end of the seventh century it was reduced to a small Christian enclave surrounded on all sides by the rising tide of Islam. As we have seen, many biblical calculations identified the seventh century as likely to herald the End Time, so there were two possible interpretations of Islamic success. One argument was that Mohammed was the Antichrist himself. In that case, the predictions of prophecy were right and the Day of the Lord was indeed imminent. But on the other hand, how could the Day of the Lord take place while Jerusalem was in Islamic hands? And if Augustine was right, how could this be happening in the middle of the Christian millennium? Was this a punishment from God and if so, for what sins?

At this time, a Syriac text appeared, claiming to be by Methodius of Olympus, a long dead third/fourth century bishop, that tackled these contemporary issues in ways that exhibited supernatural prophetic powers. We now know (of course) that it was a pseudonymous forgery, but at the time its contents were extraordinarily powerful. Methodius had no doubt that the sins that were being punished were sexual in nature, from infidelity and promiscuity to deviancy and perversion. Muslims are described as 'sons of Ishmael' who would emerge from the desert to inflict God's punishment upon Christianity, which has 'slipped into depravity'. The text leans heavily on the eschatological themes of Daniel and Revelation to establish the case that the spread of Islam is in fulfilment of scripture and heralds the End Time. But it also introduced a new variation: a Messianic figure who will defeat Islam and save Christendom, and he will be a Roman Emperor. This was not a new interpretation of existing apocalyptic themes but an addition to the usual account because contemporary events were felt to be so devastating that some sort of extra divine intervention was needed. The text prophesied that the Roman Emperor Messiah, with angelic assistance, would defeat the combined forces of Islam and Gog/Magog. However, this would trigger the rise of the Antichrist, who would beat the emperor back to Jerusalem, at which point Christ would return and defeat the Antichrist, as prophesied in Revelation. This interpretation of current events, and its hope of Earthly salvation, ensured enormous popularity for this text. By the early eighth century it had been translated into Greek, Latin and other languages. And in subsequent centuries it was to re-emerge time and again as a comfort to Christian peoples suffering from invasion in the medieval period.

The hope of an Earthly Messiah in the shape of a new Roman Emperor may seem strange given that the classical Roman Empire had by now been defunct for several centuries. However, the eighth century saw the rise of a new empire, based in France, but under the aegis of a new Holy Roman Emperor, Charlemagne, who saw his role as the defence of Christendom from outside incursion. Charlemagne was crowned Emperor by the Pope in AD 800, more than 300 years after the demise of the last classical Roman emperor. It must have seemed at the time that God was intervening again in the historical process to ensure the forward march of empire and its state religion. But Charlemagne's success did not follow the course prophesied in the *Apocalypse of Pseudo-Methodius* as it is now known: yet again, history did not end as prophesied and this non-canonical text, popular though it has often been, plays no part in modern apocalyptic thought. But as the first millennium drew to an end, time and again it seemed as if the End Time had arrived, as Christendom went through constant convulsions and upheavals. The power of the new Holy Roman Empire shifted from France to Germany in the tenth century, but any hopes of a unified Christian state were unfulfilled.

Indeed, the failure of a Messiah, Roman or otherwise, to make an appearance as the first millennium drew to a close resulted in a resurgence of interest in eschatology. The endless political convulsions seemed to indicate strongly that this was the End of Days. There was increasing speculation about the Antichrist, whose expected appearance would be a sure sign. Islam was now several centuries old itself, so neither Mohammed nor any of his early successors could be identified as the false Messiah. But there were other candidates. In the popular imagination, many now believed that rather than some regal or imperial figure, the Antichrist would arise from obscurity – the satanic offspring of the Devil himself, in union with a young virgin perhaps, or again, the unnatural issue of a perverted Jew and his own daughter. Meanwhile, the incursions of Germanic tribes earlier in the millennium were now replicated by similar incursions of Magyar peoples from Hungary. These were not merely pagan in belief, but sufficiently different in appearance and ferocity to make them likely candidates for other eschatological figures – Gog/Magog and the army of locusts predicted by Revelation. Bishops and priests were conflicted in their responses to these events. The temptation to declare them as sure signs that the Day of the Lord was imminent was overpoweringly tempting. But they also knew that to say so categorically would be to create expectations and panic that would inevitably exacerbate the situation. Luckily, scripture was very clear on the issue: Jesus had said, and the Apostles had confirmed, that no one, not even the angels, knew when God was going to call Time, so they had a perfect excuse to prevaricate on the subject. Yes, the times were dire, and yes, one might think that the end was near, but it was forbidden to speculate on dates, so best to carry on as normal.

The degree to which eschatological fears escalated as the millennium turned has long been a matter of scholarly debate. It was at one time fashionable to believe that fear of the Apocalypse reached fever pitch in the year 1000. Then the academic pendulum swung the other way, and it was argued that there is little real evidence that this was the case. In fact, of course, there is some truth in both these polarized positions. It seems hard to believe, having lived through the turn of the second millennium with its apocalyptic fears, that something similar did not happen at the first millennium. Indeed, it can be argued, surely the less sophisticated turn of the early medieval mind would ensure this was the case. But it is also true that, as I have already pointed out, we have little evidence of how the laity felt about anything at the time, let alone eschatological matters. Indirect evidence is provided by a series of false Messiahs who arose at different times and places throughout the second half of the first millennium. Their claims to Messiahship all flew in the face of scriptural description of how Christ would return, yet to varying degrees ordinary people flocked to them, showing perhaps how ignorant the laity in general was about scriptural detail. It certainly seems that throughout the first century apocalyptic expectation, vague though it was in detail, bubbled under the surface; it was inherent in the essence of the Christian message, and it could burst to the surface on the least provocation at any time, irrespective of scholarly calculations.

Personally, taking all this into account, I think that the truth is somewhere in the middle. On the one hand, Augustine had said that the millennium was not to be taken literally, but on the other he could have been wrong, and he might have taken a different view if he had lived at the time of Hungarian invasions and political disintegration. Equally, even if the end time was at hand, was this necessarily a cause for fear? Surely for the good Christian believer it was a time of hope and anticipation for a better world to come? And there was nothing magical about the number 1,000 either. Jesus had been born in AD 1 but he had died in or around AD 33, and surely his death and resurrection were more important than his birth. So perhaps 1033 was the date, not that anyone should assert absolute knowledge of this or any other date! So, it seems likely that a mingled dread and anticipation would have been in the background of people's thoughts in the decades before and after the year 1000. The day-to-day grind of medieval life, and the efforts of the clergy to allay panic, would have served to hold down the fears, but it is probably true to say that at no time since the lead up to the first Jewish uprising against Rome in the mid-first century had there been such a period of eager expectation.

Triggers for panic could be religious or natural. For example, the Church then and now celebrates events of impor-

Pre-Reformation Eschatology

tance in the Bible on different days of the year. Many of these are 'moveable feasts' – the date varies from year to year because they are dependent on days of the week or the phase of the moon. When two or more of such feasts fell on the same date in a particular year, this was seen by the superstitious medieval mind as indicative of something portentous – and as the millennium approached, this could only be the End of Days. Natural events could reinforce the panic or act entirely separately. These could be as simple as uncommonly severe weather, rather as today people ascribe freak weather to apocalyptic ideas of climate change. Or more obviously unusual events such as solar eclipses, comets, floods and earthquakes: all the 'signs' that the Old Testament prophets had adduced as evidence for the Day of the Lord. A particularly notable example was the appearance of Halley's Comet in AD 989, which had people scurrying for hilltops or deep caves, or for the churches – depending presumably on the individual's judgement of their state of grace at the time and whether as a result they saw the Day of the Lord as opportunity or threat.

Whatever the reality, yet again of course, nothing happened: the strong got stronger, the weak weaker, and the poor poorer, as always. And the Church settled down to a new millennium and the challenge of identifying its continuing role in a world that was not supposed to have lasted this long at all. Some of the most distinctive elements of medieval life now arose as a result, the first of which being the Crusades. At the turn of the millennium, Islamic expansion in the West had been halted and even in places reversed, and the Eastern Empire was now at its height. But it was not to last. In 1071, the Byzantine defeat at the hands of the Turks in the Battle of Manzikert marked the beginning of the long decline of Byzantium. In 1095, the Eastern Emperor Alexios I Komnenos called on the various individual western kingdoms of Christendom to provide help. The West responded with the Crusades. Although originally conceived to relieve Byzantium, the aim of the crusades rapidly became to eject Islam from the Holy Land. The call to the first Crusade was met with extraordinary response across western Christendom. Motives as ever were extremely mixed, economic and political as well as religious, but it is not often recognized that they were powerfully reinforced by apocalyptic hope. As noted earlier, the occupation of Jerusalem by Islamic forces was seen as a barrier to the Second Coming; all the prophecies seemed to involve an important role for the holy city in the Last Days, and it was hard to see how this could happen without Christians in control. Indeed, many participants in the first Crusade seem to have believed that by sweeping Islam out of Jerusalem they were clearing the way at last for the much-delayed return of Jesus, and that there would be a mass ascension to Heaven as a result. For such people, the Crusade was a divinely appointed mission to usher in the Millennium. And for a while, they seemed to be right. The first Crusade established four Crusader states in the Eastern Mediterranean, including the Kingdom of Jerusalem itself. But it was not to last; Christians were finally expelled from the Holy Land 200 years later, never to return, and apocalypse was postponed again.

The world did not come to an end with the establishment of a Christian Jerusalem, so of course, it was not long before other dates were sought, in defiance of church prohibition of such presumption of divine prerogative. The first notable attempt at such was by Joachim of Fiore, who was one of those who, taking advantage of the first Crusade's success, went on a pilgrimage to Jerusalem in 1159 and there underwent a profound spiritual experience that seems to have convinced him that he could unlock eschatological secrets hidden from everyone else. His fundamental perception was that the history of the world could be divided into three equal and symmetrical ages, corresponding in turn to the three parts of the Holy Trinity. He did the usual calculation of the period between Creation and the birth of Christ, working his way through all the Old Testament genealogies; but unlike virtually all his predecessors who were influenced by the six days of creation/6,000 years analogy, he came up with a much shorter period of just 1,260 years for his first age which he called the Age of the Father. The 1,260 figure derives from the prophecies in Daniel based on a mystical half week or three and a half days; because a day equals a year for God, 3½ x 360 gives the mystical 1,260. This was to be followed, he argued, by another 1,260-years age: the Age of the Son: the period between the birth of Christ and the Apocalypse. So, the Day of the Lord would be 1260 or thereabouts. Joachim died in 1202, so missed out on the great day, but his followers, Joachists, were legion and whipped themselves (literally as we shall see) into a fury as the great day approached. What exactly he and they expected to happen is not totally clear, although Joachim's version of End Times events diverged significantly from the orthodox view of the time; it prophesied no role at all for the Church after 1260, which needless to say did not commend his ideas to that institution and they were regarded as heretical. Nevertheless, in a move to be copied again and again since then, his followers redid the calculations after the 1260 prediction failed and rescheduled the end of the world to 1290, then again to 1335, and finally to 1378, by which time, presumably, even the most optimistic of Joachists must have given it up as a bad job. Apocalypse Postponed indefinitely it seemed.

Joachim was never actually branded a heretic, presumably because, unlike many others, he did not claim to make new prophecy; he merely believed himself to be in possession of a unique understanding of the meaning of scripture. His complete immersion in scripture meant that, however wild his apocalyptic conclusions, he came to recognize the chasm between the beliefs and practices of the early Church as alluded to in the New Testament, and the beliefs and practices of the Catholic Church of his day. In particular, he deplored its corruption and wealth, and identified both it and the Pope with apocalyptic figures like the Whore of Babylon and the Antichrist. He is not much remembered today, but in many ways his nonconformity anticipated the growing dissent within the Catholic Church that was ultimately to lead to the Reformation. Less obviously, perhaps, he can be seen as fathering a growing interest in mysticism that gained pace from his day right up until the present time. This stems from his depiction (following his analogy with the Trinity) of the coming third, apocalyptic age, as the Age of the Spirit. He did not elucidate what exactly would take place in this third age, but it would generally be characterized by intense spirituality. As we have noted before, once you allow individual communion with, and interpretation of, the world of 'Spirit', the theological possibilities become as many and varied as the number of individuals so communing. From the time of Joachim, throughout the fourteenth century, mysticism grew as believers sought enlightenment beyond the scriptures in arcane disciplines such as astrology, numerology and the Jewish Kabala. An apposite parallel is with the concept of the new Age of Aquarius celebrated by hippies in the 1960s. A feeling that a new age is about to be born in which carnal man is to be reunited with his spiritual being, and all things become possible. The idea of the Age of Spirit also had the advantage of postponing the (presumably) final apocalypse when that age came to an end in or around the middle of the third millennium.

The fourteenth century's sense that something momentous was about to happen, fomented by dissatisfaction with the established Church and excited by mystical revelations, seemed to be confirmed by what we would now regard as natural occurrences, but which to the medieval mind were filled with more supernatural portent. In the 1340s, the Black Death was rampaging through Europe, devastating populations and causing many to believe that this was the End Time plague long prophesied. By the end of the century, it is calculated that a third of the population of Europe had disappeared and whole communities had been destroyed. At the same time, Europe was going through what we now refer to as the Little Ice Age: extreme winters and cold summers led many then to think in terms of apocalypse.[7] The weather, of course, led to famine, disease and death on an unprecedented scale. It certainly seemed that the Horsemen of the Apocalypse from Zechariah and Revelation had been unleashed. One extreme reaction to all this was the rise of public flagellation as a social phenomenon. Joachim's followers had been known to self-flagellate, but the concept gained in popularity as the fourteenth century progressed. Thousands of people would gather, led by clergy, marching from city to city and whipping themselves to appease their seemingly angry and imminent God. Ironically, this peregrination of bloodied bodies probably contributed to the spread of the very plague they sought to ameliorate. And the perceived holiness of the flagellants, their willingness to eschew physical comfort to emulate Christ's own agony, threw into further sharp contrast the luxury and extravagance of the clergy and the Church.

The next notable Catholic dissenter was to have a more lasting legacy: the English John Wycliffe was and is rightly regarded as the forerunner of the Protestant Reformation.

---

[7] As indeed the coincidence of the COVID-19 pandemic and climate change leads many fundamentalists to a similar conclusion today.

He is remembered as an early champion of the translation of the Bible into modern languages, but the roots of his beliefs were grounded firmly in apocalyptic expectation. Wycliffe was an Oxford scholar when the plague hit Britain and it had a profound effect on him. He too concluded that this must be the Last Days and that conviction was to drive him for the rest of his life. He regarded the Black Death as divine punishment for the sins of a Church hierarchy that he saw as depraved by worldly luxury, and his life was spent denouncing the Catholic Church and its practices. In the end, unlike Joachim, Wycliffe *was* denounced as a heretic, although only some decades after his death. But his ideas were taken up by followers across Europe (notably the Lollards and the Hussites) and fed naturally into the Reformation itself, which can thus be traced right back to Wycliffe's apocalyptic fears. In many of his writings, Wycliffe verges on denouncing the Papacy itself as the Antichrist – an identification that has been made on a regular basis by Protestants of varying hues, and in relation to almost every Pope, in all the centuries since then. In modern times, the identification of the Pope as the Antichrist is the default position of many fundamentalist sects.

Wycliffe died in 1384, around the time that the Western Church split into two for about four decades, with rival popes in Avignon and Rome, both claiming holy authority and dividing allegiances throughout Europe. Yet again, it seemed that the End of Times was near and it was easy, depending on your allegiance, to identify one or other of the contending popes as the Antichrist himself. The schism was resolved finally at the Council of Constance (1414–18), but in doing so in favour of Rome, it simply sought to rubber stamp the traditional medieval status quo, with all its decadence and corruption, and effectively made the Reformation inevitable. The miracle is that it did not finally erupt for another 100 years, until Martin Luther visited Rome, witnessed for himself the depths of depravity to which his Church had sunk, and prompted him to post his 95 Theses on the door of All Saints Church in Wittenberg in 1517.

2

The Reformation

In the centuries before the Reformation, the Catholic Church controlled biblical interpretation, and its concerns were with sin and the ways in which salvation could be sought via its clergy and rituals, rather than with obscure and abstruse apocalyptic texts. There was a flurry of fearful expectation at the turn of the first millennium, prompted by Christian scholars who speculated that the Apocalypse would occur around then. The precise date identified depended entirely on the dates for Jesus' life, so there was plenty of room for uncertainty in the years leading up to and after the year 1000. This scholarly uncertainty seems to have resulted in anxiety among the uneducated masses, but the historical evidence is lacking to determine how deep or wide this phenomenon went. Three requirements were necessary for real apocalyptic panic: the availability of scripture to the masses, literacy, and a religious context that sanctioned individual and independent interpretation of scripture. These only came into place gradually over the centuries following the Reformation.

While the Catholic Church regarded the Reformation as the work of Satan, many of the early Reformers saw their movement as foretold in scriptural apocalypse. It will be recalled that Augustine's allegorical interpretation of the Millennium as referring to the history of the Church, rather than to a future return to Eden, had won the day over the early literal view. This view is now called **Historicism**. The Reformers inherited this tradition but developed their own interpretations of the key symbols. In particular, the 'little horn' of Daniel, the Beast and the Antichrist were all now regarded as identifiable within the history of the Catholic Church and its ungodly, materialistic popes. The Reformation itself was a strong indication that the Day of the Lord was at hand: the forces of Satan were now revealed to be masquerading as the Church, and in the battle between the forces of reform and the Catholic system was to be seen the great final conflict between good and evil, foreshadowed in scriptural apocalypse.

At first, the Catholic Church took the same view as the Reformers, but in reverse – *they* were the Antichrist, indicating the Last Days. But over time, as the Catholic Church organized its counter-Reformation, it found it convenient to begin to move away from the Augustinian symbolism entirely, since this had opened the way for the Protestant attack. If it was so easy to interpret the history of the Church to the detriment of Catholicism, perhaps the whole idea that apocalyptic prophecy was being played out in history was wrong. Perhaps the literalists had been right all along and the millennial events were still in the future. Or perhaps, these events *were* historical – but they had all occurred long ago, in the first century AD. The first of these alternatives has become known as **Futurism** and really took off in a big way in the nineteenth century and ever since. The second alternative is now known as **Preterism** and characterizes Catholic and some Anglican belief down to the present day. Either way, the argument ran, eschatology could not be used as an indictment of the history of the Catholic Church as the

Reformers argued. Nowadays, all these approaches can be found in fundamentalist rhetoric: historicism, futurism and preterism are the currency of modern apocalyptic speculation and we shall take a closer look at them in Part Three. But at the time, both sides used the same rhetoric, based on the same symbols, to attack and malign the other. Neither side wanted to name the Day, any more than the old Jewish prophets, but no one in the sixteenth century doubted that they were living in the Last Times and that Christ's return was imminent.

The rapid spread of reform is directly attributable to the printing press and the availability of scripture in the vernacular languages of Europe. But widespread literacy was still some way off, and the masses were still dependant on religious leaders to guide the new theology. Furthermore, the mindset of the great reformers – Luther, Zwingli, Calvin – was as authoritarian as the Catholic Church they set out to replace. Calvin laboured long and hard to produce definitive commentaries on almost all the Books of the Bible, and a monumental set of 'Institutes' of the new religion he sought to found. The new Protestant states that sprang up across Europe were founded on new orthodoxies that had little toleration of dissent. And those orthodoxies were concerned to define themselves against the teachings of Rome; the controversies they sought to settle were about sin and redemption, baptism and the mass, the who and how of scriptural interpretation, rather than empty speculations about the end of the world. Indeed, Calvin never wrote a commentary on the Book of Revelation, and all the Reformation leaders seem to have had real doubts about the inclusion of that Book in the biblical canon. However, as always, history in this regard is written by the winners. At the outset of the Reformation, there were figures whose religious outlook was shaped by apocalypse, as had been that of Wycliffe.

The Reformation

Wycliffe lived through a period of social unrest across Europe as feudalism began to decline. In England, for example, the unsuccessful Peasant's Revolt attempted to redress extreme social ills; yet Wycliffe did not support it and restricted his life's mission to Church reform. But for many, the cause of social reform and religious reform were two sides of the same coin. After all, the extreme luxury of the Church was at the direct expense of the peasantry, and the role of the Church was inextricably bound up with the whole feudal power structure that left the masses in plague-ridden poverty. Wycliffe's emphasis on the Bible as the arbiter of Christian values, combined with the rapid spread of Gutenberg's printing inventions, meant that the Bible became accessible to more and more people, and within it they found not just new religious ideas, but social ones as well. Jesus had, of course, taught that all men were God's children, but more specifically, the early Church had clearly interpreted this as requiring a form of communal living that resembled in its essential aspects a form of what we would today call communism. So not only Church hierarchies could be seen as unchristian, so could social hierarchies. And this kind of thinking could justify social revolution in an age when social inequality was deep and institutionalized. The drive to social reform at the time was reinforced by humanist and alchemist thinkers who arrived at similar conclusions from observing the world around them, rather than from scripture. Dissent and revolution were in the air.

As the Reformation took hold, its originator, Martin Luther, became afraid of the social forces he had unleashed. He had never set out to destroy the Catholic Church, but merely to reform its worst abuses. Deeply conservative at heart, he regarded the alliance of Church and State as the way in which Christianity had and should evangelize the world. But, by rejecting Church innovations in theology and resting his faith solely upon scripture, he had unleashed a Pandora's Box of unlicensed, individual interpretation of those same scriptures. Indeed, the authoritarian nature of the early Protestant states can be seen as the inevitable reaction to this doctrinal chaos. The history of Christianity since then has been one of an imposed Protestant orthodoxy vainly trying to keep a lid on the inevitable consequences of Protestant emphasis on individual interpretation of the Bible. Orthodoxy, of course, would claim the Holy Spirit as endorsement of its view. But experience of the Holy Spirit being by definition an intensely personal experience, often accompanied by an extreme sense of emotional compulsion, this has never been an effective restraint on doctrinal innovation and schism. As in the period of the Church Fathers, religious orthodoxy, in league with state power, would pronounce such dissent as heresy and its adherents were often suppressed with unbelievable violence and pious conviction.

For many social reformers, the idea of a new kind of society based on social equality rang specific biblical bells. Certainly, there was the example of Eden – the Paradise which man was created to inhabit. And there was the promise of a new Eden as part of a new Heaven and Earth following Christ's Second Coming. But there was also the biblical idea of the Millennium. The Church Fathers had originally believed this to be literal. Augustine had declared it to be an allegory. But one way or another, it seemed to describe an Earthly paradise available to man could he but reach out and grasp it. As a new religious system was arriving, surely it should be possible to bring about a social Millennium also. And if the Pope was the Antichrist, perhaps the Millennium was indeed just around the corner. Luther did not like the idea, but others did: one of the earliest dissenters from the new Protestant orthodoxy in its German homeland was

Thomas Müntzer. At first a follower and associate of Luther, he was more mystically bent, and his apocalyptic views soon moved far beyond those of his master. Luther regarded scripture as the ultimate authority and elevated it above the teachings of the Church. Müntzer regarded scripture as only a guide, subject to the divine inner inspiration of the Holy Spirit, which manifested often through dreams and visions, as with the Old Testament prophets. However, he did not believe that anybody could simply arrive independently at personal ideas; he believed in a collective truth, led by teachers like himself. His reaction to social unrest was to see it as further evidence that the world had reached its Last Days when an idealized Christian commonwealth, with absolute equality among persons and the community of goods, would be established. When peasant uprisings occurred right across Germany in 1524/5, while Luther threw his weight behind authority and suppression, Müntzer offered himself as one of the leaders of the violent Peasant's Revolt – and lost his head as a result.

The Protestant reformers emphasized scripture over Church, internal inspiration over external theology, and informed faith over blind ritual. Salvation from the fires of hell on judgement day was to be had only through individual acceptance of Jesus Christ as personal saviour. Such persons were the Elect – the people God now regarded as his chosen ones to replace the Jews in his affections. Straightforward enough, one might suppose. But dig a little deeper and it was found that scripture was vague about the finer detail. For example, did it not matter at all how one behaved if one had saving faith and/or was one of the Elect? Why bother to be good? How could you ever be sure you were one of the Elect? How should one regard Catholics? Could they be Elect but just sadly misinformed, or were they followers of the Papal Antichrist, doomed to perdition? Did the Jews have any role to play now? What about babies who died before they could be expected to have faith? What role did baptism play in salvation? What was the role, if any, of priests? How should the new Protestant church(es) be structured? Was ritual good or bad? What exactly did happen when Christians ate the bread and wine; in what sense was it the body and blood of Christ? From the very beginning, all these issues and many more arose and were to be the cause of endless schism and sectarianism right down to the present day. And these were just the possibilities arising from the imprecision of scripture. As soon as one admitted the importance of the Holy Spirit as Müntzer had done, the theological possibilities became literally endless. As endless as the number of people receiving individual divine revelations. Not surprising then, that it took no time at all for the new Protestant churches to align themselves with secular power structures and impose their own dogmas and statutes of approved religion, against which all interpretations and individual revelations could be measured and declared either acceptable or heretical. This also applied to apocalyptic ideas, especially when they took a Millennial turn and advocated dissent not just from religious orthodoxy but against the social status quo.

Of course, as we have seen, schism was nothing new. It characterized the early centuries of the Christian era until the Roman Empire adopted Christianity as state religion and various synods subsequently pronounced on orthodoxy and outlawed heresy. But in the post-Reformation era, although much the same was true, the powers of orthodoxy were themselves from the start fractured and internally riven by debate; certainly, the monolithic status of the medieval Catholic church, east and west, has never been replicated in Protestantism. Two things were responsible: the availability of printed Bibles in vernacular languages, and a new emphasis on the

Holy Spirit. The cat was well and truly out of the bag and there was no putting it back in again. To track this veritable maze of schism and heresy over the next 500 years would be well beyond the scope of this book. The Bible is a very long book indeed, and it seems as if almost every verse in it has been the cause at some time or place of the sort of hair-splitting that leads to yet another separate congregation of believers. Some of these congregations would remain isolated in time and place, often dying out with the demise of their leaders through natural or unnatural causes. Some would catch on because their core beliefs somehow would be well attuned to the spirit of the times, and these would spread far and wide and endure even down to present times. Even if we were to restrict ourselves to just those schisms that were occasioned by apocalyptic hairsplitting, this book would be twice as long.

Given that the modern home of fundamentalists is without doubt the United States of America – and it is in America where, given that country's vast resources and influence for good or evil in the world, the consequences of belief in imminent apocalypse are most to be feared – then in the rest of Part Two of this book we shall trace the key apocalyptic ideas as they arose first in Britain and then were exported to the New World by the Protestant dissenters who travelled there to establish their own Millennial communities. The Reformation in England dates from 1527 when Henry VIII, until then a committed Catholic, petitioned the Pope for divorce from Catherine of Aragon. The Pope's refusal led, over the next few years, to a range of measures that effectively converted England to a Protestant state. Henry's death in 1547 ushered in a century of confusion in which Protestantism and Catholicism fought for supremacy, until the English Civil War of 1642–1651 settled the matter. Until 1642, few people were thinking about eschatology, but as

Protestantism gained the ascendancy, people focused more on exactly what kind of Protestantism was correct, and the result was inevitably a proliferation of sectarian belief. And for some sects, eschatology became one of the ways in which they defined themselves. The most conservative (i.e. extreme) Protestants in England in the sixteenth century were the Puritans, so called because they sought purity of religion. Remembered now for their dour opposition to any form of secular entertainment, their unrelenting commitment to a life of drab conformity to the dictates of an unsmiling, unforgiving deity was conceived and sustained by a parallel belief in the imminence of the Day of the Lord. Like the Apostle Paul, whose teachings lay at the heart of the Calvinism that they embraced, they believed that eternal judgement was just around the corner and there was, therefore, no time for fun, which could be had only at the expense of the immortal soul.

One eschatological topic that preoccupied many during the seventeenth century was the forever vexed problem of the Jews. Scapegoated throughout history as the murderers of the Christ, scripture seemed nevertheless explicit that their return to the Holy Land was a necessary prerequisite for the return of that same Christ. And since the dashing of such hopes with the failure of the Crusades, leaving the Holy Land in the hands of Islam, some new thinking was clearly required. One possibility was that the Jews would undergo a mass conversion to Christianity. The Puritans in particular re-examined the role of Jews in the Christian world. They found much to admire in Hebraism, with its stoical adherence to stern Old Testament morality when compared with the lax corruption of the Catholic Church. By modelling their own behaviour on aspects of Judaism as God's new 'chosen' people, they were able to maintain animosity to Jews themselves, and the desire to relocate Jews to the Middle East had the happy consequence of removing them from Europe and fulfilling prophecy at the same time. The dark shadow of this feat of convoluted thinking is cast across the holocaust of the twentieth century. Another possibility was that the Jews of Europe were not the Jews that would repossess the Holy Land. The sixteenth century was also a time of exploration and discovery. Columbus hit land to the west in 1492 and, suddenly, the constricted world view of the medieval period was exploded, and new imaginative possibilities opened up. How did these new lands fit into God's purposes?

One important possibility was that this was where the lost Ten Tribes of the Northern Kingdom of Israel had been hiding; if they could be located and identified, perhaps their return to the Middle East would follow swiftly. Belief in the continued existence of the Ten Tribes seems to have lasted from the time of Amos, throughout subsequent centuries right down to the Christian era, although there are only isolated and scattered references to it in Jewish texts, indicating perhaps that the fate of the Lost Tribes did not worry people too much until more recent times. The idea seems to have been that the Ten Tribes were exiled in unknown lands but all would eventually return to the Holy Land in the Last Days. Throughout the Middle Ages there were various claims regarding the existence of the Ten Lost Tribes as well as attempts by scholars and explorers (both Jewish and non-Jewish) to discover them and/or to identify different peoples with them. But with the discovery of the New World in the seventeenth century, and its exploration by Christian explorers and missionaries, the search took on a new impetus. In particular, a Jewish Portuguese traveller, Antonio de Montezinos, reported that some of the Lost Tribes had survived as indigenous people in South America. This news was picked up by Menasseh ben Israel, a Dutch Jew, who in 1649, published, *The Hope of Israel*, in which he expounded the theory that the indigenous people of America were descendants of the Lost Tribes. An English translation was published in London in 1650 and aroused interest, partly because the year 1666 was approaching and the last three digits were regarded as apocalyptically significant. From these events ultimately stem many apocalyptic cults, notably Mormons and British Israelites, that we shall trace later in this book. One possibility was that the indigenous Americans could be descended from the ten tribes; this idea resurfaced prominently in the thinking of Joseph Smith, the founder of the Mormons two centuries later. And a corollary to that idea was that the American continent was itself a new Eden: that the Millennium would find its home there. This concept of the New World as the basis for the new Heaven and Earth of Revelation was to inspire many Puritans and other Protestant sects to brave the Atlantic in small boats in search of social and religious salvation.

All of these ideas and more created a ferment of apocalyptic speculation and excitement throughout the seventeenth century, and those not prepared to look for the new Eden in America sought to create it in England. A full survey of all these radical social and religious groupings and sects would require another book, but perhaps we can take time to look at a few of the more curious. The Ranters, for example, who based their ideas on Joachim of Fiore's teachings about the New Age of the Spirit. For them, Christ's Second Coming was manifested symbolically in the conversion of the believer to new life in the Spirit, leading to complete freedom from any consequences of sin. Many of them seem to have taken their liberty to extremes: public nudity and sexual licence abounded, apparently with God's full approval. Similarly, the Adamites also favoured public nudity as evidence of their Edenic innocence. The Seekers on the other hand, conducted themselves more soberly, but in their search for a new, purer

The Reformation

form of Christianity were happily tolerant of all other sects and religions until Christ returned and put everyone straight on just exactly what He wanted a church to be. Most or all these strange sects have long dwindled away to nothing. The main exception is the Quakers, who began at this time and of course survive to this day, partly because they seem to have absorbed some of the other sects. They too believed in the pre-eminence of the Holy Spirit within each believer, and that this frees the believer from behavioural requirements; but they somehow square this belief with a requirement nonetheless to behave in accordance with traditional Christian values.

All these groups were founded by individuals whose reading of scripture and/or personal inspiration by the Holy Spirit, led them to their convictions. Sometimes, their convictions led them to believe that they were themselves apocalyptic figures from scriptural prophecy. In the 1630s, even before the Civil War, a pair of weavers, Richard Farnham and John Bull, made the extraordinary claim that they were the two witnesses prophesied in Revelation Chapter 11. These twin characters feature prominently in Futurist interpretations of End Time prophecy; I shall return to the subject later. Ironically, Farnham claimed on scriptural grounds to be immune from the plague but, after incarceration in Bedlam Hospital, died of it. Another such was Thomas Tany, who was typical of the type. Born Thomas Totney, he changed his name to Theaurau John Tany, following some sort of revelatory experience, and claiming descent from Aaron (the supposed brother of Moses) he presented himself as the last prophet, sent by God to declare the final Day of the Lord. The claim to be the 'final' prophet has been repeated over and over again from John the Baptist onwards and, of course, reaches its apotheosis in the claims of Islam's Prophet Mohammed. Unlike the latter, however, Tany failed to establish lasting fame or followers and died without seeing the doomsday he proclaimed. Another again was John Robins, who went one better than Tany and declared himself to be not just a prophet but, in reality, an incarnation of God himself, with supernatural powers commensurate. Following a period of imprisonment, he seems to have regained a sense of proportion and retired quietly back into the obscurity from which he came.

These, however, were but an overture to the main act of one Lodowicke Muggleton, a London tailor born in 1609, who founded the wonderfully named Muggletonians. Like many of the leading characters in the story of eschatological belief, his ideas about the end of the world, and his sense of religious conviction, were rooted in an earlier period of spiritual confusion and search. A Puritan in his earlier years, Muggleton was, like many Puritans, much troubled by a sense of personal sin and a lack of conviction that he was one of the Elect: those according to Calvinist belief who are chosen by God from the beginning of time for salvation. In his mid-twenties, by then having lost two wives and several children, he found himself falling away from the Puritan faith altogether. However, fifteen years later, in 1850, his interest in religious matters was reawakened by contact with some of the other Protestant sects and flamboyant preachers flourishing in London at the time, including Thomas Tany. Muggleton was for a time mesmerized by these and other charismatic religious figures, and in 1651 began to experience his own personal revelations from God, particularly concerning the meaning of scripture. By some extraordinary coincidence, or perhaps not so extraordinary given the religious fervour of the times, he discovered that his cousin, John Reeve, was experiencing similar revelations. They compared notes and determined that *they* must be the 'two witnesses'. Suddenly, eschatological prophecy was centre stage and appeared to be being enacted, not in the dim and distant past of the Holy Land, nor sometime in a hazy future, but here and now, on the streets of the capital city. Their joint 'witnessing' continued for six years, broken only by a six-month spell of imprisonment for blasphemy – an experience that seems to have done nothing to cool their ardour. But then Reeve died in 1658, and for the next 40 years Muggleton travelled the country building followers. He wrote several books and pamphlets, setting out the tenets of what became known as Muggletonianism. It is an extraordinary fact that the last Muggletonian only died in 1979, presumably still awaiting the postponed apocalypse.

Most of these deluded people did little harm to anyone except themselves. They may have preached an imminent Millennium, but they did not personally take up arms to institute it, nor incite their followers to insurrection. The exception was the Fifth Monarchy men, who based their ideas on the five empires prophecy of Daniel, Chapter 2. They believed the 'fifth empire' to be a reference to the Millennium, which was imminent, and they regarded Cromwell as God's instrument in this. When Cromwell executed Charles I, they welcomed it as the first step towards the abolition of human government and the establishment of a new world order. They now looked forward to the conversion of the Jews, the destruction of Islam and the Second Coming, all led by Cromwell from his new position of political power. Unfortunately for them, events took a different turn and Cromwell pursued a more moderate course, outlawing the Fifth Monarchists in so doing. In response, a Fifth Monarchist group led by Thomas Venner attempted their own glorious revolution in 1657 and failed. Venner was jailed for a couple of years, but on release attempted a second coup in 1661. With about fifty followers, he violently attacked strategic positions in London but was again put down and this time hanged. There were no further attempts to bring about the Millennium by force, but social and religious Millennial ideas continued and subsequent generations sought to create their new Edens in the new world.

Millennial expectation, which had been building in the first half of the seventeenth century, erupted fully in 1666. Simple arithmetic, if not common sense, suggested that 1,000 years plus 666, the sign of the Beast, gave 1666. And right on cue, the Black Death made a devastating reappearance in that year. What further signs were needed that at last the Day of the Lord was at hand? It is hard to comprehend the sheer scale of the devastation, but for a populace with no modern understanding of the causes of disease, the plague yet again seemed to be the punishment of a wrathful deity and the harbinger of worse to come. And indeed it came, in the shape of the Great Fire of London – a biblical judgement if ever there was one, echoing the fire and brimstone of divine retribution. And yet, with the benefit of hindsight, we now know that of course, the world did not end. And in fact, 1666 was in many ways a turning point. The great fire did more than anything else to halt the plague in its tracks. But more fundamentally, the second half of the seventeenth century saw the beginning of what we now regard as the advent of scientific reason. Even while the fire burned, Newton was discovering the fundamental laws of physics, and while it would still be many years before the true causes of the plague were understood, nevertheless a new spirit was abroad in the land. Not Joachim's Age of Spirit but the Age of Reason. For a time, it seemed that blind superstition would give way to scientific understanding and that apocalyptic lunacy would fall by the wayside along with other pre-scientific fears and bogeymen. Unfortunately for us all, this is not how it eventually played out.

3

Post- Reformation Eschatology

The latter half of the seventeenth century in England, after the turmoil of 1666, saw apocalyptic interest subside. Political, economic and religious stability (relatively speaking) created a favourable environment for the new, rational ideas of the Enlightenment, and the Anglican compromise reduced Christianity to the state religion we have come to know: more concerned with the comfort of the clergy and the physical wellbeing of parishioners than the salvation of immortal souls. The Apocalypse that had seemed so imminent receded again. But as always, new religious leaders arose to stir the waters, the most notable being the Wesley brothers, John and Charles, in the first half of the eighteenth century. They were uninterested in the economic progress of the nation. The only thing that mattered to them was the need to save souls from damnation and, with their followers, they set about awakening the nation to its spiritual peril. Revivalism as it is known became a recurring feature of Christianity in the UK from that time to this, working both within and without the established Anglican Church to refocus religious effort away from the physical concerns of today towards the spiritual concerns of eternity. The emphasis was on the experience of being 'born again' followed by a righteous life guided by the indwelling influence of the Holy Spirit. This was, of course, a Protestant phenomenon. Catholic Europe saw no such need for revival and pretty much carried on as it had always done, sowing the seeds of its own destruction at the end of the eighteenth century when, for a time, the French Revolution swept it away in the name of Reason.

Revivalism went hand in glove with a new eschatological interpretation of the Millennium. We have seen how the early Church took a literal view of the matter: Christ would return, establish his thousand-year reign, and then final judgement and a new Heaven and Earth. The timing of Christ's return was unknown, but no one doubted it was imminent. Except, of course, it did not happen. Augustine dealt with the unfortunate postponement of the Day of the Lord by arguing that it had all been a misunderstanding. The Millennium was not a future event – it was happening now. It had started with Christ's life and was the thousand-year period in which Christianity, in tandem with the Roman Empire, would evangelize the world before Christ came again. Following Augustine, the Catholic Church took the view that the Millennium was not a physical thousand-year reign but a symbol for the reign of the Catholic Church itself as, hand in glove with the Roman Empire, it would gradually extend the era of God's grace and Pax Romana across the world. Clearly, for Protestants after the dust settled on the Reformation, this interpretation would never do. But a parallel could be drawn between the gradual extension of the Catholic Church (now regarded as the work of Satan) and the gradual extension of the Protestant Gospel through evangelism. Revivalism was clear evidence that, given a focus on the work of the Holy Spirit, the evangelizing of the world could be a reality and a true Millennium on Earth could be created, preparing the ground for Christ's Second Coming. Preaching the Gospel to the unconverted had the dual objective of bringing individual souls to salvation and hastening the process necessary for Christ's return. This 'post-millennial' understanding as it is known, characterizes many evangelicals in the UK and America down to the present day. However, it fails to deal with the other necessary prerequisite for Christ's return: the need for the Jews to return to Jerusalem, rebuild the temple, and convert to Christianity. This knotty problem required nifty intellectual footwork and did not receive its solution until the nineteenth century, with the emergence of what became known as Dispensationalism.

The idea that God's dealings with mankind can be divided into separate dispensations was not new; for example, it is not dissimilar to Joachim of Fiore's division of history into different ages or eras. But the assumption had always been that these dispensations were sequential and that when one ended, another began. In very simple terms, the First Dispensation was that based on God's Covenant with the Jews; it stretched from the Mosaic Covenant down to the crucifixion and is characterized as the Dispensation of the Law. The Second Dispensation, that of Grace is that initiated by Christ through his sacrifice on the cross and continues to this day. The Third Dispensation (the Millennium) will be that ushered in on the Day of the Lord. (The period between Creation and Moses is divided by Dispensationalists variously into between one and five extra dispensations, but we can ignore those for the purposes of understanding the apocalyptic implications). Under the traditional view, the Dispensation of Grace replaced that of Law. In other words, Christians replaced Jews as the chosen people, with all the unfortunate implications that has had for Jews over the centuries since. But as we have seen, there was no escaping the biblical implication that, nevertheless, the salvation of the Jews and their return to Jerusalem was somehow involved in the advent of the Millennial Dispensation. And the Second Coming would be delayed until then. For those thirsting for the Day of the Lord, this seemed like an immovable obstacle.

Dispensationalism solved the problem neatly by arguing that the mistake is to assume that Grace supersedes Law; that all God's promises to the Jews were transferred to Christians. Instead, it argues, God's Covenant with the Jews remains in place and will in time be fulfilled. It is just that it is put on hold during the Dispensation of Grace. Law and Grace overlap. This then neatly allows not only a separation between the nation and people of Israel on the one hand, and the spiritual nation of Christians on the other, but it also separates the Rapture of Christians from the physical Second Coming and the Millennium. Under the new scheme of things, Christ will gather up the faithful at a stroke, thus ending the Dispensation of Grace; this will be followed by the Millennium, in which period the Jews will find salvation and return to Jerusalem; and then will come the physical Second Coming, the final judgement, and the new Heaven and Earth.

There are endless nuances to this new Dispensationalist scheme. For example, will the Great Tribulation precede or succeed the Millennium, or even occur sometime in between? And there is the issue of the status of Jews who convert to Christianity in the Dispensation of Grace – including, of course, the New Testament Apostles: some Dispensationalists believe that Jews can still be saved by obedience to the Law because they will be judged under the rules of that Dispensation; others believe that everyone, including Jews, needs to be converted. But these hairsplittings need not detain us here. The key point is that at one bound, Dispensationalism freed Christians from the requirement for the identification of the Lost Tribes of Israel, the conversion of the Jewish people to Christianity and the problematical usurpation of the Holy Land from an entrenched Islam. And it gave a new prominence in eschatological thinking to the Rapture.

Dispensationalist hopes could now focus on a magical moment when Christ will miraculously raise the living and dead faithful to join him in the sky: a devastating moment that could occur at any time and providing Dispensationalist fiction writers with endless opportunity to explore the effect of this 'Rapture' on those 'left behind' in driverless cars and pilotless aircraft.[1] These ideas were in the air as the nineteenth century dawned, but they were thought through, codified and promulgated by one extraordinary man – John Nelson Darby. The sect he founded, the Plymouth Brethren, survives to this day in two main forms: the cultish Exclusive Brethren and the milder Open Brethren. The former hit UK headlines in the 1960s and 1970s as its teachings tore families apart. Believers were taught to cut themselves off completely from unbelievers, including their own parents and children. The cult still exists today but the media seem to have lost interest in its appalling excesses, focusing on more successful and prominent sects.

But Darby's real legacy is Dispensationalism and the concomitant belief in the Rapture as the central focus for Christian belief. Many evangelical, fundamentalist Christians today would subscribe to Dispensationalism in one of its varied forms. What drives their faith is the belief that the Dispensation of Grace could end at any second in a single, decisive event, after which anyone not 'saved' will be catastrophically left behind. Any event that seems to suggest that the Millennium might be approaching, notably the creation of the modern state of Israel, is welcomed as evidence that the End Times are upon us all, but the Rapture is not dependant on any such event and can happen anytime, and then, woe betide anyone, professing Christianity or not, who is

---

[1] The prime example being the 'Left Behind' series of pretribulation, premillennial, dispensational novels by Tim LaHaye and Jerry B. Jenkins.

caught with his or her soul in anything but a state of Grace. Darby died in 1882 but spent the preceding fifty years promulgating his new scheme around Britain and Europe and, crucially, in 1862 and again in 1871, in missionary crusades across America, where he found a receptive audience among the various evangelical and fundamentalist sects that proliferated there. His ideas preceded him through American disciples like James Inglis who, in 1854 began to publish a monthly magazine – *Waymarks in the Wilderness* – which drew on Darby's ideas. By the end of the nineteenth century, Darby's Dispensationalism was firmly established as the predominant eschatological view among Protestant dissenters in the USA. Its emphasis on the urgent need for repentance and salvation in the face of imminent Rapture, dependent on nothing but God's whim, provided the perfect spur to evangelical effort.

As essentially a fundamentalist phenomenon, Revivalism wherever it is found tends to take a keen interest in apocalypse. And from its ranks at times emerge new leaders with new visions, founding new sects, some of which still thrive today. One of the earliest such is worth looking at in some detail because most of the characteristics of such sects can be discerned there. The story starts with one Richard Brothers, who in the last decade of the eighteenth century declared himself to be the direct descendant of the biblical David and the Apostle of a new sect that regarded England as the new Israel. He ended up in a lunatic asylum, but from him stem several British sects. The first of these was led by Joanna Southcott who, following the incarceration of Brothers, and supported by seven of his followers (her 'Seven Stars'), declared herself to be the incarnation of female apocalyptic figures from Revelation.[2] At the age of 65 she declared herself

---

2 The woman arrayed with the sun in Revelation 12 and the Bride of Christ from Revelation 19.

pregnant with the Messiah, but died a few months later having failed to deliver – physically or spiritually. Nevertheless, she had succeeded in attracting about 100,000 adherents, who, rather than renege on their beliefs, decided that her Messianic pregnancy must be interpreted as a spiritual event: the desperate refuge of many a disappointed prophet of the Apocalypse. There then ensued a squabble over her succession. The sect split as a result. Some followed a John 'Zion' Ward, who declared *himself* to be the awaited Messiah, but the bulk of believers followed George Turner, who regarded himself more modestly to be the Baptist figure to the coming Messiah. He wrote new scriptures mimicking the English of the King James Bible. On his death, another visionary emerged from the Southcott ranks – a John Wroe, who on the basis of angelic visions, declared his mission to be the gathering of the Ten Lost Tribes and the subsequent inauguration of the Millennium. He also declared that God had appointed seven virgins for his use, and that when one of them then became pregnant she would give birth to the Messiah. Unfortunately, the subsequent birth of a girl rather undermined his credibility.

The story of the Southcottians would be played out again and again right down to today. An individual arises and declares himself – or herself – to be anointed by God to some key task in the apocalyptic scheme. His motives may or may not be sincere: he may be driven by delusions, or by idiosyncratic interpretations of obscure scripture, or by more earthly goals. One way or another his pronouncements turn out to be false, but his followers explain this away, usually by spiritualizing what began as historical prophecies – literal interpretation yet again giving way conveniently to metaphorical explication. New leaders then arise. Usually schism occurs at this point, as the new leaders struggle for supremacy. New scripture of some sort is produced as the basis for the beliefs of the new sects, usually written in the belief that God's own language is Jacobean English, and there is no evidence for the supernatural origin of these texts other than the word of the leader himself. Then, at some point, sex raises its ugly head. For some reason, the Christian God who throughout history seems to have a problem with human sex, decides that, nonetheless, His appointed representative on Earth must have access to the sexual objects of his choice. In the case of John Wroe, this seems to have been a step too far, resulting in his eclipse, but there are plenty of examples where the sect leader is able to sustain his sexual requirements for years and even decades.

Of course, most Christians were not led astray by this sort of nonsense. But throughout the eighteenth century most believers did subscribe to the assumptions that underlay all these sects: that Protestantism in all its forms was sounding the death knell for Catholicism and that the downfall of the Catholic Church was an apocalyptic event that evidenced the Last Days as prophesied in scripture. But yet again, history did not meet expectations. The world went on, as did the Catholic Church. Pope succeeded pope, and none turned out to be the Antichrist. As the Jews had done after the destruction of the Northern Kingdom; after the Babylonian Exile; after the predations of Antiochus; after the Roman destruction of Jerusalem and the Holy Land. And as Christians also had done time and time again as, despite all expectations to the contrary down the centuries, the End of Days never arrived.

The legacy of the evangelical revival has been the last 300 years in which Christianity in Britain has become more and more polarized between fundamentalist evangelicalism, both within and without the established Anglican Church, and traditional, moderate Christians, suspicious of the 'enthusiasms' and 'extremities' of the evangelicals. As the progress of reason

Post-Reformation Eschatology

continued into the nineteenth century and after, the whole basis of belief in a supernatural Christianity came under attack and this led to increasing polarity. At first, in the nineteenth century, that polarity led some traditionalists back to the welcoming arms of the Catholic Church, but increasingly over time, the polarity has become between, on the one hand, evangelicals, fundamentalists, salvationists and their ilk, who cling to a literal interpretation of the Bible against all the odds, and the vast majority of professing Christians who take little or no interest in the foundations or even the ultimate truth of their faith, but who trust that a good life is sufficient, and for whom churchgoing is a social rather than a particularly religious act. Eschatology is now a minority interest in the UK, pursued by fundamentalists who get a thrill from the intellectual exercise of trying to reconcile the conflicting biblical accounts of the End Time events. Unfortunately, as we have seen, when their findings occasionally surface in general consciousness, they stir ancient feelings of fear and uncertainty until, for the umpteenth time, their prophetic certainties are shown to be no more substantial than the wind, and things settle back down again to comfortable disinterest. In America, however, things are different. Protestant revivalism found fertile soil for its ideas in America, where fundamentalism of one kind or another was the legacy of the founding fathers who had sought to create a new Eden on those western shores. What the British call the Evangelical Revival is known in the US as the First Great Awakening, and historians of religious developments there discern Second, Third and even Fourth Great Awakenings stretching down almost to the present day. Indeed, Revivalism has been and is a strong feature of American religious life, and this has created the intellectual environment for endless eschatological speculation.

The Second Great Awakening spawned two figures whose

importance to doomsday thinking in America cannot be overestimated: William Miller and Joseph Smith. Miller was born in Massachusetts in 1782. Raised as an orthodox Baptist, he rejected revealed religion in his early twenties on the grounds of its myriad inconsistencies and, heavily influenced by European rationalist thinking, became a Deist. Deism was a popular philosophy before Darwin showed that there might be other explanations for human existence. Deists believe that there is a God, as evidenced by the existence and wonder of the natural world, but that we can know nothing about Him and He in any case does not intervene or concern Himself in any way with human affairs. However, Miller's participation in the American War of Independence caused a change of mind; his personal experience of deliverance from death during one battle, combined with the deliverance of the American people, gave him a new perspective on God's intervention in human history. The deaths of his father and sister soon after the war deepened his seriousness about human destiny, and he rediscovered his faith in an emotional conversion experience. He sought to reconcile his new commitment of faith with all the rationalist doubts he had previously espoused, by undertaking a lengthy and exhaustive study of the Bible, convinced that, properly understood, the inconsistencies would melt away and he would be able to re-establish its inerrancy. This was a major new idea. Previous theologians had been largely content to rest on faith that all would be revealed in eternity; Miller set out to define revealed Truth here and now.

He worked his way through the Bible from cover to cover, only moving from verse to verse when he felt he had a full understanding. The result of this effort was that he began to believe not only that the truth generally was available to anyone diligent enough to study scripture as he had done, but that, specifically, it was possible to pinpoint the precise time of Christ's Second Coming. By 1618, when he was in his mid-thirties, he had it nailed. The method he used was to use prophecies in the Book of Daniel that we shall examine in detail later. Suffice to say here that by this method he arrived at the date of 1843 when the world would end, and Christ would return in glory. The movement he founded became known as Adventism for this reason. He thus had twenty-five years left in order to prepare himself, his family and others for the great moment.

The first few of those years were taken up with checking and rechecking his calculations and eventually in September 1822 he went public for the first time. But he did not begin to actively promote his ideas until ten years later when, in 1832 he published a series of articles in a Baptist newspaper, followed by a tract in 1834. From then onwards, he found himself a celebrity, and Millerism over the next decade became a national religious movement. Every time his date for Christ's return passed without (apparent) incident, he revised his calculations and announced that Christ would return 'sometime between March 21, 1843, and March 21, 1844'. This then shifted to 18 April 1844, and then finally to 22 October 1844. This last date became known to his followers as 'The Great Disappointment' and some of them dealt with it by deciding that Christ did indeed return as scheduled, but it happened invisibly in Heaven. Amazingly, the Adventist movement that Miller founded has millions of adherents right down to the present day. As usual, the Adventist movement manifests itself through a whole range of sects stemming from Miller's original teachings, but each differing on some matter of doctrine. These include Seventh Day Adventists and Christadelphians as well as dozens of smaller sects. One of the latter you may have heard of. A sect called Shepherds Rod split off from the Seventh Day Adventists in the 1930s. In time this became known as the Davidian

Seventh Day Adventists: an offshoot of this is the Branch Davidians. A group of these split off again, led by one David Koresh, and seventy-six of them died at the Waco Siege. Reminding us, if any such reminder were necessary, that these crazy ideas kill people.

If Adventism regards itself as still Christian, deriving its doctrines from the Bible, the same cannot really be said of Mormonism. Mormons regard themselves as Christians because they believe in the atoning power of Christ's sacrifice on the cross, but in almost every other respect their specific beliefs are at variance with those of mainstream Christianity. The sect was founded by Joseph Smith who, like Miller, began his career in Revivalism, but went on to 'discover' new scriptures of his own and to take his followers off in new directions entirely, although still with their roots in the eschatological concerns and ideas of mainstream Christianity. Born and raised in New England, Smith was caught up in the feverish excitement of the countless revival meetings in the area and began from an early age to have visions of his own. In 1823, at the age of 18, by his own account, he was visited by an angel called Moroni who directed him to the hidden location of several religious artefacts. He visited the location several times over the next four years and eventually translated a new scripture, inscribed on golden plates among the artefacts, that was eventually published as the *Book of Mormon* in 1830. It is the key scripture of the movement he founded, now known as the Church of Jesus Christ of Latter-day Saints or Mormonism. Mormon eschatology runs counter to mainstream Christianity in that it most resembles the literal understanding of the early Church: that Christ will return and personally rule on Earth for a Millennium before the final judgement. The distinction in this, as in most aspects of the teachings of the sect, is that all prophecy is interpreted in a North American context. The

Post-Reformation Eschatology

Lost Tribes of Israel landed up in America in the sixth century BC; Christ appeared to them there after his resurrection; God has now chosen to re-establish his church in America through Joseph Smith;[3] Mormons are the new Israel; and Christ's Second Coming will be in America – probably Missouri! But none of this is going to happen any time soon: Mormons believe that the Gospel must be brought to Israel before Christ will return and as of now, by agreement with the Israeli government, Mormon teams do not knock on doors in Israel.

Smith died in 1844 and his movement was subsequently developed and led by Brigham Young. A few of the beliefs established by Young, notably God's favourable attitude to bigamy, have led over the years to various revisions to Mormon belief, and sectarian splits as a result. But in total there are about 15 million Mormons of one kind or another across the world and, as long as you are not an Israeli, there is a fair chance that they will be knocking on your door at some point. If the knock turns out not to be Mormons, chances are it will be a Jehovah's Witness. This sect traces its origins back to a man called Charles Taze Russell. Born in 1852, he was too late for the Second Great Awakening, but this did not prevent him initiating another successful cult: there are only 7 million of them (half the number of Mormons) but this does not prevent them vying with the latter vigorously for your soul. As with Mormonism, Jehovah's Witnesses regard themselves as Christians because of their belief in salvation through faith, but would be rejected as such by mainstream Christianity. Not that this worries them overmuch; their fears of doctrinal contamination keep them separate from the rest of humanity (as with Darby's Exclu-

---

[3] Effectively a new 'dispensation' though Smith predates Darby and dispensationalists would not recognize Smith's Latter-Day dispensation.

sive Brethren) and impervious to any pleas of common sense.[4]

Russell was raised a Presbyterian, became a Congregationalist and then, at age 18, came under Adventist influence that convinced him he was living in the Last Days. Unlike Smith, he did not have visions of his own but sought to understand the Truth through a close study of scripture: the original movement he founded was the Bible Study Movement. In this, he resembled people like Miller and, indeed, his early Bible study groups involved people with an Adventist background. One Adventist in particular, Nelson Barbour, perhaps influenced by Darby, predicted that an invisible rapture would take place in 1873, and then in 1874. Like the Millerites before them, Barbour's followers dealt with their own great disappointment by arguing that the invisible return of Christ had indeed taken place on schedule and would be followed imminently by a visible return in 1878. The response of Russell, who met Barbour in 1876, was to sell up all he had (his family clothing stores, worth around 7 million dollars in today's money) and devote the two years before the Second Coming to fomenting a new revival. The non-appearance of Jesus in 1878 led to a split with Barbour, but Russell retained belief that Jesus had indeed returned invisibly in 1874 and that he now reigned in Heaven. His personal fortune meant that he could spend his life in Bible study and in the promulgation of his findings through publications that were to become *The Watchtower* magazine, hawked by his followers on street corners to this day. He did not die until 1916, and over the 40 years until then made many predictions about End Time events, none of which of

---

4 I have had personal experience of this. My father's brother became a Jehovah's Witness and isolated his family from his mother, brothers and sisters. The isolation continues to the present day, down to the third and fourth generations.

course materialized but all of which were explained away by his followers by the usual expedient of claiming them to have occurred spiritually or symbolically.

The movement today acknowledges that many/most of these predictions were plain wrong, but, nevertheless, maintains that Christ has been reigning from Heaven since 1914, and although they will not be drawn on dates again, they regard the End of Days as imminent. In their scheme of things, they give considerable weight to the idea of Armageddon which they understand to include the destruction of all earthly governments by God. After Armageddon, will come the Millennium, but again, not a Millennium that any other Christian sect would recognize. The peculiar belief of Jehovah's Witnesses is that there will be a sort of two-tier eternity. They interpret the reference in Revelation 14:4 to 'the 144,000' as a reference to their own sect. These people will reign with Christ over everyone else for a Millennium, during which the dead will be resurrected. The final judgement at the end of the 1,000 years will be based, not on past deeds, but on the way people conduct themselves over the Millennial period. At the end of the 1,000 years a final test will take place when Satan is brought back to mislead a perfected mankind. The end result will be a fully tested, glorified human race. So, when you next encounter a Jehovah's Witness on the doorstep or the street corner, you know that their evangelical zeal is driven not just by the belief that we live at the End of Days, but by the more personal conviction that there are only 144,000 places available in the top tier of eternity, and with 7 million of them vying for those places, the only way they can be sure of their own place is to save more souls than the rest of their congregation.

The twentieth century has seen even more proliferation of new sects in Christianity, all of which have distinctive eschatological views and in many cases were founded precisely because of those views. Two perhaps worth picking out from the crowd are Pentecostalism and British Israelism. Both have their roots in earlier times but picked up adherents and influence in the early decades of the twentieth century, although the former continues as a strong force in mainstream Christianity down to the present day, while the latter has receded.

British Israelism is exactly what it sounds like: the literal belief that the British peoples are directly descended from the lost Ten Tribes of Israel. We have seen how the issue of the role of the Jews in End Time events has bedevilled eschatology from the beginning; also, how after the Reformation this led to a love/hate relationship between some Protestant sects and the Jewish people. These contradictions can be traced right back to the seventeenth century, but British Israelism as a movement began in the 1880s in Britain, spread rapidly to the USA and the Empire, and had its heyday in the racialism and anti-Semitism of the 1930s. The idea behind it is simple enough: if modern Jews are all descended from just the two tribes of the Southern Kingdom,[5] the vast majority of real Jews are missing, descended from the Northern Ten Tribes. By the twentieth century, it had become pretty clear that they could not be lurking in some as yet undiscovered part of the world: there might be Neanderthals, Yeti, and Loch Ness Monsters still surviving, but not the millions of descendants of the Ten Tribes. So they must be hiding in plain sight.

The impetus to identify them with the British derives from the unprecedented success of the British Empire and the explicit belief among many that this reflected a God-inspired destiny to evangelize the world and bring about the Millennium. One such, for example, was Alexander James Ferris who wrote a couple of dozen pamphlets before, during and

---

5 And one of those, Benjamin, was the smallest tribe of the twelve.

after the Second World War, in which he argued for the inevitability of British and American victory on the grounds that the Allies would be fulfilling scripture in relation to Israel.[6] The evidence was sought for in scripture and archaeology, but the foundation stone of the belief was in the amateur linguistic and racial theories of the time. To summarize a great deal of speculative association, the Lost Tribes were regarded as re-emerging into history as the ancient Scythians. Some ancient sources called them the Sacae, and from this was discerned the name Isaac from whom, of course, all Jews are said to be descended. From Sacae comes the Saxons (Isaac's sons) who invaded England from their homeland in Denmark (the home of the biblical Tribe of Dan). Similar word association linked the Sacae with the Scotii of Scotland. Needless to say, none of all this stands up for even a second to modern scientific scrutiny. We have known for a long time that Hebrew, a Semitic language, has totally distinct roots from English, which belongs to the Indo-European family of languages and any similarity of sounds are accidental. And of course, modern genetics disproves the theory entirely. Yet such is the strength of this sort of belief that the British-Israel-World Federation, founded in 1919, still exists and has members across the world.

The founders of the movement were by and large people who had respect for the Jews, believed in their continuing role in God's eternal plan, and genuinely sought a solution to the problem of the Lost Tribes and the Last Days. Indeed, in its early days, the movement numbered some prominent

---

[6] *Why the British are Israel: nine conclusive facts proving that the Anglo-Saxons represent the House of Israel of scripture* (1934) is representative. I possess a copy of his bestseller – over 60,000 copies sold – *When Russia Bombs Germany* (1940) which argues, among other lunacies, that the aerial bombardments of the war were prophesied as the seventh vial of Revelation: 'And the seventh angel poured out his vial into the air.'

Jews and rabbis among its adherents. But the early decades of the twentieth century were a time of unscientific racial theories that legitimized pogroms and eventually led to the Holocaust, and in this environment the crazy but relatively benign ideas of early British Israelism mutated for many into justification for the anti-Semitism that always lurked just below the surface of British religious belief. For these people, it was a relatively small step from the idea that the English are the Lost Tribes to the idea that the English are indeed the only *real* 'Jews' and that the people in Europe who styled themselves Jews were just imposters. It was then easy for such people to become Nazi sympathizers, sharing their perverted ideals of racial purity. Like the Nazis too, they linked their beliefs to all kinds of mystical nonsense to do with ancient Egypt, the pyramids and Celtic mythology; and like the Nazis in *Raiders of the Lost Ark*, went hunting for the Ark of the Covenant and other mystical archaeological treasures, seriously damaging sites like the Hill of Tara in Ireland in the process. The worst of these people formed a movement called British Identity and went so far as to conclude that only people of the 'Caucasian' race possess souls and therefore are candidates for salvation: the rest of humanity being, in effect, on the same level as animals. And from there to the Holocaust was not even a small step. The fact that there are some, not without influence, in America today who believe something similar would be cause for merriment were it not so horrifically chilling.

Many Christian sects in the twentieth century became infected with the ideas of British Israelitism. One will have nostalgic resonance for British readers of this book who like me were young in the 1960s. Strict government control of broadcasting meant that for many years the only source of consistent contemporary pop music on the radio was Radio Luxemburg – a station based outside UK jurisdiction but that beamed its programmes at the UK mainland. A ubiquitous advertiser on that channel was an American, Herbert W. Armstrong who, with his son Garner Ted, every night broadcast an advertising segment in which they brought 'the good news of the world tomorrow'. Originally Adventist in belief, Armstrong split with them when he became convinced by British Israelism and established his Worldwide Church of God with that belief at its heart. He felt himself called by God to evangelize the Lost Tribes in Britain before the imminent Day of the Lord and via both his radio broadcasts and his free *Plain Truth* magazine,[7] did just that. He continued to preach the usual apocalyptic, prophetic inanities, interpreting every world event in terms of signs of the times, until his death, when his Church inexorably became riven by schism, not least over the issue of the Jews.

Another notable convert to the British Israelism cause was George Jeffreys, who founded the Elim Pentecostal Church. He split from his own church when, like Armstrong, he became convinced of British Israelism, but Elim continues strong to this day. Pentecostalism, of which Elim is a prominent version, was the other major innovation at the turn of the twentieth century, although it too, like British Israelism, has its roots far back in Christian history. As the name implies, it focuses on the day of Pentecost, described in Acts Chapter 2, where the Holy Spirit descends as fire on the disciples in Jerusalem and results in them preaching in different 'tongues' to the crowds gathered for the Jewish Feast of Weeks. This concept of baptism by the Holy Spirit is developed in the

---

7 I remember as a teenager, along with my friends, receiving this through the post regularly – not because we bought into its obvious nonsense, but because we just could not believe that such an expensively produced, glossy magazine could be distributed absolutely free. It was the first experience Britain had of the sheer monetary resources of American evangelism before Billy Graham brought his mass crusades to the UK.

early Church as something available to all believers and is regarded as bestowing various 'Gifts' of the spirit, including healing and prophecy as well as speaking in tongues. We saw earlier that ongoing prophecy was accepted in the early Church in contradiction to the Jewish faith, which regarded the age of prophecy to have ended centuries before. However, as we also saw, prophecy became increasingly uncomfortable to the established Church as it could undermine or conflict with the emerging doctrinal consensus, and together with the other Gifts of the Spirit it gradually fell by the wayside. With the advent of Revivalism and fundamentalism in the nineteenth century, an interest in these ideas was reawakened. And as the challenges to Christian belief grew during that century, some people sought refuge from growing secularism in these doctrines that supported inner certainty in the face of exterior challenge. The logical arguments of scientific secularism could be met with inner conviction, born of the Holy Spirit Himself. And insofar as the Gifts of the Spirit could be manifested to the world at large through incontrovertible acts of healing, or the extraordinary exercise of the Gift of Tongues, this provided 'proof' of a kind more than enough for fundamentalists.

The founder of Methodism, John Wesley himself, lay the foundations for this. He taught that following the conversion experience in which the sinner accepted Christ as his personal saviour and his sins were remitted – the first 'act of grace' – there should follow in the life of a true believer a second 'act of grace', as at Pentecost, in which the believer receives the Holy Spirit in his life and exhibits the Gifts of the Spirit as an external signal to the community of believers that his conversion was real and he is progressing along a spiritual path. Where the Pentecostal path could lead ultimately was a matter for fine debate. For some, the next step was a third work of grace. In some churches and for some

Post-Reformation Eschatology

individuals, this might manifest as speaking in tongues. For others, as the gifts of healing or handling snakes with impunity. For some, even the return of prophecy – although, the Bible is still regarded as fixed and finished and modern prophecy is fallible, to be tested by the congregation for conformity with accepted doctrinal interpretation of scripture. Indeed, restricted in this way, as we saw before, prophecy effectively becomes just powerful preaching; as with the ancient Jewish prophets, foretelling the future is only a minor element in prophecy.

And for most, the path was believed to lead eventually to a sort of spiritual perfection in this life, a oneness with God that is conceived as the very reason for Earthly existence, and a preparation for the life to come. The phenomenon of speaking in tongues is a strange one, that no doubt has a secular psychological explanation. When witnessed today by a critical, rational observer, it appears bathetic: absurd, repetitive nonsense syllables babbled by a person in some sort of semi-trance state, brought on by ecstatic absorption into communal ritual. But when experienced within the context of those rituals by an emotional believer, feeling an intimate connection with deity, it must be an extraordinarily uplifting and inspiring experience. Certainly, that experience has fired the growth of Pentecostalism down to the present day as a vibrant, living religious experience that contrasts markedly with the bread and water, formulaic and vitiated version of Christianity perpetuated by the established churches.

The influence of these ideas emerged in the early twentieth century as a Holiness Movement: a form of Revivalism that regarded the Day of the Lord as imminent and the evangelization of the world as urgent imperative. Because believers felt themselves to be living at the End of Days, they, like countless Christians over the previous two millennia, looked for signs. Most if not all of them were followers of Darby's

Dispensationalist ideas: they believed there would be a sudden Rapture and that would precede all the other apocalyptic events like the Millennium and the Tribulation, so there was no point looking for the Lost Tribes or the Antichrist. For them, the sign of the Last Times was the increased activity of the Holy Spirit generally, and a restoration of the Gifts of the Spirit to believers specifically, as had been the case in the early Church. The Pentecostal Movement proper is usually reckoned to have begun in America, through the work and ideas of an African American preacher called William J Seymour who conducted a long-running revival in Azusa Street in Los Angeles, during which all the Gifts of the Spirit seem to have poured down in a way never seen before. The movement, energized by these unprecedented emotional events, spread like wildfire across the Atlantic and eventually round the world. At first, it was practised in separate Pentecostal churches, each with their own brand of apocalyptic and theological ideas. For the most extreme, the second and third works of grace are actually necessary for salvation; the first work of conversion is not enough to ensure a place in Heaven. Over time, it infiltrated the staid, unemotional established churches as the Charismatic Movement, eventually in the 1960s penetrating into the very bastion of established orthodoxy, the Catholic Church. Today, half a billion people around the world subscribe to and practise some form of 'charismatic' belief.

Pentecostalism, Dispensationalism and belief in the very imminent Rapture characterize the most visible manifestation of apocalyptic belief today: the American-style TV evangelists. So many have been caught over the years with their pants down, their fingers in the till, and their phoney deceits exposed to the public that it seems almost impossible that they survive, let alone thrive as they do. But it is the 'Gifts of the Spirit' that lie behind it: all the scientific evidence in the world, and all the logical argument of the best minds of our time are completely disarmed by these simple emotional tricks. Healing ministries abound; speaking in tongues is spectacular as ever; the claim to modern prophecy provides authority to preaching; and all the old Revivalist manipulations of gullible crowds are revitalized and given an emotional turbocharge, no longer restricted to Revivalist tents, but broadcast across the airwaves and the internet as never before. The message has come full circle. Believers of an eschatological bent may pour over their Bibles looking for indications of the Apocalypse, and they may debate with one another endlessly in their chatrooms about the fine detail of the apocalyptic events; but for the televangelist, all this is put aside in favour of the 'old, old story': the Rapture could happen at any second; give, give, give to secure your shelter from the coming storm, and woe betide anybody 'left behind'.

And so we end our brief canter through the weird and wonderful world of apocalyptic belief. This has only been the tip of the iceberg. In every generation for the last 2,000 years there have been individuals coming forward with new, personal predictions about the end of the world. Some have had visions, some have been given new scriptures, some have devoted their lives to disentangling the scriptures they already have. I have related the story of some of them, and through that have endeavoured to pick out the highlights and the general movement of eschatological thought. But for every individual I have highlighted there have been hundreds more who have played their part in the story. My intention here has not been to catalogue them all, or to provide a guidebook to every nuance of thought and interpretation, but to provide a broad historical framework for the next section of this book, in which I shall take the twenty-four topics identified in Part One and exemplified in Part Two, and examine each for the truth of its origins and meaning.

PART THREE

TRUTH

I

Preliminaries

We have traced the key topics of Christian eschatology as they developed among the Jews and then the earliest Christians, as revealed by the prophetic writings of the Old and New Testaments. Then we surveyed the myriad ways in which these issues have been interpreted over the two millennia since. Now we must turn to the topics themselves and examine what lies behind them: what did the original writers have in mind, and what sort of texts did they think they were writing? In short, what are we to make of it all? For the layman, expositions of Christian apocalyptic ideas can be impenetrable because of the language used. Even the description of this branch of study seems unnecessarily pompous; why it has to be called 'eschatological hermeneutics' instead of simply 'interpretations of the End Time' or some such phrase is beyond me. But academics of all disciplines are fond of their jargon because it keeps the uninitiated and, crucially, other academics off their turf. And in this case, of course, impenetrable jargon serves to disguise the pseudoscientific nature of most Biblical Studies.

At bottom, what we saw in Part One was a bunch of old prophecies, made by a large number of different people and recorded by another large number of writers who may or may not be the same people as the prophets themselves, over two millennia and then all collected together in a book we call the Bible, with no attempt at all at reconciliation of repeated or overlapping or contradictory texts. And in Part Two we saw another bunch of different people making their own sense of it all, either by dedicated reconciliation and harmonization of discrepancies, or by visions, inspirations and/or new scriptural writings of their own, over another two millennia. The problem, of course, is harmonization. Why on earth would you attempt it? Only if you have an *a priori* belief that what we have here is the infallible word of God and that, contrary to all appearances and plain common sense, harmonization and reconciliation of abounding conflicts must be possible. And at the end of all this effort, do we have a harmonized account that satisfies everybody or even a majority of believers? As Part Two has shown, we have the exact opposite: more interpretations, versions, sects and cults than you can shake a stick at. Either God really doesn't want us to know what he has in store for humanity, or all these texts have no more validity as prophecy than the horoscopes you read in the daily paper.

In among all the bogus scientific jargon (some of which we shall elucidate over the coming pages) theologians have in particular coined three basic terms to cover all the possible believer responses to biblical prophecy. We met them briefly before in the context of the Reformation, but it would be as well to survey them now.

Preterism regards prophecy in general as being fulfilled in the past, especially in the second half of the first millennium BC and in the first century AD. Full Preterists believe that all our twenty-four topics took place then, including the Second Coming. This has the advantage of dealing with Jesus' embarrassing comment that 'this generation will not pass away until all these things have happened', but requires some considerable ingenuity to explain all the topics in these terms. More common is the *Partial* Preterist view that there is a Second Coming still in the future but most/everything else has already happened. Preterism as a concept goes right back to the seventeenth century and arose within the Catholic Church as a response to the Historicist views of the Reformation theologians who, seeing prophecy fulfilled in the history of Christianity, labelled the popes of the time as Antichrist, rather than some future eschatological figure.

Historicism was the prevailing view among Protestants until the nineteenth century. It regards prophecy as being fulfilled in the past, present and future: some prophesied events occurred during the period of the Bible's composition; some have taken place since then in the two millennia of Christian Church history; and some have yet to take place. The Book of Daniel is particularly influential in Historicism and, in particular, adherents of this position base their ideas about chronology of apocalyptic events in history on the numerical prophecies made in that Book, of which more later. A key identification is the period of papal hegemony with the Antichrist, against which Jesuit counter-reformation thinkers erected Preterism that ascribed such eschatological characters to a future time. I am not sure where Partial Preterism ends and Historicism begins. In reality, these terms seek to straitjacket a range of opinion and interpretation that is really a wide spectrum.

Futurism regards most if not all apocalyptic prophecies as referring to events which have not yet been fulfilled but will take place at the end of the world. It was by definition the position of early Christians, awaiting the imminent return of Jesus, but lost favour as time passed. It revived again in the fundamentalism of the nineteenth century and, in its literalism, can perhaps be seen as the inevitable result of the democratization of biblical interpretation. Futurism is the approach that is most dangerous for the future of us all, not because the Futurists may turn out to be right, but because many of them both welcome, and work towards that outcome. Futurists are by and large the extreme fundamentalists that welcome Zionism, Middle East unrest, and the rise of fundamentalist Islam because all these are seen as fulfilment of apocalyptic prophecy.

These three approaches are all concerned with timings: past, present and future. Overlaid on top of these are two possible ways of interpreting apocalyptic events, whenever they take or took place.

Literalism simply takes the Bible at its word. If scripture says there will be a Millennium, this is taken to mean exactly 1,000 years. Futurists tend to be literalists; just because supernatural events of this sort have not been witnessed in the past is, for them, no reason to suppose they cannot happen in the future. If this means that the future looks more like a fantasy novel of magic and sorcery than the real world as we know it, this is no barrier at all to belief. Indeed, for the literal Futurist, it is all rather exciting.

Idealism sees apocalyptic descriptions of doomsday scenarios as just colourful images expressing more mundane historical events and processes. Preterists and Historicists tend to be idealists. They have to be in order to wrench historical fact to fit prophetic hyperbole. If an apocalyptic event seems so far-fetched that it really cannot in all honesty be squared through symbolism or allegory with any real historical event, the idealist Preterist simply assumes that the event did indeed take place, but on a spiritual plane inaccessible to mortal man. This symbolist 'get out of jail free' card has been used countless times to explain the postponement of predicted eschatological events.

As we proceed to dissect each apocalyptic topic, I shall give a brief summary of the Preterist, Historicist and Futurist position for each. I do this with considerable trepidation. There is probably no 'pure' version of any of the three. We are dealing with a continuous spectrum of belief here, muddled by the literalism/idealism issue. However I define the views of the three main positions, I will leave myself open to objection from fundamentalists who could split hairs until the cows come home. I hope that, in broad terms, my summaries represent the central, most common belief of each position, and if I get anything wrong in anyone's eyes, they have only themselves to blame, since there is absolutely no agreement among fundamentalists about any of this, and the debates are utterly unresolvable.

The stance that I shall take in this book is that all the above are in any case complete nonsense because the very idea of prophecy is flawed. At the risk of overkill let me repeat myself one more time: extraordinary explanations require extraordinary proof. As we have seen, there is not a shred of evidence that any prophecy made by the Bible constitutes proof – ordinary, let alone extraordinary – that these prophets knew anything more about the future than the rest of us. Imprecise assertions about future events are proof of nothing except that anyone can make predictions based on current events and some will turn out to have been correct. The assertions of prophets who got it wrong are unlikely to have survived. Furthermore, many, if not most, biblical prophecies were written down *after* the events they purport to predict; like many things in life, correctness is easy with hindsight. Whether you take the view that the prophets were deceiving themselves as well as others or were cynically playing on the fears of their hearers is irrelevant to all this. Hearing voices from God is evidence of psychiatric illness rather than divine inspiration, and the more extreme the symbolic actions of the prophets became, the more one can be sure that they exhibit severe psychoses.

We have identified twenty-four topics in all. They fall into two distinct groups. The first dozen can be characterized as Jewish apocalypse:

No. 1: The Day of the Lord.
No. 2: The Return and Exaltation of the 12 Tribes.
No. 3: The New Heaven and Earth.
No. 4: The Fall of Elam.
No. 5: Gog and Magog.
No. 6: The Four Horsemen of the Apocalypse.
No. 7: The Two Men of Oil.
No. 8: The Great Tribulation.
No. 9: The Battle of Armageddon.
No. 10: The Apocalypse of Daniel.
No. 11: The Abomination of Desolation.
No. 12: The Original Apocalypse of John the Baptist.

By this I mean that they originate in Jewish eschatology and then find their way, transmuted, into Christian eschatology. This a vital point to understand. As we shall see, time and again, this process of transmutation is what I characterize below as forcing a square peg into a round hole. Jewish theology is essentially historical. God has a pact with the Jews, going back to their ancestral patriarchs: if they observe His rules of behaviour, He will respond by protecting them from their enemies and allowing their nation to prosper. The pact has nothing to do with eternity. The Day of the Lord is only necessary because the Jews have broken the rules and are being punished for it; the Day will come when God will intervene in History and reset the Jews back on their path again. This will involve tribulation and judgement but will result in a new Eden. Christian theology wants to know none of this. It is about a different kind of pact – spiritual not historical – in which an individual's eternal destiny is determined by his faith or otherwise in the salvation on offer through Jesus Christ. The two pacts are diametrically opposed, no matter how Christians attempt to obscure that fact, and the strain shows constantly as soon as one starts to try to reconcile the two different kinds of Day of the Lord. Topics 1–12 all originate in Jewish theology and are incorporated into Christianity with varying degrees of difficulty that we shall unpeel in coming pages.

Topics 13–24 are purely Christian:

No. 13: The Mother and Child and Dragon.
No. 14: The Beast from the Sea.
No. 15: The Beast from the Land.
No. 16: 666.
No. 17: The Seven, Eight and Ten Kings.
No. 18: The Great Harlot.
No. 19: The Millennium.
No. 20: The Rapture.
No. 21: The Great Apostasy.
No. 22: The Man of Sin.
No. 23: The Restrainer.
No. 24: The Antichrist.

By this I do not mean that they are wholly uninfluenced by Old Testament prophecy; in many cases, they clearly are. But they are really introduced as major topics of eschatology only in the New Testament, particularly in Revelation but elsewhere as well. In some cases they are invented in order to deal with the problems alluded to above. John B can be seen wrestling with this sort of problem and inventing new symbols to deal with it. But, in others, they are veiled references to contemporary people and events.

This is an important distinction. Time and again with Topics 1–12, we shall see that although often expressed in the course of 'historical' narrative, these apocalyptic topics are pure symbolism: attempts to identify them with characters and events in Jewish history are doomed to failure. But with Topics 13–24, the writers from which these topics are drawn are commenting on contemporary events that they were convinced were evidence that the Day of the Lord was imminent. In this respect they were like modern Futurists seeking clues from contemporary events, but with one huge difference. Today's Futurists seek to equate contemporary events with biblical symbols; the writers of the New Testament were creating those symbols to describe contemporary events. The purpose of this book is to unmask these correspondences in the first century. In that respect, I am not dissimilar to Preterists and Historicists, but with one enormous difference. They start from a belief in prophecy. They seek to identify prophecy fulfilled in the past. I start from a rationalist belief that prophecy does not exist, and when we find correspondences between symbols and historical events this is evidence that the text involved was written after those events, not before.

I shall now take each of these topics in turn to demonstrate, not only that these are not prophecies for our own time (Futurism), nor even are they prophecies already fulfilled (Preterism or Historicism), but that they can only be truly understood in the context of who wrote them, when they wrote them, and what events current at that time prompted them. Some of them will then be seen to be history masquerading as prophecy; some will be seen as predictions that luckily came true; and some will be seen to have just got it plain wrong. None of them represent anything to worry or concern us today and all should by rights be consigned now to the domain of scholars in the history of religious ideas.

2

The Dozen Jewish Apocalyptic Topics

APOCALYPTIC TOPIC NO. 1: THE DAY OF THE LORD

Preterism: The Day of the Lord was the destruction of Jerusalem by the Romans in AD 70. Full Preterists hold that this was the Second Coming of Jesus; that we are now living in the Kingdom of God; and that this will last for as long as the Earth lasts. Partial Preterists believe that there *will* be a final intervention – a Second Coming.
Historicism: Agrees with the Partial Preterists.
Futurism: The Day of the Lord is sometime in the future when God will finally call a halt to time and judge the world for eternity. No one knows when this will be, but it is generally held to be imminent, and the Bible is endlessly scrutinized for clues. Futurists tend to be Literalists on this topic. All the dire events described by the prophets will actually happen, no matter how mad and deranged they seem.

This topic is where it all begins. In Part One, we saw how the concept was introduced by Amos, probably the first of the old Jewish prophets to come down to us in the Bible, but was almost certainly not invented by him. It is implicit in the most basic elements of Jewish belief. Mankind is fallen. God cannot allow a fallen creation indefinitely. At some point, He must call a halt, pass judgement, and then redeem Creation once again as a new Heaven and Earth, in line with his original intention. God has a Covenant with the nation of Israel that this redemption will favour them over others, but only so long as they are obedient to God's Will, as expressed in His Law. Prophets down the centuries have picked up on this theme and seem to have regarded the Day of the Lord as imminent, but dual edged:[1] it is to be both feared and welcomed. Feared because for sinners it will herald the last judgement and welcomed because for those shielded from God's righteous wrath, it will herald a return to Paradise. So far so simple. And at this simple level, its adoption as a concept by Christians seems unproblematic:[2] the Day of the Lord arrived (sort of); the Jewish Messiah came, walked the Earth, but was rejected by the Jews; he will return for a second time and it will be then that the *real* Day of the Lord will happen. But as we have seen, as soon as you delve below the surface the cracks appear. By proposing two Days of the Lord, and by not only seeking to retain all the Jewish developments of this idea, but also by adding to it embellishments of their own, Christians have saddled themselves with an insoluble problem of harmonization. This emerges most pointedly when one tries to pin down the exact chronology of End Time events now that we must deal not with a single Day of the Lord, but two or, as we shall see, possibly three, or even four!

---

[1] Isaiah, Jeremiah, Ezekiel, Joel, Amos, Obadiah, Zephaniah, Zechariah and Malachi.

[2] See Acts 2:20, 1 Thessalonians 5:2 and 2 Peter 3:10. Also 1 Corinthians 5:5 and 2 Corinthians 1:14 where the phrase becomes 'the day of the Lord Jesus'.

The dimension to eschatology not covered by the broad categories defined above is precisely this – the *chronology* of apocalyptic events. As we have seen, there are different descriptions in different parts of the Bible and all the problems arise when you try to combine them. This is particularly true of events like the Great Tribulation, the Millennium, the Rapture, and so on. How they fit together is problematical and has been the cause of more than a few sects to arise over the centuries. We shall deal with each in turn below. But as we have also seen, there have been historically two broad ways of tackling the issue of chronology.

Supersessionism. This is the term used by theologians to characterize the interpretation of chronology accepted by virtually everyone in the Christian faith down to the nineteenth century. Under this view, crudely speaking, God had a Covenant with the Jews that they abrogated; he *replaced* this with a new Covenant with those who accept Christ's atoning sacrifice; Christ will return at some unknown future date – the Day of the Lord – initiating a succession of End Time events concluding with a new Heaven and Earth. The clear implication of this simple understanding is that the Christian era of Grace *supersedes* the Jewish era of Law. Christians are now God's chosen people, replacing the Jews, and the Jews are now irrelevant to God's eternal plan. There are different versions of this basic understanding, depending on what view you take of God himself – whether he effectively changed his mind about the Jews (Covenant Theology) or whether he always intended Christ's sacrifice, which is therefore the focus of all history (Kingdom–Dominion Theology), but these quibbles need not detain us. The problem with supersessionism is that it is contradicted by the biblical theme that the Jews *are* central to God's plans – past, present and future. Obviously, this is true in the sense that, as we have traced earlier, most of the eschatological themes of Christianity have their roots in Jewish belief and it is therefore hard to isolate them from that context. But as we have also seen, many New Testament texts insist on a continuing role for the Jews at the end of time – notably that all the tribes of Israel will be gathered together in Jerusalem, the Temple will be rebuilt, and one way or another a new Edenic Earth will be created and ruled from there.

Dispensationalism. Formulated by Darby in the nineteenth century and developed in various ways over the decades since, particularly in America, this concept seeks to solve the Jewish/Israel problem. It does so by arguing that the different dispensations, particularly the period of Jewish Law and the period of Christian Grace, are not always supersessional (i.e. one succeeding the other) but are superimposed one on top of the other. The Dispensation of Law did not end with the arrival of Christ, it was merely suspended; when Christ returns, he will remove from the picture all those saved by him and, at that point, those 'left behind' will be subject once again to the Dispensation of Law until that dispensation is in its turn ended. At one stroke, this clever piece of sophistry solves the Jewish/Israel problem because the prophecies that make them central to End Time events can be fulfilled after the Christians have disappeared (literally). But it does so only by creating new problems of its own. Now, it seems, we have two Second Comings. The first (known as the Rapture) has some scriptural authority if you want to read the texts that way, but it introduces more complexity still to the chronology of End Time events and, as we shall see, no one can then agree at all as to precisely how to fit the Tribulation, Millennium, Second Coming, and other related events into a coherent chronology. It is like squeezing a balloon:

you get one bit under control, but the balloon just bulges out somewhere else. Each different interpretation of these complexities has its own vocabulary, its own adherents and their own sects, cults and movements.

We shall tease out these implications and complexities as we work our way through the remaining topics. But as any Jew will tell you, the Christian interpretation of their Day of the Lord is perverse and wrong. Christianity has appropriated the concept and sought to integrate it into its belief system, but in doing so has created a mare's nest. The dispensationalist solution is the craziest of all; we now have Christ coming three times (the life of Jesus, the Rapture and the Second Coming) not to mention the 'coming' of the Holy Spirit at Pentecost, which some Preterist sects regard as fulfilling the prophecy of the Second Coming of Christ (since they are both mysteriously part of the Trinity). Other Preterists take the view that Christ returned in glory to watch the defeat of the Jews in AD 70. To meet the reasonable objection that the Bible speaks of the Second Coming as a highly visible, glorious event, they take refuge in a couple of reports by contemporary historians of supernatural omens at the time. According to Josephus:

> chariots and troops of soldiers in their armour were seen running about among the clouds and surrounding of cities.[3]

According to Tacitus:

> In the sky appeared a vision of armies in conflict, of glittering armour. A sudden lightning flash from the clouds lit up the Temple. The doors of the holy place abruptly opened, a superhuman voice was heard to declare that the gods were

---

3 *Wars of the Jews*, 6:296-300

leaving it, and in the same instant came the rushing tumult of their departure.⁴

Certainly, commentators at the time, Roman and Jewish, understood the religious significance of the events of AD 70. Jewish conviction and belief were widely known and understood and even respected by many; it is hardly surprising at all that there should be reports like this. Supernatural appearances are a commonplace of war, from the Iliad, to Constantine's battlefield vision, to the Angel of Mons. Minds under immense stress will play strange tricks.

So far as the original Jewish idea is concerned, I would ask only that you consider this: the promise of the Day of the Lord was made by Amos more than 4,000 years ago and almost certainly predates even him; every prophet that has iterated it has regarded it as imminent in his own time; since its first conception, the Jewish nation has been divided, conquered, exiled and scattered countless times and still the 'great and terrible day'⁵ has not come. Nowadays, the Jewish faith has split broadly into two, but neither camp seems to regard the Day of the Lord as imminent. Indeed, even conservative Orthodox Jews are free to interpret Jewish texts about the Day of the Lord as metaphorical, rather as Christians in the Idealism camp do about the Second Coming of Christ. How many take such a view it is hard to say, but as the world becomes ever more secular and supernatural belief atrophies, I suspect that those who choose to believe in a personal Messiah will decline, while the predominant view will become belief in some sort of future 'Messianic age' of peace and harmony. In this, they will come into alignment with the progressive 'Reformed' Jews of today, who

---

4 *Histories*, Book 5, v. 13.

5 Joel 2:31.

already hold that view. Personally, looking at the world of today, I would not be holding my breath for that either.

APOCALYPTIC TOPIC NO. 2: THE RETURN AND EXALTATION OF THE 12 TRIBES OF ISRAEL

Preterism: If the destruction of Jerusalem in AD 70 is the Day of the Lord, then this prophecy refers to those that survived the destruction. Preterists are divided over whether these survivors are Diaspora Jews, Jewish Christians, or all Christians who now form the 'new Israel'.
Historicism: As Preterists. Or as Futurists.
Futurism: The modern state of Israel in one way or another fulfils the prophecy or makes the prophecy's fulfilment possible.

It is, of course, one of the great ironies of the Christian Faith that its adherents need the Jews, whom they claim to have replaced as God's chosen ones, and who rejected and crucified Jesus, to play a key role in their Christ's return. The problem is solved for Preterists and many Historicists, because in one way or another they can explain the concept away in terms of first-century events. But Futurists have somehow to allow for a key Jewish role in their eschatology. We first came across the idea in Micah, who envisaged a time when the nations of the world would look to an exalted Jerusalem for spiritual guidance and God would introduce a time of peace and harmony. The theme is picked up again and again across the Bible; here is just one example:

> And it shall come to pass in that day, that the Lord shall set his hand again the second time to recover the remnant of his people, which shall be left, from Assyria, and from Egypt,

and from Pathros, and from Cush, and from Elam, and from Shinar, and from Hamath, and from the islands of the sea. And he shall set up an ensign for the nations, and shall assemble the outcasts of Israel, and gather together the dispersed of Judah from the four corners of the Earth.⁶

There are two elements to this prophecy. First, that Israel will become a nation once again. And second, that all the Lost Tribes of the Diaspora will gather once again in the new Israel. Of course, this has happened a number of times in Jewish history, most notably when they returned from Exile in Babylon and during the Maccabee period. The waxing and waning of the fortunes of the Jewish nation over 2,000 years means that all these various passages can be argued to apply to a range of historical events, rather than some future eschatological one. Scholars debate endlessly these sorts of issues, but they all pale into insignificance in the eyes of fundamentalists in the face of one, indisputable contemporary fact: the establishment of the modern state of Israel after the Second World War in 1948.

The prophecy is as old as the concept of the Day of the Lord itself. We have traced how this concept has caused no end of trouble for Christianity down the ages because it seemed impossible, and yet many passages of scripture in the Old and New Testaments reinforce the idea so it cannot be ignored. Of course, Christianity itself started out as a Jewish Messianic sect, looking to the fulfillment of this prophecy in the context of the Roman occupation of Judæa. As Micah had looked to the triumph of Israel over the mighty empires of his own time, so the Jews of the first century AD shared the same hope. It seems, unsurprisingly, that from the very beginning God's decisive intervention in history was

---

6 Isaiah 11:11-12.

The Dozen Jewish Apocalyptic Topics

conceived by Jews as centring on the apotheosis of their own race and religion. But there has been no Jewish 'homeland' in the Middle East or anywhere else for 2,000 years. Israel had already been reduced from twelve tribes to two by the first century AD and had become merely a small, unimportant province of the Roman Empire. Indeed, there were more Jews by far living outside Judæa by then than were living in the province. Then in two successive uprisings against Rome, in AD 64 and AD 132, the Jews sealed their fate. At the end of the second war, Rome decided they had had enough and scattered the Jewish nation to the four winds. The state of Israel ceased to exist for two millennia. Yet, against all the odds, we now have a modern state of Israel which, with its nuclear capabilities and uncompromising attitude to its Arab neighbours, seems perfectly willing to initiate Armageddon as the price of its continued existence. The Futurist fundamentalists are delirious with joy.

And it is indeed a remarkable historical reversal. But some prophecies can be self-fulfilling: the very existence of the prophecy secures its fulfilment. Take the Greek myth of Oedipus. It was prophesied that he would kill his father and marry his mother. So, his father abandoned him on a mountainside as an infant. The result was that he neither knew nor recognized his parents when he stumbled across them, killing his father and marrying his mother in ignorance. The tragedy ends when he blinds himself in despair. The point of the story is that of course if his father had ignored the prophecy in the first place it would never have been fulfilled. The prophecy was the cause of its own fulfilment. And so, of course, as I have argued with the story of Jesus. He too fulfilled prophecy. Would he have ridden into Jerusalem (or be described as doing so) on an ass if there had not been a prophecy to that effect. Otherwise, what a strange thing to have done. The creation of the modern state of Israel is a perfect example of self-fulfilling prophecy. At the end of the day, if you want to see the hand of God in it, nothing I say here will convince you. But for those more inclined to natural rather than supernatural explanations for unlikely events, there are plenty of reasons why this particular unlikelihood turned out to be less unlikely than one might imagine.

First, the nature of the Jewish religion makes it likely. The fierce racial identity of the Jewish people ensures that no matter how geographically scattered they are, Jews never fully integrate with their surrounding Gentile culture. Their dietary, attitudinal and behavioural characteristics (and particularly their ban on 'marrying out') ensure they keep themselves to some extent separate. And in their racial and religious enclaves they nurture among themselves the history of their race, its unique relationship with their God, and their divine destiny. They invented the very idea of multiculturalism, rather than racial integration. And the fact that, at times in their past, their nation has re-gathered in Palestine lends moral support to their belief in an Israeli state. In the late nineteenth century, the Zionist Movement got underway, seeking through political means to establish a new Israel. This would have been ineffective as a movement if this were just, for example, the Roma people of Eastern Europe seeking a new homeland. But Jews were in positions of power and influence throughout Europe. Indeed, through their prominence in European banking, some Jewish families were able to affect political policy in the very nations, particularly Britain, that had the power to make the Zionist dream a reality. And the reasons for this state of affairs point us to the second cause of self-fulfilling prophecy: the persecution of Jews.

Jews have been denigrated throughout modern European history as the people who crucified Christ. No matter that Jesus himself was supposed to be a Jew. The Gospel stories were written by believers seeking to make their beliefs palatable to the Roman authorities, and the depiction of the Jews baying to Pilate for the blood of Jesus owes everything to that context rather than to any historical reality.[7] Yet the Jews had their uses. Judaism permits usury (the lending of money at interest), which for the Catholic Church was a sin, and since modern economies are founded on the money creation of credit, the modern banking system was created by Jews who became rich and vilified in equal measure. As a result, pogroms against Jews have been a feature of all European countries over the last millennium, culminating in the Nazi Holocaust. The final unveiling of the horrors of the Nazi extermination camps at the end of the war provided an environment of revulsion and guilt that boosted the Zionist cause. It powerfully influenced politicians responsible for redrawing the maps after 1945 to create a new homeland for the surviving Jewish people, who had suffered so much. Thus, ironically, the Holocaust, which had its roots in biblical fiction, served as the second cause of turning prophetic fiction into political fact.

The third reason why the establishment of the new Israel was self-fulfilling prophecy, was the religious naivety of the politicians involved. Britain was responsible for administering the Palestinian region before and after the Second World War and key British politicians, brought up to believe the Bible, not only wanted to compensate for the Holocaust, they actually wanted to fulfil biblical prophecy themselves. The fact that the region had been populated by Arabs not Jews throughout the previous 2,000 years, and that the twentieth century Arab occupants of those lands would be

---

[7] The old joke runs thus: a Jew and a Gentile had been friends for years, until one day the Gentile hit the Jew to the ground. The Jew asked why and was told it was because the Jews had killed Jesus. 'But that was thousands of years ago!' replied the Jew. 'Yes, but I only found out today,' responds the Gentile.

disenfranchised and disenchanted by this imposition from outside was ignored. The Zionist cause was successful because Lord Balfour and his successors had been brought up from infancy on oversimplified, romantic Bible stories about the 'Holy Land'. Influenced by their conviction of Britain's own eschatological destiny, and in some cases excited by the ideas of British Israelism, they believed that, as with the British Empire itself, they were fulfilling God's purposes. Similar people with similar ideas are now influential in Washington. The fact that this event can be seen to fulfil biblical prophecy is just facile. In the end, it was not pure coincidence that saw the prophecy 'fulfilled' – it was self-fulfilled. The whole process is circular: prophecy begetting its own fulfilment. If the prophecy had been the exact opposite; if it had predicted that the Jews would be destroyed rather than reassembled, I suspect that those same politicians would have seen the hand of their God in Hitler's work and no doubt with much shaking of heads, concluded that that after all was the prophecy and left the Jews to their fate.[8]

Even if you want to believe that the modern state of Israel is fulfilling prophecy, the fact is that the ten missing tribes are still missing and likely to remain so. Reuben, Simeon, Dan, Naphtali, Gad, Asher, Issachar, Zebulun, Manasseh and Ephraim. For as long as half the world remained to discover, they could be imagined lurking somewhere. But there remain

---

8 I write the above paragraphs with some trepidation, in the midst of the Labour Party's crisis over alleged anti-Semitism in its ranks. Nothing I say here or anywhere else should be taken as an endorsement in any sense of anti-Semitism: any racism is loathsome and unacceptable. For a more detailed rejection of anti-Semitism and racism, see the Preface to Volume I. But to recognize and even regret the long-term effect on world peace of Zionism is not anti-Semitic, nor is it the same thing as saying that Israel should not exist. Israel does exist, and we all – including the Labour Party in the UK – need to deal with the consequences as best we can.

very few corners of the planet where they could be hiding, waiting to return in triumph to Jerusalem. One wonders what the reaction of the xenophobic Israeli government would be to any such claim. Joseph Smith thought he had solved the problem in indigenous Americans,[9] and British Israelites fondly imagined themselves to be descended from ancient Jews. As we watch the hegemony of the Anglo-Saxon nations shrink before the inexorable growth of China and India, the idea that the Lost Tribes can be found in the UK and USA seems more and more unlikely. The reason we do not have a flourishing Chinese-Israel or Indian-Israel movement is, of course, that no one in those lands feels the need to justify their economic emergence in terms defined by a western document that is 2,000 years old. Nevertheless, search for the concept and it can be found somewhere in the vast eschatological literature. For example, Jesus and/or the Apostle/Brother James are supposed to have travelled to India in search of the Lost Tribes.[10] And others have suggested the Chiang-Min of Szechuan as candidates.[11]

There is hardly a place on Earth where the Lost Tribes have not been spotted – based on dubious linguistics, cultural parallels and that other twentieth century pseudoscience, physiognomy. Indeed, the Jewish Diaspora over the last 3,000 years has resulted in Jewish enclaves in the most unlikely of places, and the peculiar Jewish cultural chauvinism means that many of these have retained Jewish characteristics and traditions. But pinning any of these down to specific Lost Tribes as understood by fundamentalists defies

---

9 Every Mormon is baptized into membership of one of the twelve tribes of Israel.
10 *Jesus Lived in India*, Holger Kersten (Element: 1994).
11 Notably the Rev. Thomas Torrance in his 1937 work, *China's First Missionaries: Ancient Israelites*.

all modern endeavours. The truth is simple. As with the Day of the Lord itself, in taking over this particular Jewish religious idea Christians have saddled themselves with an absurdity. The problem can only be solved by the missing tribes turning up out of the blue somewhere or by promoting impossible modern descent.

APOCALYPTIC TOPIC NO. 3: THE NEW HEAVEN AND EARTH

Preterism: We are all living on a New Earth now. It does not feel much like that because sin and pain and death continue as ever. But if we view it through spiritual eyes, we will see that it is entirely different, because the eternal consequences of sin have been removed by Jesus' crucifixion and death. For believers in that spiritual vision, even death itself has no meaning anymore because it just marks the transition to eternal life in the New Heaven, prepared for us by Jesus.

Historicism: As Futurism.

Futurism: The Second Coming will usher in a New Heaven and Earth sometime in the future, although the precise chronology of events depends on the view you take about the Millennium.

It will be recalled that we owe this topic to Isaiah, building upon Micah. The problem it addresses is what happens the day *after* the Day of the Lord. No one knew exactly when that Day would be, but for most prophets down the ages it has been imminent and will usher in a New World. Isaiah's own take on this was that it would be in effect a return to Paradise – a new Eden where hunger and pain are unknown and where the wolf lies down with the lamb (so presumably a vegetarian or even vegan Eden). Unfortunately, the Bible is pretty vague about the detail, leaving room for infinite speculation. Will the whole universe be recreated or just the Earth? Will Earth be transformed or will there be a completely new planet? Will there be a new Jerusalem and if so, what role will it play? And would there be more communication between Heaven and Earth? Would it all last forever? Is mankind ultimately intended to live in Heaven with God and His angels or forever on Earth? Who would get to live in the new Earth: Jews, Gentiles, sinners, saints? Would they have physical bodies? Sex and marriage? What about all those dead before the Day of the Lord? And would there be babies born on the New Earth? I could go on. Whole books could be written on this topic alone, and indeed, have been. The lack of specificity in the Bible leaves things open to any and every answer to these questions and more.

For the Jews, the answers are reasonably straightforward. The concept of Heaven or the Heavens in Judaism is the realm of God, not Man. For ancient Jews, Creation is divided into three: the Heavens, the Earth and Sheol. The last is the underworld, the abode of the dead. Isaiah is quite clear on the New Earth: a man of a hundred will be still in his youth; babies will no longer die in infancy; and there will be peace and plenty for all. It is a simple vision: death will not be abolished but life will be longer and happier. Isaiah has virtually nothing to say about Heaven and Sheol. As for all ancient Jews, these are unknowable. God's various covenants with mankind are to do with life here and now. The problem for Christianity was how to fit this materialistic scheme into its new spiritualized religion in which God's covenants concern righteousness, sin and eternal destiny. Christians read Isaiah Chapter 65 and read into it the Christian concept of what happens after the Day of the Lord, but they are more concerned with a New Heaven in which the righteous will live than a New Earth which speaks of extended mortality rather than eternal spiritual bliss. Not for the first time, there is a huge disconnect here that commonality of language obscures. The Jew looks towards a future time when human life returns to an Earthly paradise; the Christian looks to a time when he spends eternity with Christ. How can the two become reconciled? This knotty problem clearly preoccupied John B; the answer he came up with, of course, was the concept of the Millennium. We shall examine this in more detail later, including the specific biblical references that suggested the period of 1,000 years. But there is a clue in the passage from Isaiah quoted in Part One:

> For, behold, I create new Heavens and a new Earth: . . . And I will rejoice in Jerusalem, and joy in my people: and the voice of weeping shall be no more heard in her, nor the voice of crying. There shall be no more thence an infant of days, nor an old man that hath not filled his days: for the child shall die an hundred years old; but the sinner being an hundred years old shall be accursed.[12]

Isaiah's hundred-year-old youth implies an average age for man of 1,000 years or so – and that is where the whole idea of a Millennium originates.

The logic of the Christian concept of the Day of the Lord is that Christ returns, judges the living and the dead and consigns to Heaven or Hell accordingly. That is the central message of Christianity, and for virtually all the New Testament that simple schema is all we get. It is only in Revelation that

---

[12] Isaiah 65: 17-20.

we find the Millennium inserted incongruously,[13] and it seems inescapable that it is an attempt to reconcile the different Jewish and Christian ideas about the Day after the Day of the Lord. The concept of Hell evolves from the Jewish Sheol and Heaven is Heaven in both faiths. But how to fit in this New Earth of Isaiah's? The writer of Revelation solves his problem by inserting the Millennium – a thousand-year period in which man lives in a New Earth, just as Isaiah prophesied. Then, with that out of the way, the serious business of eternal fate can begin. Neat. But of course, as we have seen, this clever solution just creates a whole bunch of new problems, much more intractable and requiring all the ingenuity of Christian theoreticians from Augustine to Darby to tease out and unravel. It is here more than anywhere where the problems of fitting the square peg of Jewish eschatology into the round hole of Christian theology become painfully evident. The idea of the Millennium otherwise makes no sense. There is nothing in Christian belief that requires it and it just gets in the way of, and delays, the unfolding of God's plan as conceived by Christianity.

Personally, I find the idea more attractive than an eternity of disembodied spirituality in Heaven. Living longer, happier lives – is that not what science strives towards? Death might well be more palatable after 1,000 years of happy life. Who knows? But an eternity telling God how wonderful He is does not seem to me to be a particularly attractive reward for spending this life on my knees doing the same thing.

---

13 Christian commentators will read the Christian idea of the Millennium backwards into the Old Testament texts about the new Heaven and Earth in order to flesh out exactly what the Millennium will be like, since the writers of Revelation offer few clues. But circular arguments like this prove nothing except the ingenuity of biblical scholars in reconciliation and harmonization between vastly different texts.

APOCALYPTIC TOPIC NO. 4: THE FALL OF ELAM

Preterism: Fulfilled when Elam fell, either to the Assyrians, the Medes or the Persians.
Historicism: As Preterists.
Futurism: Being fulfilled in the Middle East right now.

It will be recalled that this prophecy was made by Jeremiah:

> The word of the LORD that came to Jeremiah the prophet against Elam, in the beginning of the reign of Zedekiah king of Judah, saying, "Thus says the LORD of hosts: Behold, I will break the bow of Elam, the foremost of their might. Against Elam I will bring the four winds from the four quarters of Heaven, and scatter them toward all those winds; there shall be no nations where the outcasts of Elam will not go. For I will cause Elam to be dismayed before their enemies and before those who seek their life. I will bring disaster upon them, my fierce anger,' says the LORD; And I will send the sword after them Until I have consumed them. I will set My throne in Elam, And will destroy from there the king and the princes,' says the LORD. But it shall come to pass in the latter days: I will bring back the captives of Elam,' says the LORD."[14]

This prophecy claims to have been made a little after 597 BC, dated by reference to the reign of Zedekiah who ruled from that date until 586 BC. In fact, by that date the nation of Elam, situated in modern Iran, had already been conquered by the Assyrians in 647 BC and then incorporated a little after into the Median Empire. On that basis, this was already old news by around 597 BC. However, Jeremiah is more likely to be referring to the subsequent incorporation of

---

[14] Jeremiah 49:34-39.

Elam into the Persian Empire of Cyrus the Great. It will be recalled that it was this Cyrus who allowed the Jews to return from their Exile in Babylon at the end of the sixth century. Jeremiah had prophesied that too. As we have noted, the Book of Jeremiah is a composite text, written by different hands at different times and finally redacted much later, so if these prophecies relate to events at that time (as I am sure they do), we can also be sure that they were written after the fact.

Indeed, one has no need to look any further than the Book of Ezekiel for confirmation:

> There is Elam and all her multitude round about her grave, all of them slain, fallen by the sword, which are gone down uncircumcised into the nether parts of the Earth, which caused their terror in the land of the living; yet have they borne their shame with them that go down to the pit.[15]

But for the Futurist fundamentalist this is all beside the point because the Elam prophecy is applied to our own times, heralding the imminent Day of the Lord. The 'bow' of Elam is a symbol of Iran's desired nuclear capability; the four winds are a combination of western nations, perhaps under the UN; the 'outcasts' are the flood of refugees; and so on. The reason fundamentalists must argue this way is that if this is a sign of the End Times, it cannot be applied to the sixth century BC because the Apocalypse did not take place then. In fact, of course, the simplistic equation of Elam with Iran has no more basis than a coincidence of geography. The Elamites were, unlike modern Iranians, regarded by Israel as a Semitic people. They took their name, at least in ancient Jewish etymology, from their patriarch, Elam, the son of Shem, the son of Noah.

---

15 Ezekiel 32:24.

Genesis Chapter 10 lists the three sons of Noah – Shem, Ham and Japheth – and asserts that all the nations of the Earth are descended from these, everyone else of course having perished in the Flood. (We shall return to this in the next section where we identify Gog and Magog). All Semites were believed to be descended from Shem.[16] But not all Semites were Jews; some were Arabs and uncircumcised, hence the shame that Ezekiel refers to. All this prophecy is saying is that Elamite Arabs as well as Jews will suffer Exile as punishment for their wickedness. But just as Jeremiah promises that the Jewish Exile will end, so too will that of the Elamite Arabs. In the final sentence he confirms that 'in the latter days: I will bring back the captives of Elam.' So, if fundamentalists are looking for signs in this text that the Day of the Lord is imminent right now, they should presumably be looking for a time when the current Persian population[17] of Iran is ousted by Arabs. A likelihood I leave to the reader to judge.

This passage and fundamentalist interpretation of it is far from the mainstream of fundamentalist eschatology, and perhaps many such would find it one step too far. But it neatly demonstrates the way such interpretation works. As I have said in other contexts, it is hard to understand why Christians resist as absurd similar interpretative techniques by ancient Jews that resulted in the stories of Jesus, when they are at the same time quite happy to take similar liberties with Old Testament texts like this one. The allegorical techniques of *Midrash* and *Pesher* that seem so outrageously laughable to the rational mind of today, nevertheless continue to thrive in this sort of fundamentalist interpretation. Let me just reprint here something from the website of one such:

---

16 Shemite = Semite.
17 'Caucasian' not 'Arab'.

It was March 29, 2014, in Orlando, Florida when prophecy experts Chuck Missler and Gordon McDonald, of Koinonia House Ministries were reminded of a long-forgotten Bible prophecy concerning Iran. They, along with yours truly, were seated alone together at the head table of the Prophecy in the News conference banquet. While patiently awaiting the auditorium doors to fling open, and the masses to flood in for the feast, I humbly inquired,

'Have you gentlemen taken a serious look at the vastly overlooked prophecies identified in Jeremiah 49:34-39 concerning Elam?'

With heightened interest, they turned their undivided attention toward me and replied, 'No, we haven't.' Pleased to have piqued their curiosities, I took the liberty of unpacking the prophet's predictions. Apparently, they liked what they heard because they invited me to author this article, and their ministry is offering you my new book entitled, *Nuclear Showdown in Iran, Revealing the Ancient Prophecy of Elam,* which takes an in depth look at Jeremiah's prophecies concerning Elam.[18]

These 'prophecy experts', enjoying a 'conference banquet' at a 'Prophecy in the News Conference' are enthusiasts for prophetic texts, vying with one another to spot the most obscure such, and apply them tortuously to the headlines of today. The conference and seminar industry of today, providing the perks of international travel and banquets to university scholars is bad enough in this sort of respect, but these are not scholars, they are like twitchers or trainspotters – members of a hobbyist club, delighting in 'humbly' pointing out to their peers the rare birds and trains that they only have

---

18 http://www.prophecydepotministries.net/2014/elam-irans-forgotten-prophecy/

had the privilege to spot. And if they can make money from a book based on their decodings, all the better. It is like the daily newspaper horoscope: check out all the predictions, not just the one under your own birth sign, and you will find most if not all can be made to fit your 'unique' personal experience; given a propensity to allegorize, any event can be made to fit the prediction. The account of the destruction of Elam is so generalized, it can be made to fit almost any conflict. What war does not involve destruction of weapons, alliances between powers and floods of refugees? Whatever happens in Iran in the coming years and decades, I guarantee there will be new fundamentalist commentators who will see it fulfilling scripture in new ways, equally inane.

APOCALYPTIC TOPIC NO. 5: GOG AND MAGOG

Preterism: Fulfilled either in the Temple desecration of Antiochus and the subsequent Maccabean wars and/or in the persecution under Nero and the Roman/Jewish War of the sixties AD.
Historicism: As Preterism.
Futurism: The view Futurists take on this is crucially dependent on its position in the chronology of the Millennium, the Great Tribulation and Armageddon and whether, as a result, the Gog/Magog battle is identical with Armageddon or different.

Gog and Magog appear in the apocalyptic tradition in an obscure passage in Revelation:

> And when the thousand years are expired, Satan shall be loosed out of his prison, And shall go out to deceive the nations which are in the four quarters of the Earth, Gog and

Magog, to gather them together to battle: the number of whom is as the sand of the sea.[19]

Fundamentalists who take a Futurist view will seek to identify Gog and Magog with this or that nation, whichever seems at that moment to be the bad guy on the world stage. The most common Futurist interpretation is a coming invasion of Israel by Russia and various allies. Certainly, the writer of Revelation sees Gog and Magog as symbols of the bad guys (the enemies of God), and without a convincing identification of them with characters or states in Jewish/biblical history, it seems natural to those who regard all biblical prophecy as infallible to take the Futurist view and look to contemporary events or trends for clues. And many fundamentalists regard Gog and Magog indeed as one of the most, if not *the* most, important clue of all to the imminent Day of the Lord. So, we need to take some time to understand exactly who or what Gog and Magog were, or were thought to be by the writers of the relevant biblical texts.

We first came across these two strange characters in Part One in Chapter 38 of Ezekiel. That passage falls in the middle of a self-contained sequence of chapters in Ezekiel dealing with God's future intentions towards Israel and its neighbours. The sequence begins with Chapter 29 and continues to the end of the Book in Chapter 48. The reference to the destruction of Elam that we dealt with in the previous section also falls within this sequence, so it is a particularly important set of prophecies for fundamentalists. It will be my contention that this sequence represents a definitive expression of Jewish eschatology at the time. One cannot extract sections from this and interpret them out of context. The Elam passage

---

19 Revelation 20:7-8.

examined in the previous topic is a case in point, as we shall see. As we observed with the issue of the Earthly Millennium, the problem here will turn out to be that of shoehorning Jewish expectation of Earthly paradise into the Christian concept of eternal salvation. The culprit again is John B, who is struggling to make sense of his Jewish heritage in the face of new Christian ideas.

Over four chapters,[20] God tells Ezekiel in graphic detail (and not a little repetition) that he is going to destroy the power of Egypt because of its historic animosity to Israel:

> I will make the land of Egypt utterly waste and desolate, from the tower of Syene even unto the border of Ethiopia.[21]

But He will not do it by direct supernatural intervention; He will work as he often does through human agency. In this case, the human agent will be 'Nebuchadnezzar, king of Babylon' – presumably, Nebuchadnezzar II, the Babylonian ruler mentioned in the Book of Daniel whose dates (634–562 BC) fit with a supposed dating for Ezekiel's prophecy of 587 BC. This prophecy can only refer to the Battle of Carchemish (*c*. 605 BC), in which the Egyptians met the full might of the Babylonian and Median army led by Nebuchadnezzar II and the Egyptian forces were destroyed. From that point, as Ezekiel says, Egypt ceased to be a significant force in the Ancient Near East. The reference to Elam, noted above, is in Chapter 32 alongside references to Assyria, Edom, the 'princes of the north', the Zidonians (Lebanon), Meshech and Tubal. It is not clear from the text whether these are being held up to Egypt as examples of kingdoms God has already destroyed,

---

20 Chapters 29-32.
21 Ezekiel 29:10.

or whether Ezekiel is prophesying that they too, like Egypt, will be destroyed. I think the latter, for reasons that will presently become clear.

After the Battle of Carchemish, Nebuchadnezzar besieged Jerusalem, setting in train the events that were to culminate in the Jewish Babylonian Exile, which began in 597 BC. And that is when, according to Ezekiel, he is receiving these prophecies. God speaks to Ezekiel 'in the tenth year'. It will be recalled that Ezekiel's conversations with God began 'in the beginning of the reign of Zedekiah king of Judah', who reigned from 597 BC. So, the tenth year is presumably 587 BC or thereabouts – the year of the Exile. And that is exactly the subject to which Ezekiel now turns in Chapter 33. In the 'twelfth year' of the Exile – so, 575 BC – God says that as a result of the Jews not observing God's laws, He will make Judah 'most desolate'. But he also promises in Chapter 34 that:

> I seek out my sheep and will deliver them out of all places where they have been scattered in the cloudy and dark day. And I will bring them out from the people, and gather them from the countries, and will bring them to their own land, and feed them upon the mountains of Israel by the rivers, and in all the inhabited places of the country... I will seek that which was lost, and bring again that which was driven away, and will bind up that which was broken, and will strengthen that which was sick... And I will set up one shepherd over them, and he shall feed them, even my servant David; he shall feed them, and he shall be their shepherd... And I will make with them a covenant of peace, and will cause the evil Beasts to cease out of the land: and they shall dwell safely in the wilderness, and sleep in the woods... and they shall be safe in their land, and shall know that I am the Lord, when I have

broken the bands of their yoke, and delivered them out of the hand of those that served themselves of them.[22]

This passage is clearly about the Day of the Lord, and the Millennial period that will follow it, under the kingship of a descendant of David. But it is not something that will happen in *our* future; it is not the return of Christ as fundamentalists envisage; it is quite clearly, in context, the return of the Jews to their land from the Babylonian Exile, and the promise by God that he will forgive them and allow them to live in peace and prosperity once again. And in evidence, he declares in Chapter 35 that he will desolate Mount Seir and the surrounding country of Edom that sought to exploit the Jewish Exile by appropriating their lands. We have seen this prophecy before in Part One: Obadiah also foresaw the destruction of Edom. Both he and Ezekiel got it wrong. Then as now, Israelis have no love of Arabs and their fight over the same Palestinian lands is as old as these texts. But for the last 2,000 years it has been the people of Edom who have inhabited the land, and the establishment of a new Israel has not settled the issue at all, as we read in our papers daily. Chapter 36 then restates God's intention, not only to return the Jews to their homeland, but to make it a paradise:

> And they shall say, This land that was desolate is become like the garden of Eden[23]

And Chapter 37 reinforces the point with the famous image of the valley of dry bones that return to life.

It will be recalled that Edom was in the list of nations alongside Elam that were held up to Egypt as examples of

---

22 34:12-27.

23 Ezekiel 36:35.

what happens to nations that upset God. I said that I think this list was a future threat rather than a historical reminder. The prophecy about the future destruction of Edom in Chapter 35 bears this out. As does the following passage from Chapter 38 that introduces us to Gog and Magog:

> And the word of the LORD came unto me, saying, Son of man, set thy face against Gog, the land of Magog, the chief prince of Meshech and Tubal, and prophesy against him, And say, Thus saith the Lord GOD; Behold, I am against thee, O Gog, the chief prince of Meshech and Tubal: And I will turn thee back, and put hooks into thy jaws, and I will bring thee forth, and all thine army, horses and horsemen, all of them clothed with all sorts of armour, even a great company with bucklers and shields, all of them handling swords: Persia, Ethiopia, and Libya with them; all of them with shield and helmet: Gomer, and all his bands; the house of Togarmah of the north quarters, and all his bands: and many people with thee.[24]

Meshech and Tubal in line three of this passage, were, like Edom, also mentioned in the list in Chapter 32, which clinches the point. These are all the traditional enemies of Israel. In that earlier chapter, we were told that all these nations are to be destroyed. Here in Chapter 38, we are told that it is God himself who will cause these nations to revolt against the restored nation of Israel, only so that (in Chapter 39) He can utterly destroy them – as proof of His power, and as a sign to Israel that henceforward they will live in Millennial peace and prosperity. Ezekiel is saying, in effect, that when Israel has undergone her punishment and has returned to her Promised Land, then God will remove future threats by subduing all surrounding nations. No doubt modern

---

24 38:1-6.

Israel would like the same, but it seems hardly likely. Chapters 40–48 are devoted to detailed descriptions of the New Jerusalem, and the new Temple that will crown the new state of Israel. But again, who are Gog and Magog?

To untangle this, we need to turn back to Genesis Chapter 10, which lists the offspring of the three sons of Noah, Shem, Ham and Japheth, who were regarded by the Jews as the remote ancestors of the various tribes and nations known to them in the Middle East. It will be recalled that the Elamites and other Semites including themselves were descended from one son – Shem. The sons of Ham were regarded to be the ancestors of the peoples of Asia and Africa, and the sons of Japheth similarly founded the peoples of India and Europe. Magog, Meshech, Tubal and Gomer mentioned by Ezekiel are all the sons of Japheth and Togarmah (also mentioned) is Gomer's son, so all are Japhites. The syntax is a little unclear but it seems that Gog is the 'chief prince of Meshech and Tubal' and this is confirmed in Chapter 39, verse 1, where he is again described thus. This seems to mean that Gog is not the prince of those places, rather, a prince of somewhere else but superior to the princes of Meshech and Tubal. In fact, it seems that he is the prince of a place called Magog – called here the 'land of Magog' and in Chapter 39, verse 6, Ezekiel says that God will send fire on Magog so, again, presumably a place. So, to recap, we have here a confederation of States, all named after descendants of Japheth, and led by a chief prince from the state of Magog who is called Gog. This confederation is joined by 'Persia, Cush and Put' – African, Arabian and Asian nations, all descended from Ham. In other words, the whole Gentile world from all continents and directions is here seen as gathering in one united mass to annihilate the Jewish nation. We are told that God Himself is behind this – He draws them out like hooking a fish out of water – in order that He can then destroy them utterly, securing at one stroke His own reputation and the security of His people.

The key point to notice here is that, unlike the destruction of Egypt, which took place through the human agency of Nebuchadnezzar, the destruction of this armed confederacy of all the nations of the world will be wrought through God's own supernatural intervention:

> Therefore, son of man, prophesy and say unto Gog . . . thou shalt come up against my people of Israel, as a cloud to cover the land; it shall be in the latter days, and I will bring thee against my land, that the heathen may know me, when I shall be sanctified in thee, O Gog, before their eyes. Thus saith the Lord God; Art thou he of whom I have spoken in old time by my servants the prophets of Israel, which prophesied in those days many years that I would bring thee against them? And it shall come to pass at the same time when Gog shall come against the land of Israel, saith the Lord God, that my fury shall come up in my face. For in my jealousy and in the fire of my wrath have I spoken, Surely in that day there shall be a great shaking in the land of Israel; So that the fishes of the sea, and the fowls of the Heaven, and the Beasts of the field, and all creeping things that creep upon the Earth, and all the men that are upon the face of the Earth, shall shake at my presence, and the mountains shall be thrown down, and the steep places shall fall, and every wall shall fall to the ground. And I will call for a sword against him throughout all my mountains, saith the Lord God: every man's sword shall be against his brother. And I will plead against him with pestilence and with blood; and I will rain upon him, and upon his bands, and upon the many people that are with him, an overflowing rain, and great hailstones, fire, and brimstone. Thus will I magnify myself, and sanctify myself; and I will be

known in the eyes of many nations, and they shall know that I am the Lord.[25]

The only fighting it seems will be the enemy forces falling upon each other. The Jews will need to do nothing to defend themselves; God will send earthquakes, pestilence, flood, hailstones, fire and brimstone to utterly destroy the forces of Gog. There is nothing new in this prophecy. As Ezekiel says in the passage above, the prophets had been saying just this for many years. This is all standard Jewish apocalypse, as it appears in most of the Old Testament prophets: the Day of the Lord will see the Jews (all twelve tribes) re-gathered in the Promised Land, the temple re-established in Jerusalem, and all their enemies destroyed, making possible a new era of peace and joy. The only puzzle is none of the prophets have ever mentioned this character called Gog. So, is he *new*, or have we met him before under a different name?

There is another Old Testament character with a similar name (remembering Hebrew's problem with vowels) : Agag, the King of Amalek, who was captured by the Jewish King Saul and subsequently hacked to pieces by the prophet Samuel.[26] The etymology of Agag is uncertain, but some scholars suggest it means 'high' and was probably not a personal name but the title for the kings of Amalek. Either way, Amalek itself is named after a descendant of Esau of that name and the Amalekites seem to have lived in the same sort of region, south of Israel, as the Edomites. Scholars debate endlessly the historicity or otherwise of these two peoples and the relationship between them, but we need not get into any of that. Basically, these were Arabs and the Jews came to regard them as their archetypal enemies. Agag and the

---

25 Ezekiel 38:14-23.
26 I Samuel, 15.

The Dozen Jewish Apocalyptic Topics

Agagites, Amalek and the Amalekites; these all become interchangeable symbols for the quintessential enemies of God and his chosen people. The requirement for their utter destruction was always implicit in Jewish understanding of the Day of the Lord and the events that follow it. There can be no doubt that Agag and Gog are one and the same. In Numbers 24:7, there is an End Time prophecy that the future King of the Jews will be exalted above Agag and there is a variant reading of this verse in other manuscripts (Septuagint, Samaritan Pentateuch and others) that reads Gog in the place of Agag, although standard texts use Agag. So, Gog/Agag was an established prophetic shorthand for the enemy who would be annihilated following the day of the Lord. The Jewish writer of Revelation, prophesying about a Christian Day of the Lord, but concerned as always to square his account with the old Jewish prophets, uses Gog and Magog in the same way: either as individuals, or as lands named after them, they symbolize the ultimate triumph of Good over Evil as a guarantee of Millennial peace.

Futurists want to interpret Gog/Magog as symbols for modern enemies of the Jewish State or of Christianity but their origin in Ezekiel was in a prophecy about a Jewish apocalypse in which God brings the world to its collective knees through fire and brimstone. Ezekiel thought it was imminent in his day, but clearly it did not happen. Historicists usually argue that the prophecy was fulfilled by the Maccabean revolt against the Seleucids, although this gives them major problems, not least being that Ezekiel describes the destruction of Gog before the rebuilding of the Temple, not after. And as I have pointed out, according to Ezekiel, the destruction of Gog's forces will not require the Jews to lift a finger in battle; their sole role will be to bury the dead. This last gives Preterists the biggest problem of all. They want to believe that the Word of God is infallible and therefore prophecies must have been fulfilled in the past; therefore, in some way or another, the Gog confederacy must have taken place in the sixth century BC as described in Ezekiel. *But there is no historical evidence whatsoever that anything like that took place.* The destruction of Egypt can be ascribed to the activities of Nebuchadnezzar, but not the destruction of Gog and his forces, whoever they were. In desperation, some Preterists have located the answer in their Bibles. There is a biblical story about an assault on the Jews at this time, and it is found in the Book of Esther.

The Book of Esther tells of a king called Ahasuerus. His palace is in Shusha which can be identified with certainty as Susa, the capital of Achaemenid Persia, so we know he is one of the kings of that Empire. He is often identified with Xerxes, but there are other candidates, particularly Ataxerxes III, and in truth, almost any of the first dozen kings of the Achaemenid Persian Empire can be made to fit the bill. He marries a Jewess called Esther, although he is unaware of her racial background. Esther is the adopted daughter of Mordecai, a Jew whose forebears had arrived in Susa at the time of the Babylonian Exile and had stayed rather than return to Israel when the first Achaemenid ruler Cyrus the Great conquered Babylon and ended the Exile. At the same time an important character called Haman enters the scene. This Haman is favoured by the king and promoted to be a sort of Grand Vizier to whom all are expected to bow. But Mordecai refuses to do so and, as a result, as the Book of Esther tells the story, Haman resolves to kill all Jews and casts lots to decide when it will be propitious to undertake his planned genocide. Then he approaches Ahasuerus for permission to carry it out and offers to pay for the pogrom from his own funds. Ahasuerus (unaware still of the race of Mordecai and Esther) tells him to keep his money in his pocket and do what he pleases with the Jews. Haman then,

The Dozen Jewish Apocalyptic Topics

in the king's name, sends out edicts to all the king's provinces to have all Jews, men women and children, killed on the day that the casting of lots had indicated.[27] The edicts were not kept secret; the Jews were informed in advance of their fate. Mordecai urges Esther to intervene with the king and (cutting a rather long story short) she does so at real risk to her own life. The king has Haman killed but (we are told) cannot stop the pogrom because a king's edict cannot be revoked. So, a new set of edicts are sent out granting the Jews the right to assemble, bear arms and defend themselves. They do so, killing upwards of 75,000 people, including Haman's ten sons. The story is celebrated by Jews everywhere in the annual Festival of Purim, Purim meaning the casting of lots, as carried out by Haman.

The planned pogrom and its defeat are offered by some Preterists as evidence that Ezekiel's prophecy was indeed fulfilled. Apart from the convenience if this were true, the justification given for making the connection between Haman and Gog is that Haman is described in Esther as 'the son of Hammedatha the Agagite' and there is a late manuscript that refers to Haman as a 'Gogite'. And I think to that extent, the connection is valid: Mordecai is descended from King Saul ben Kish, who overthrew the original Agag, so both protagonists – good and bad – are descended from historical symbols of the Jewish nation and its enemies. Haman may well be based on Gog/Agag, the archetypal Jewish enemy. But the connection points to the reality here, which is that Esther is a fiction. The story is implausible to say the least. The protagonists are symbols not historical figures, and there is absolutely no evidence in the Bible or anywhere else that the events described happened. The story was almost certainly concocted from other Babylonian and Persian sources – the

---

27 The thirteenth day of the twelfth month.

very names Esther and Mordecai seem to be derived from the Babylonian gods Ishtar and Marduk – and was probably written to provide a justification for the Festival of Purim rather than the reverse.

Purim itself is a strange festival; unlike other Jewish festivals it seems more secular than religious and involves a considerable element of food, alcohol and merrymaking, and almost certainly entered Jewish life from pagan festivals they encountered in Babylon and Susa. Esther was written to give it a pseudo-historical context and rationale, and the writer of that romance brought in the Gog/Agog connection to add symbolic depth. The writer may even have had in mind the need to provide evidence of a sixth-century pogrom. But what is certain is that even if there is historical truth to the story of Esther, the resistance of Diaspora Jews in the Persian Empire to an attempted pogrom is something very different indeed from the supernatural onslaught envisaged by Ezekiel in his Gog prophecy. Fundamentalists – be they Preterist, Historicist or Futurist – share a common belief in scriptural infallibility and prophetic inexorability that makes them impervious to the common-sense view that what we have in Gog/Magog is a prophecy of End Time events, envisaged to take place a millennium and a half ago, that just never happened. Seeking to attach it to a fictional novella, or looking for its fulfilment in unrelated historical events, or looking to a future event that hasn't happened yet and seems unlikely to happen to say the least, are all tricks that fundamentalists use to bolster their belief in scriptural inerrancy. The truth is that Ezekiel, like the prophets before him, got it plain wrong; the writer of Esther was seeking to justify a strange festival rather than provide pseudo-historical evidence for an event that never happened; and John B was just trying to shoehorn into his visions a set of symbols that were wholly Jewish and tangential to the central concerns of the new Christian religion.

APOCALYPTIC TOPIC NO. 6: THE FOUR HORSEMEN OF THE APOCALYPSE

Preterism: Fulfilled one way or another in the turmoil and wars between the Jews and Rome throughout the first century AD.
Historicism: As Preterism.
Futurism: To be fulfilled in the Last Day events – the Great Tribulation and Armageddon.

There are few if any images in the Bible that can compete with this one for its sheer power to evoke terror. From Sleepy Hollow to Middle Earth, writers have delighted in the symbol of skeletal figures of Death and Destruction riding the land, and Hollywood has, on countless occasions, written those images large and lurid on the big screen. The immediate source for all this is, of course, Revelation:

> And I saw, and behold a white horse: and he that sat on him had a bow; and a crown was given unto him: and he went forth conquering, and to conquer. And when he had opened the second seal, I heard the second Beast say, Come and see. And there went out another horse that was red: and power was given to him that sat thereon to take peace from the Earth, and that they should kill one another: and there was given unto him a great sword. And when he had opened the third seal, I heard the third Beast say, Come and see. And I beheld, and lo a black horse; and he that sat on him had a pair of balances in his hand. And I heard a voice in the midst of the four Beasts say, A measure of wheat for a penny, and three measures of barley for a penny; and see thou hurt not

the oil and the wine. And when he had opened the fourth seal, I heard the voice of the fourth Beast say, Come and see. And I looked, and behold a pale horse: and his name that sat on him was Death, and Hell followed with him.[28]

But as we have seen, the writer of those New Testament passages was raiding the larder of Old Testament eschatology and, as ever, shoehorning Jewish images into a proto-Christian context. In Part One, we came across this symbol in the Book of Zechariah, where there are in fact two sets of equine imagery. The first comes right at the beginning of the Book:

> I saw by night, and behold a man riding upon a red horse, and he stood among the myrtle trees that were in the bottom; and behind him were there red horses, speckled, and white. Then said I, O my lord, what are these? And the angel that talked with me said unto me, I will shew thee what these be. And the man that stood among the myrtle trees answered and said, These are they whom the Lord hath sent to walk to and fro through the Earth.[29]

The context here is that Zechariah is asking his God when the Day of the Lord will arrive – when the Babylonian Exile will be ended and God will reinstate the people of Israel in their Promised Land. These four horsemen are angels, messengers of God, who rove the Earth and report back to Heaven. At this stage they are not apocalyptic figures, but their angelic identification here informs the concept as it then develops.

The second equine reference in Zechariah comes a little later, in Chapter 6:

---

28 Revelation 6: 2-8.
29 Zechariah 1:8-10.

> And I turned, and lifted up mine eyes, and looked, and, behold, there came four chariots out from between two mountains; and the mountains were mountains of brass. In the first chariot were red horses; and in the second chariot black horses; and in the third chariot white horses; and in the fourth chariot grisled and bay horses. Then I answered and said unto the angel that talked with me, What are these, my lord? And the angel answered and said unto me, These are the four spirits of the Heavens, which go forth from standing before the Lord of all the Earth. The black horses which are therein go forth into the north country; and the white go forth after them; and the grisled go forth toward the south country. And the bay went forth, and sought to go that they might walk to and fro through the Earth: and he said, Get you hence, walk to and fro through the Earth. So they walked to and fro through the Earth.[30]

The symbolism has changed a little here; the horse riders have become charioteers, but the identification is confirmed by the reference in both passages to them walking 'to and fro through the Earth'. There are four of these Heavenly beings – spirits or angels – and their role seems to be simply to watch and report. But by the time we come to Revelation, their role has become harbingers of destruction:

> And power was given unto them over the fourth part of the Earth, to kill with sword, and with hunger, and with death, and with the Beasts of the Earth.[31]

The link between Zechariah and Revelation is found in Ezekiel:

---

30 Revelation 6:1-7.

31 6:8.

> For thus saith the Lord God; How much more when I send my four sore judgments upon Jerusalem, the sword, and the famine, and the noisome Beast, and the pestilence, to cut off from it man and Beast?[32]

Here God is speaking of his punishment of Israel, but the fourfold nature of it corresponds precisely with that of the four horsemen and clearly provided the writer of Revelation with the idea to turn these four spirits into avenging angels.

They are also analogous to the four winds:

> And after these things I saw four angels standing on the four corners of the Earth, holding the four winds of the Earth, that the wind should not blow on the Earth, nor on the sea, nor on any tree.[33]

Zechariah is a primary source for Revelation, or, to be more precise, for John A, who can be identified with some confidence as John the Baptist. The idea of the four winds being in effect the breath of God, through which He imposes His Will directly on Earth (rather than through human agency) is found in many Old Testament prophets and enters Revelation directly via Zechariah. Let me emphasize again here that on the Day of the Lord, God will require no human agency to defeat the forces of evil: His four horsemen/winds/angels will do all the work. According to Revelation, God pours out His vengeance and judgements from a series of vials or bowls into the air. In the Second World War, which seemed for many to be the final apocalypse, a common interpretation of this prophecy was that it was being fulfilled by aerial bombardments of civilian populations by all the major armed combatant nations. I guess that

---

[32] Ezekiel 14:21.
[33] Revelation 7:1.

if you were living through the hell of the Blitz or the firestorm of Dresden, you could be forgiven for such imaginings. But the twentieth century, for all its horrors, did not see the Day of the Lord arrive, any more than it is likely to now.

The first horse in Revelation is white and its rider wears a wreath or crown; he carries a bow and is described as a conqueror. Fundamentalists are completely divided on this one. Some argue that this is a symbol of Christ riding out to meet and destroy Evil. And indeed, later on in Revelation Chapter 19, verse 11, Christ is unequivocally symbolized in just this way. But others argue that the similarities are either coincidence or a reflection of Satan's propensity to appear deceitfully in holy guise. One must wonder about the likely validity of visions that are so vague they can be interpreted in such diametrically opposed ways. Preterists, of course, have their usual problem of trying to identify this character with some historical personage or event; they point for example to the Parthians who (apparently) rode white horses, carried bows, and in AD 62 did in fact have some limited success against Rome. The truth of course is that one of the horses has to be white because that is how Zechariah described them, and this is a symbolic figure of death and destruction like the other three who will appear on the Day of the Lord, if and when that ever happens.

The second horseman is less contentious. He rides a red horse, carries a large sword and has been given the power to provoke civil war. The source here is Ezekiel. It will be remembered that in the great battle against Gog:

> I will call for a sword against him throughout all my mountains, saith the Lord God: every man's sword shall be against his brother.[34]

---

34 Ezekiel 38:21.

The third horseman presented a problem for many years until quite recently. His identity is clear enough: he rides a black horse and carries scales, a symbol here not of justice but of famine. But why does the voice say, 'see thou hurt not the oil and the wine.'? This obscurity was only explained when the Dead Sea Scrolls revealed,[35] for the first time, the central importance in Temple ritual of twin Feasts of Oil and Wine. God may be intent on destroying most of the planet, but not at the expense of rituals necessary to maintain appropriate divine worship.

The final horseman rides a pale horse and is, of course, the pale rider, Death. The personification of Death in this way more than any other of these symbols, influences high art and popular culture alike – from Durer's engravings to Terry Pratchett's Mort and He-Man's foe, Skeletor. Preterists and Futurists alike can and will try to identify all these with people and events from the past or in the present. But they ignore the obvious truth that they are not fresh, prophetic insights by the writer of Revelation about a Christian apocalypse, but reworkings of old Jewish symbols about how God will intervene in history. The events they presage are entirely supernatural in nature, so it is pointless to look for human agents. And whether you choose to believe in them or not hinges entirely on your attitude to the supernatural generally. Personally, if God works in this kind of way, I see no reason to respect, let alone worship Him. Such a concept of deity derives from Jewish belief in their special relationship with God and their despair at their subjugation to pagan peoples; only supernatural intervention on a grand scale could not only reverse history but secure a permanent safety for Israel. Apocalyptic-minded Christians find it comfortable to appropriate the same symbols because they feel the same

---

35 In the Temple Scroll.

way about themselves: they have pinned their faith on a set of beliefs and a way of life that sets them at odds with the rest of humanity, and they relish the Day of their Lord when he proves them to have been right all along. The four horsemen give a symbolic finger in the air to unbelievers.

APOCALYPTIC TOPIC NO. 7: THE TWO MEN OF OIL

Preterism: Moses symbolizing the Jewish Law and Elijah symbolizing the Prophets, or the Old and New Testaments symbolizing the Dispensations of Law and Grace.
Historicism: As Preterism. Both positions take an Idealist view.
Futurism: A literal prophecy of two eschatological characters who will appear in Jerusalem in the Last Days and preach the Gospel.

We first met these twin characters in Zechariah:

> And the angel that talked with me came again, and waked me, as a man that is wakened out of his sleep. And said unto me, What seest thou? And I said, I have looked, and behold a candlestick all of gold, with a bowl upon the top of it, and his seven lamps thereon, and seven pipes to the seven lamps, which are upon the top thereof: And two olive trees by it, one upon the right side of the bowl, and the other upon the left side thereof. So I answered and spake to the angel that talked with me, saying, What are these, my lord? . . . Then said he, These are the two anointed ones, that stand by the Lord of the whole Earth.[36]

I argued in Volume II that these two anointed ones were the twin Messiahs of Jewish eschatology: the King Messiah and

---
36 Zechariah 4:1-14.

the Priest Messiah. I showed how in the early decades of the first century AD, Judas the Galilean and John the Baptist sought to associate themselves with these two eschatological roles and I traced how Christianity arose from this. The problem with this interpretation is that when these two apocalyptic characters resurface in the Book of Revelation (in the first Apocalypse of John A – specifically in Chapters 10 and 11) as it has come down to us, they have been downgraded from twin *Messiahs* to two *Witnesses*:

> And there was given me a reed like unto a rod: and the angel stood, saying, Rise, and measure the temple of God, and the altar, and them that worship therein. But the court which is without the temple leave out, and measure it not; for it is given unto the Gentiles: and the holy city shall they tread under foot forty and two months. And I will give power unto my two witnesses, and they shall prophesy a thousand two hundred and threescore days, clothed in sackcloth. These are the two olive trees, and the two candlesticks standing before the God of the Earth. And if any man will hurt them, fire proceedeth out of their mouth, and devoureth their enemies: and if any man will hurt them, he must in this manner be killed. These have power to shut Heaven, that it rain not in the days of their prophecy: and have power over waters to turn them to blood, and to smite the Earth with all plagues, as often as they will. And when they shall have finished their testimony, the Beast that ascendeth out of the bottomless pit shall make war against them, and shall overcome them, and kill them. And their dead bodies shall lie in the street of the great city, which spiritually is called Sodom and Egypt, where also our Lord was crucified. And they of the people and kindreds and tongues and nations shall see their dead bodies three days and an half, and shall not suffer their dead bodies to be put in graves. And they that dwell upon the Earth shall rejoice over them, and make merry, and

shall send gifts one to another; because these two prophets tormented them that dwelt on the Earth. And after three days and an half the spirit of life from God entered into them, and they stood upon their feet; and great fear fell upon them which saw them. And they heard a great voice from Heaven saying unto them, Come up hither. And they ascended up to Heaven in a cloud; and their enemies beheld them.[37]

The reference to olive trees and candlesticks surely confirms that these are indeed the two Men of Oil of Zechariah. There can be no doubt about this: the writer of Revelation is drawing on Zechariah here. In Revelation as we now have it, they appear on Earth after the Day of the Lord when seven seals have been opened, and the seven trumpets have been blown, and God has destroyed most of Creation in preparation for a new Heaven and Earth. Whatever they are doing then, they do not appear to be Messianic figures – as understood either by Jewish or by Christian tradition. I believe this is a key issue. The problem arises because of the ordering of events in the First Apocalypse of John A. We shall resolve this under Topic No. 12 below, where we shall see that John's text has become corrupted, trace exactly how this has happened, and show how when appropriately re-ordered, Zechariah and Revelation cohere (as they surely must, if one is the source of the other).

APOCALYPTIC TOPIC NO. 8: THE GREAT TRIBULATION

Preterism: The Jewish War against Rome in the sixties AD.
Historicism: The centuries of papal dominance in Europe.
Futurism: A future End Time event.

---

37 Revelation 11:1-12.

This is, of course, along with the four horsemen, one of the scariest concepts in Christian eschatology: the idea that the Day of the Lord will be accompanied by worldwide death and destruction. Jesus himself talks of it and gives the topic its name in the Olivet Discourse:

> For then shall be great tribulation, such as was not since the beginning of the world to this time, no, nor ever shall be. And except those days should be shortened, there should no flesh be saved: but for the elect's sake those days shall be shortened.[38]

And it is the first topic we must deal with that really distinguishes the different schools of thought on Christian eschatology. Preterists and Historicists generally focus on the Olivet Discourse rather than Revelation. The former regard the Great Tribulation as the events of the Jewish War against Rome in the sixties AD. The latter take a longer historical view and usually ascribe this topic to the period of papal power prior to the Reformation: a period when they believe the Catholic Church perverted Christian truth and various popes were antichrists.[39] How they square this with the graphic descriptions in Revelation and the Old Testament prophets of devastating natural disasters and war is difficult to see; even the Olivet Discourse does not gloss over the disagreeableness:

> For nation shall rise against nation, and kingdom against

---

38 Matthew 24:21-22.

39 The specific period identified by Historicists is 1,260 years, arrived at from numbers in the Book of Daniel. See Topic 10 for details. The end date for this period is usually taken as 1798, when Napoleon ordered the Pope taken prisoner, but this gives 538 as the start date and Historicists have some trouble identifying this with any specific person or event.

kingdom: and there shall be famines, and pestilences, and Earthquakes, in divers places.[40]

But it is the Futurists that really get themselves snarled up over this topic: those that believe that this prophecy and the related ones regarding the Apocalypse lie some time in the future, perhaps the immediate future.

As we now work our way through the different Futurist interpretations, do not worry if you get confused; most fundamentalists get confused too in this quagmire of speculation. Futurists see the Great Tribulation as a relatively short period, but a devastating one in that, through a combination of every cataclysmic hardship imaginable – disasters, famine, war – around three-quarters of the world's population will be wiped out. Only then will Christ return for the final judgement. The burning question of course for fundamentalists that believe this is whether *they* must go through all the pain and suffering along with the rest of us, or whether God will spare them in some way: do they get to sit on the sidelines applauding the devastation or do they too have to be players on the pitch? I guess it must be hard for them to positively welcome this genocidal expression of God's divine Will if they are not in some way miraculously excluded from the pain and suffering. This is where the concept of the Rapture comes along, to much relief of the righteous. Unfortunately, as we have observed, the biblical references here are none too clear about how and when the Rapture fits into the divine scheme of things. There are three main takes on this among fundamentalists (although such is the welter of speculation, I could well have missed some nuances, and I have certainly simplified some of the infinite hair splitting for the sake of clarity).

---

40 Matthew 24:7.

Pre-Tribulationists are the real sadists. They grab the idea of the Rapture as the ultimate 'get out of jail free' card. The Rapture of all believers, alive and dead, takes place before any Tribulation begins. They get to sit with Jesus in Heaven with smug smiles on their faces. Unfortunately, comforting though this is, it is quite hard to maintain as an interpretation, given the many texts that suggest that Christians too will have to go through the Tribulation. The Olivet Discourse is one such; immediately following the announcement of the Great Tribulation above, Jesus says:

> All these are the beginning of sorrows. Then shall they deliver you up to be afflicted, and shall kill you: and ye shall be hated of all nations for my name's sake... But he that shall endure unto the end, the same shall be saved... And except those days should be shortened, there should no flesh be saved: but for the elect's sake those days shall be shortened.[41]

These words certainly seem to suggest that we are all going to be in it together, but notice that there are a couple of caveats, and these feed into the other interpretations. First, there is a reference to the 'beginning of sorrows', so perhaps the Great Tribulation will come in phases and believers will be spared the worst phase? And second, the period of tribulation will be 'shortened' for the sake of believers, so again, perhaps they will be spared the worst?

Mid-Tribulationists seize on these caveats and postulate that there will be two periods: the 'beginning of sorrows' followed by the 'Wrath of God'. As always, opinions divide over exactly where the dividing line falls: early, halfway or late. The Rapture is again the idea that makes this possible:

---

41 Matthew 24:8-13.

Jesus will come and yank out the believers so they avoid the worst of what is to come, before his final 'return' at the end of time. Ironically, this interpretation is made possible because of the redaction of the Book of Revelation itself. It comprises two documents relating the same events; this makes possible the division into two that many 'Mid-Trib'[42] believers cling to.

Post-Tribulationists are the pessimistic masochists. They will have none of this namby-pamby Rapture nonsense. There is a Great Tribulation coming when God will vent his wrath on a sinful Earth and we shall all – believers and non-believers alike – be up to our necks in it together. The only good news is that if you are a believer, when it does all finally come to an end you will find yourself in Heaven rather than Hell.

So, what can we make of all this? First, it must be emphasized that the whole concept of a Great Tribulation is a Jewish one, not a Christian one. To make the key point yet again: Earthly punishment and reward fits with the Jewish concept of God and his relationship with Man; Christianity regards Earthly life as a mere antechamber to the eternal spiritual life, and Earthly happiness or misery are equally irrelevant in the grand scheme of things. Why would an eternal God choose to rain bloodshed and terror on just one generation of people when there have been billions who have lived their lives, well or badly, without having to endure such wrath? Bad luck indeed just to happen to have been born at the wrong time. It makes sense to the Jewish mindset. At the very beginning of 'history', God, despairing of the sinful state into which His creation had sunk, destroyed all of it in the

---

[42] Fundamentalist hobbyists love to use terms like this – Pre, Mid, and Post 'Trib' – in their endless splitting of imaginary hairs.

Flood, sparing just one breeding pair of all animals (including humans) to start again. Given this sort of mindset, it does not seem unreasonable that God would do it again. Indeed, the second time round, he is only going to destroy three-quarters of creation. Such grace![43]

But it makes no sense at all in the Christian scheme of things, which is why outside of the fundamentalist community, most Christians just gloss over all this. Jesus is coming back in glory to take believers to Heaven. What more do you need to know? The Catholic Church teaches that before Christ returns, there will be some sort of tribulation that will shake the faith of many believers, but they downplay the importance of this beside the much more serious threat of eternal damnation for those without the sacred rites of the Church. Protestant denominations uninfected by fundamentalist ideas mostly take a similar tack, though of course downplaying the role of church rites and emphasizing more the need for Faith. But there can be no doubt that any reader of either the Old Testament prophets or of Revelation will be left with a clear impression that at some stage in history, God intends some pretty serious infliction of his divine Wrath on an unsuspecting sinful world, on a scale of destruction not dissimilar to Noah's Flood, before he finally calls an end to it all and institutes a new Heaven and Earth. Can we trace how this idea has arisen?

As we have seen, from the very beginning the Jewish idea of the Day of the Lord has been double edged: relief that God will end the sufferings of his people but fear also that he will vent his righteous wrath on a world of sin. Quotation at this point would be superfluous. We have seen this Jewish idea of God venting his wrath time and again – sometimes

---

[43] Although 75% of the 8 billion currently inhabiting the Earth is a trifle more than the putative population at the time of Noah.

through human agency, but on the Day of the Lord itself, directly through his angelic emissaries. And the Jews had no trouble accepting that they would suffer too. It goes to the heart of Jewish self-image. There was no miraculous Rapture for them, just suffering after suffering until the Day of the Lord arrives. This Jewish idea enters Christianity through the Book of Revelation. There is nothing in the Olivet Discourse that is not already there in traditional Jewish eschatology, notably in Zechariah and Daniel. Of course, this is not the commonly understood order of things. Christians believe that Jesus taught the concept in his Olivet Discourse and John of Patmos merely expanded on it in his prophecies. The truth is the exact opposite: Revelation precedes Mark; the Gospels are late fictions that draw upon Jewish scripture including Revelation and the Olivet Discourse is a summary of the ideas in Revelation. This then presents immense problems for Christianity as soon as Revelation is admitted to the Christian canon. What on Earth were Christians to make of all this wrath and destruction as part of a religion based on love and forgiveness? The whole problem of squaring Jewish historicism with Christian spirituality is exposed starkly in the concept of a Great Tribulation. And the problem is exacerbated by the nature of the Book of Revelation itself. Two source documents giving two versions of the same apocalyptic events are read as one document of seemingly unending misery; how could a just and merciful God inflict so much pain and suffering on a Creation he is supposed to love? But ironically, the very accident that created this problem offered the solutions we have seen: a chaotic manuscript comprising irreconcilable parts offers enough ambiguity and vagueness to allow for myriad interpretations to suit every fundamentalist perspective. And when that is compounded by the ambiguity and vagueness of all the other New Testament statements about eschatology, it becomes possible to believe anything on a spectrum between virtually nothing to worry about at all to utter annihilation, with just about every stop in between.

APOCALYPTIC TOPIC NO. 9: THE BATTLE OF ARMAGEDDON

Preterism: Fulfilled in the Jewish War against Rome in AD 70.
Historicism: As Preterism.
Futurism: Perhaps World War III?

The Great Tribulation ends with the mother of all battles between Good and Evil, Christ and Satan, with their respective Heavenly and Demonic forces, and is known as Armageddon: a term that has now become synonymous with nuclear war and devastation. It is a sort of Judaeo-Christian version of the Norse Ragnarök. And for many Futurists, the prospect of nuclear war is precisely how they anticipate that this prophecy will be fulfilled:

> And I saw three unclean spirits like frogs come out of the mouth of the dragon, and out of the mouth of the Beast, and out of the mouth of the false prophet. For they are the spirits of devils, working miracles, which go forth unto the kings of the Earth and of the whole world, to gather them to the battle of that great day of God Almighty. . . And he gathered them together into a place called in the Hebrew tongue Armageddon.[44]

Satanic forces stir up 'the kings of the Earth' to gather their forces together at a place called in Hebrew Armageddon.

---

44 Revelation 16:13-16.

The Dozen Jewish Apocalyptic Topics

Most scholars are agreed that the Hebrew etymology of Armageddon is *Har Megiddo*, meaning the hill or mount of Megiddo. And we know where that is: Megiddo is an ancient fortified hilltop city in northern Israel that drew much of its importance from its strategic location guarding an important ancient trade route between Egypt and Asia. The route passes through Mount Carmel and overlooks the fertile Jezreel Valley. Battles have been fought there throughout history right up to modern times. General Allenby's forces routed the Turks there in 1917.

All of which sounds reasonable, but for the fact that this is the only reference in the whole Bible to the final battle being called Armageddon, or indeed, of being situated at Megiddo. As we have seen, the Old Testament is full of references to this final great battle; it is the battle led by Gog *of* Magog (that became over time Gog *and* Magog) that also found its way into Revelation. But almost all these Old Testament passages refer to the location of the great Final Battle as the Valley of Kidron in Jerusalem, which, from a Jewish perspective, seems much more appropriate. There are many Old Testament references to Megiddo and the many battles there, but none of them locate the Final Battle there or have any prophetic context. In Jewish apocalypse, the Day of the Lord results in the Jews re-gathering in their Promised Land to enjoy their New Eden, and God raises up all their traditional enemies against them so that they can be defeated finally in a great battle that secures their peace and prosperity for the future. Yet again, we have a Jewish concept being shoehorned awkwardly into Christian end time theology, but how in the transfer process did the location get moved from Jerusalem to another place entirely in the north of Israel? Theologians have debated this issue for centuries and have come up with myriad solutions, none of which succeed in reconciling the irreconcilable. Driven by their conviction that the Word of God must be inerrant, they seek to harmonize the different accounts, but the truth is that the writer of Revelation got it wrong, and given the perspective of the New Paradigm set out in Volume II we can now see exactly how it happened.

The key to this mystery, as with so many in this respect, is yet again the Book of Zechariah. The Battle of Armageddon is the fourth of the apocalyptic topics, after Nos. 6-8, that come straight out of Zechariah. Zechariah must have been open in front of John A when he wrote his apocalypse.[45] Speaking of the Day of the Lord, Zechariah reports God as saying:

> Behold, the day of the Lord cometh, and thy spoil shall be divided in the midst of thee. For I will gather all nations against Jerusalem to battle; and the city shall be taken, and the houses rifled, and the women ravished; and half of the city shall go forth into captivity, and the residue of the people shall not be cut off from the city. Then shall the Lord go forth, and fight against those nations, as when he fought in the day of battle. And his feet shall stand in that day upon the mount of Olives, which is before Jerusalem on the east, and the mount of Olives shall cleave in the midst thereof toward the east and toward the west, and there shall be a very great valley; and half of the mountain shall remove toward the north, and half of it toward the south.[46]

This is clearly the Final Battle at the end of days and it is to be fought in Jerusalem. The valley referred to is not Jezreel but the Valley of Kidron below the Mount of Olives, hence that location's prominence in the story of Jesus' arrest. How-

---

45 Think scroll rather than book, but both have to be opened.
46 Zechariah 14:1-4.

ever, Zechariah does mention Megiddo too, a couple of chapters earlier:

> Behold, I will make Jerusalem a cup of trembling unto all the people round about, when they shall be in the siege both against Judah and against Jerusalem. . . . And it shall come to pass in that day, that I will seek to destroy all the nations that come against Jerusalem. And I will pour upon the house of David, and upon the inhabitants of Jerusalem, the spirit of grace and of supplications: and they shall look upon me whom they have pierced, and they shall mourn for him, as one mourneth for his only son, and shall be in bitterness for him, as one that is in bitterness for his first born. In that day shall there be a great mourning in Jerusalem, as the mourning of Hadadrimmon in the valley of Megiddon.[47]

This is another description of the Day of the Lord. The reference to Hadadrimmon is contentious among scholars, with no real consensus as to whether it refers to a place or a person, and various etymologies are available. But the overall reference seems clear: the Old Testament recalls a great battle. It was an important passage in Volume II because of the references to mourning a 'son' and 'piercing' which feed into the crucifixion story of Jesus. Here its importance is that, while the Final Battle is unequivocally at Jerusalem, the 'great mourning' that will take place is *compared* to the mourning that took place in the Valley of Megiddon. In principle, this could refer to any of the battles, but almost certainly it refers to the most important and prominent in Jewish myth: the battle in which King Josiah of Judah was killed by Egyptian forces in 609 BC.[48] Presumably when

---

47 Ch.12:2-11.
48 2 Kings 23:29 and 2 Chronicles 35:20-27.

Zechariah says 'as when he fought in the day of battle', this is the ancient battle to which he refers.

So, we have two passages in Zechariah that refer to the Final Battle. Both locate this in Jerusalem, but one compares it to an earlier battle in Megiddo. We know that Zechariah was a key source for the writer of Revelation. It takes little or no imagination to see him getting the two references confused and naming his version Armageddon. And of course, all the confusion over location serves to disguise the real issue here, which is that Jewish apocalypse is being introduced to a narrative that is embarrassed by it. There is nothing in Christian theology that requires such a concept; Christians are focused on a new Heaven, Jews on a new Earth. The latter logically requires the defeat of Earthly enemies, but for the former, it is an irrelevance. That is why Armageddon is mentioned only once in the New Testament, but the Final Battle centred on Jerusalem is found in many of the Old Testament prophets – Jeremiah, Micah, Zephaniah, Ezekiel and Joel, as well as Zechariah. Different versions of fundamentalists take different views about what all this means: Futurists scan their morning papers daily for evidence of a coming conflagration in the Jezreel Valley; Historicists generally like to just regard it all as symbolic of the ongoing struggle between Good and Evil; and Preterists regard it as prophecy that was fulfilled in the destruction of an apostate Jewish nation by the Romans in the first and second centuries. But it is none of these. It is genuine Jewish prophecy about their envisaged End Time; it foresees an imminent great battle between Good and Evil, just as it is portrayed throughout the Old Testament, and it seems, like the Great Tribulation, to be permanently postponed.

The Dozen Jewish Apocalyptic Topics

APOCALYPTIC TOPIC NO. 10: THE APOCALYPSE OF DANIEL

Preterism: A key text.
Historicism: *The* key text.
Futurism: A key text.

We now leave Zechariah to look at the various prophecies found in the Book of Daniel, a happy hunting ground for fundamentalist hobbyists and the central text for those of the Historicist persuasion. Zechariah, Jeremiah and the other prophets writing at the time of what we have called the second generation of prophets, were dealing with the Babylonian Exile and looking towards a Day of the Lord that would bring it to an end with a supernatural intervention by God. It did not happen. The Exile ended, but through the intervention of the Persian King Cyrus who, having put an end to the Babylonian Empire in 539 BC, issued an edict that allowed the Jews to return home. The Bible asserts that this, like the original Babylonian conquest of Judah, was all prompted by God, using human agents to impose his Will on history. More cynically, we might conclude as modern historians do, that Cyrus pursued a more sympathetic approach to foreign policy, recognizing that the goodwill of conquered nations was probably a better way to achieve a stable empire. Either way, this was clearly not the great and terrible Day of the Lord which would require no assistance from human agents but would be a direct intervention by God through both natural forces and Heavenly armies. As we have seen, Jeremiah knew the Exile would end, but he was as clueless as his predecessors as to the precise timing of the Day of the Lord.

A few centuries later, the Jews found themselves in the same boat again. This time, they were subject to the Seleucid Empire that in their part of the world had succeeded the

Macedonian Empire of Alexander the Great. Overall, they had found this relatively congenial, since most of the Seleucid rulers took a similar view to Cyrus and, recognizing that they ignored the strength of Jewish religious belief at their peril, took an accommodating view. But, partly as a result of this of course, many Jews were becoming 'Hellenized' – that is, they found the more relaxed attitudes of the wider Hellenic world to be more congenial than the strict dietary and behavioural requirements of a jealous Yahweh. By the time Antiochus IV Epiphanes came to the Seleucid throne in 175 BC, the Jewish nation was deeply divided. The way Jewish history then tells the story, Antiochus forced the issue and sought to do away completely with the Jewish religion, provoking the subsequent Maccabean uprising. Modern historians seem more inclined to the view that there was in effect a civil war brewing between Orthodox Jews and Hellenized Jews, and Antiochus, forced to intervene, chose not unreasonably from his point of view, to back the Hellenized faction. Either way, he has gone down in Jewish history as the man whose sacrilegious acts were responsible for the events celebrated in Hanukkah.

This was the background to the Book of Daniel, which confusingly places the eponymous hero at the time of the Babylonian Exile in the sixth century but was finally redacted at the time of the Maccabees 400 years later in the second century. As we saw, the Book comprises two quite distinct parts. The first part, Chapters 1–6, tells the stories of Daniel in the lion's den, the fiery furnace and so on. It is impossible to say with certainty when these folk tales were originally written down, but the likelihood is sometime in the third century. They were then redacted by other hands before appearing in the form we have them in our Bible. The second part, Chapters 7–12, were written around the time of Antiochus. A lot of admirable scholarly work has revealed much detail about the authorship of these chapters. In broad terms, there are four apocalyptic visions/prophecies, each written by a different author. These four authors each wrote at different times during the reign of Antiochus, so demonstrating different knowledge of the stages of his escalating campaign to bring the Jews into line with the rest of the Hellenic world. The fourth author also revised, amended and added to the previous three in an attempt to create a coherent whole. Fundamentalists usually ignore all this. The most extreme of them maintain that the Book of Daniel is exactly what it claims to be: a contemporary record of a man living through the Babylonian Exile. Even those who accept later authorship still like to believe that the Book can be read as a straightforward, unified message from God. Unfortunately, this gets them in a terrible muddle as we shall see, because the fourth author, in his final redaction of the four visions, did not cover his tracks very well. And because, as we shall also presently see, he was writing in the middle of the persecutions of Antiochus, and when he does make real prophecy rather than prophecy after the fact, he gets it hopelessly wrong.

Fundamentalists of course have their answers to this, but by imposing symbolic interpretations that could only be contemplated by someone already committed to a belief in supernatural foresight, rather than open to the possibility that whoever wrote Daniel was just a limited human being like the rest of us. In the analysis that follows, I shall for convenience refer throughout to Daniel as a singular writer of the book that bears his name - but to emphasise again, the book was the work of several authors writing hundreds of years after Daniel was supposed to have lived.

Vision 1: The Four Beasts (Chapter 7)
The first prophecy is a good example of this confusion. It is a vision of four great Beasts; clearly a precursor in some way to the various Beasts of Revelation. In the latter, one emerges

from the sea, and the others from the land; here, all four come from the sea. They are all devouring monsters, but the fourth Beast is the worst of all, that will devour the 'whole Earth' and has ten horns. Daniel is told by an angelic being that the four Beasts are four kingdoms and that the fourth and last has had ten kings. The prophecy is that God will allow the tenth to have dominion for a period until at last He destroys it and establishes His Kingdom on Earth. All scholars seem pretty at one on the interpretation of this. The first three kingdoms are the empires of the Babylonians, the Medes and the Persians, all of whom subjugated Israel. The fourth is the Greek Empire created by Alexander and then ruled by his generals after his death. Israel was part of the empire ruled by the Seleucids. The counting to ten kings is a little problematical, depending on whether you start with Alexander or with his general, Seleucus I Nicator, and whether you count in the odd regent. Prophecies like this can be interpreted in different ways, depending what outcome you seek to validate. In this case, we need not get too involved in the maths, because there is no doubt at all about the identity of the tenth king. From the way he is described as the worst of the lot, there can be no doubt that he is Antiochus IV Epiphanes – the Seleucid ruler who sought to Hellenize the Jewish people and stamp out their distinctive religion in the years 169–164 BC. The writer of this vision is saying, as so many Old Testament prophets before him, that this latest persecution of the Jews really is the last one; that God's final intervention is imminent; and the much-delayed New Eden is just around the corner. It will be recalled that this ruler's persecution reached its peak with his desecration of the Jerusalem Temple Holy of Holies itself in 167 BC, in what became known as the Abomination of Desolation. There is no mention of that action here, as there surely would have been if it had been written after that event, so this vision was almost certainly written after 169 BC but before the desecration, which took place in December 167 BC.

This much is straightforward, but problems arise because the text in our Bibles has been amended by the final redactor, who has introduced a confusing extra element: an eleventh 'little horn' that arises among the other ten and uproots three of them. This eleventh horn is confusing because it is also quite unmistakeably a symbol of Antiochus. What seems to have happened is that the redactor, coming along a little later and knowing now of the further depredation and desecration of Antiochus, failed to recognize that the tenth horn was already Antiochus and introduced the eleventh as an afterthought. It is easy to see how this could have happened, because of the difficulties in deciding which rulers to include in the count, and from which ruler the count should begin. All this confuses many and gives the hobbyists much to play with but ignores the key point: that the vision foresees an imminent Day of the Lord resulting in the utter destruction of the Seleucid Empire and, of course, it never happened. The Seleucid Empire was not destroyed at this time. It was defeated in Israel by the Maccabean uprising, but this was not the Day of the Lord either. All this of course parallels what happened in the sixth century Exile, when Daniel is supposed to have lived. Then, too, Jewish suffering was ended through human agency rather than apocalyptic intervention by God, and the Day of the Lord was postponed.

The prophecy of the four Beasts recalls an earlier prophecy in Chapter 2 of Daniel. In that case, the prophecy is in the form of a dream of the king that Daniel interprets; the same four kingdoms are symbolized as a giant statue made of four metals, each of which corresponds to the Babylonian, Median, Persian and Macedonian Greek empires. These empires, whether symbolized as metals or as beasts, are clearly envisaged as succeeding one another before the

Day of the Lord finally ushers in the fifth and final Kingdom of God. More specifically, Daniel regards the Medes as replacing the Babylonians: in the story of the Babylonian King Belshazzar's feast, the writing on the wall (mene mene tekel upharsin), clearly states that the Babylonians will be succeeded by the Medes and we are then told that on Belshazzar's death, 'Darius the Median took the kingdom'.[49] Unfortunately for believers in scriptural inerrancy, this reflects the distorted historiography of the time rather than the reality as we now know it to be.[50] In simple terms, the Empires of the Medes and Babylonians were contemporary rather than successive. Yet the Book of Daniel describes its protagonist as successively present at the court of the first three, the fourth being of course far in the future and known only to Daniel as distant prophecy. This erroneous belief occurs elsewhere in the Old Testament: Isaiah[51] and Jeremiah[52] both prophesy the destruction of Babylon at the hands of the Medes – something that never happened. The Medes were conquered, about a decade before the Babylonians, by the Persians. And Darius the Mede is unknown to history. There was a Darius, but he was a later Persian monarch who seems somehow to have become confused with Cyrus. Fundamentalists struggle badly with this one, but there really is no way round it unless we rewrite history.

Vision 2: The Ram and the He-Goat (Chapter 8)

The second vision was written a little later by another author entirely. A ram with two horns, one longer than the other,

---

49 Chapter 6.

50 The misunderstanding came from Persia via Rome. Persian sources spoke of four kingdoms but their memories were longer – they started with the Assyrians.

51 13:17; 21:2.

52 51:11; 28-9.

represents the Medes and Persians; we know, because an angel tells Daniel as much. It is overturned by a He-Goat with one horn that is also identified explicitly as the Macedonian Greeks. The goat is triumphant for a while but then its horn breaks off to be replaced by four horns, and out of one of these another little horn grows. As before, these horns are the four empires and the little horn is Antiochus IV Epiphanes, who gives 'both the sanctuary and the host to be trodden under foot'. This reference to the desecration of the Temple (the Abomination of Desolation) suggests that this vision was probably written sometime <u>after</u> that event, which took place at the end of 167 BC – presumably in 166 BC or thereabouts. What Daniel wanted to know, of course, was exactly how long this desecration and persecution would last; how long would God permit it before finally intervening and replacing the fourth empire with His fifth – the Kingdom of God. Daniel overhears two angels discussing it and gleans from this the answer: that the Temple would be purified again in '2,300 days'. He also is told that this would then herald the End Time. So, to emphasize again, this is not a miraculous prophecy of the Maccabean revolt, this is an expectation of the Day of the Lord that never materialized. The 2,300 days prophecy was almost certainly a later addition to the text. And the King James translation here is misleading. The text actually reads 2,300 'evenings and mornings'. This refers to the evening and morning[53] sacrifices in the now desecrated Temple, so the text should more accurately read 1,150 days, which is three and a bit (3.15 to be exact) years. In the first vision, Daniel is told that the Day of the Lord will come in 'a time and times and the dividing of time', which interpreted in the light of this text, must

---

53 The evening precedes the morning here because the Jewish day then and now starts in the evening.

mean 'a year plus two years plus a part of a year' or again, three-and-a-bit years. The same prediction is given again in Chapter 12, verse 7. In fact, Antiochus died in Nov/Dec 164 BC, some three years after the Temple desecration. Scholars are pretty much all agreed that the passages in all the visions referring to the three (and a bit) years were later additions, but you decide!

Vision 3: Seventy Weeks of Years (Chapter 9).
Jeremiah was told that the Babylonian Exile would last for seventy years. Whatever maths you want to use to show this to be correct, it remains the case that the end of Exile did not usher in the Day of the Lord and a subsequent new Holy Kingdom, just subjugation by the Persians and then the Greeks. In Chapter 9, we are shown Daniel pondering on this uncomfortable fact until an angel appears, promising to make all clear:

> Seventy weeks are determined upon thy people and upon thy holy city, to finish the transgression, and to make an end of sins, and to make reconciliation for iniquity, and to bring in everlasting righteousness, and to seal up the vision and prophecy, and to anoint the most Holy. Know therefore and understand, that from the going forth of the commandment to restore and to build Jerusalem unto the Messiah the Prince shall be seven weeks, and threescore and two weeks: the street shall be built again, and the wall, even in troublous times. And after threescore and two weeks shall Messiah be cut off, but not for himself: and the people of the prince that shall come shall destroy the city and the sanctuary; and the end thereof shall be with a flood, and unto the end of the war desolations are determined. And he shall confirm the covenant with many for one week: and in the midst of the week he shall cause the sacrifice and the oblation to cease, and for

the overspreading of abominations he shall make it desolate, even until the consummation, and that determined shall be poured upon the desolate.[54]

Not as clear then as Daniel or we might have hoped! But with a bit of work, we can see what this is all about. Here we have Daniel applying the *Midrash* technique to Jeremiah's scripture, seeking to interpret its hidden meaning. And the key that unlocks it is the idea he introduces, that when the scripture speaks of years it really means weeks of years. In other words, the Day of the Lord did not materialize in seventy years after Jeremiah's prophecy, so it *must* have meant 7 x 70, or 490 years.

Jeremiah first prophesied in 605 BC (the first year of Nebuchadnezzar's reign). So, 490 years on from then would be 115 BC, which of course overshoots the period of the Temple's desecration in 167 BC by half a century! Jeremiah made another specific prophecy, this time about the rebuilding of the Temple a little later, during the Exile itself, in 594 BC. Using this as the starting date reduces the error by a decade or so, but the prophecy is still way out. In fact of course, the seventy years was never meant to be an exact figure. It was the threescore years and ten of a man's life. And so also with Daniel's *midrashic* interpretation as 490 years. The significance is not the figure 490 (which Daniel does not mention) but the mystical symbolism of 7 times 70. Daniel does not care that his numbers do not add up. Only fundamentalist hobbyists care. They have a field day trying to square Daniel's prophecy with historical reality.

As a matter of fact, it cannot be done without huge distortion and wishful thinking, but it is all beside the point. The writer of this prophecy just wants an excuse to apply Jeremi-

---

54 Daniel 9:24-27.

ah's prophecy about the Day of the Lord to his own time. He knows that the prophecy expired hundreds of years ago, but he needs to believe it will be fulfilled in his own time, with God's destruction of Antiochus. That is why his breakdown of the 7 x 70 years is also into symbolic periods. The first such period is seven weeks (seven again). At that point, he says intriguingly, that 'Messiah the Prince will come'. Who or what does he mean by that? The authors of the authoritative Anchor Bible volume on Daniel have an answer: they identify the Messiah referred to here as Joshua/Jesus, the first High Priest of the new, rebuilt Temple. For anyone who doubts my identification of the High Priest Jesus of the sixth century as the source for the 'Jesus' of the Gospels, this is a key text. It is obviously an important identification in the context of Volume II's New Paradigm and we shall return to this in Topic 13.

The second period is the long one: threescore and two weeks, or sixty-two weeks of years, or 434 years. None of this is particularly symbolic, but that is because it is just the balancing period before the final, third period of a single week: the writer wants to start with the mystical 7 x 7, and end with a single week of 7 days, so the 62 weeks is what is needed to make up the 7 x 70 total. But what is the mystical significance of the final week? The answer is that it is divided into two halves of 3½ days, and we have come across that number before: it is the period given in the previous visions – 'a time and times and the dividing of time'. So, at the end of all this, he is just repeating the previous prophecy that the persecution of Antiochus will last for three-and-a-bit years. And the mystical significance of that figure is that it is half of seven. So even if the prophecy *was* made in advance, it was based on mystical numbers, not some foresight of when Antiochus would die.

Vision 4: The Final Revelation (Chapters 10–12).
This vision is the longest and most detailed. It purports to

be a vision of future events vouchsafed to Daniel while in Babylonian captivity. In fact, like the other visions, it dates from the time of Antiochus IV Epiphanes as we shall now see. The prophecy itself begins thus:

> Behold, there shall stand up yet three kings in Persia: and the fourth shall be far richer than they all:[55]

Scholars are divided about exactly which kings Daniel is referring to, but the next reference is crystal clear:

> And a mighty king shall stand up, that shall rule with great dominion, and do according to his will. And when he shall stand up, his kingdom shall be broken, and shall be divided toward the four winds of Heaven; and not to his posterity, nor according to his dominion which he ruled: for his kingdom shall be plucked up, even for others beside those.[56]

This can only be Alexander the Great and his generals who divided his empire between them on his death. The generals all vied with each other, but two emerged with the lion's share – Ptolemy and Seleucus. The former ruled the southern empire based on Egypt and the latter the northern Asian empire. Judah found itself in the Seleucid Empire but was a pawn in the ongoing rivalry between the two empires founded by Ptolemy and Seleucus, and over the next twenty verses Daniel recounts this rivalry between the 'king of the south' and the 'king of the north' over a period of 150 years or so. The tale he tells can be related with complete certainty to the events and characters of the period as we know them from history, and with one or two minor caveats, Daniel

---

55 Daniel 11:2.

56 11:3-4.

seems to get his history right, establishing presumably his credentials as a prophet. But his real interest is not in this period because of course his prophecy is being written in the second century not the sixth century. The next twenty-four verses deal in detail with the reign of Antiochus IV Epiphanes – more verses than in the whole of the previous history – down to and including the ultimate sacrilege of the desecration of the Temple in 167 BC:

> . . . and they shall pollute the sanctuary of strength, and shall take away the daily sacrifice, and they shall place the abomination that maketh desolate.[57]

This sacrilege was the final straw and provoked the first armed revolt that turned eventually into the Maccabean rebellion. Daniel seems to know of this but is not impressed, referring to it as but 'little help':

> And they that understand among the people shall instruct many: yet they shall fall by the sword, and by flame, by captivity, and by spoil, many days. Now when they shall fall, they shall be holpen with a little help: but many shall cleave to them with flatteries.[58]

These words were presumably written right at the beginning of the Maccabean Revolt, when it would have been very uncertain to say the least that it would succeed as wildly as it did. But in any case, Daniel was not interested in human action of this kind. He was convinced God would now intervene directly; the Day of the Lord was imminent. The remainder of the Book of Daniel is a prophecy about exactly

---

[57] 11:31.
[58] Daniel 11:33-34.

that, but of course, from this point on, when attempting genuine prophecy, Daniel gets it completely wrong. Fundamentalists do some amazing wriggling to avoid this – notably to identify the events prophesied at the end of Daniel to a later Roman period. But there is absolutely no basis for this other than wishful thinking; it requires for the kings of the north and south to suddenly become other empires entirely, and even then, the facts do not fit very well with the text. Fundamentalists also like to point to the fact that some manuscript references to the tales of Daniel pre-exist the second century so, it is argued, the Book must be genuine prophecy. But that is precisely the point: *parts* of the Book were indeed old tales from way back, *but* there is not a shred of evidence that any of the actual prophecies predate the events they describe. And from verse 40 to the end of the Book there is nothing historical at all. The only rational explanation that fits the facts is that Daniel as we have it was finally redacted after 167 BC and before the end of 165 BC. At that time, Antiochus was alive and well and his persecutions of Orthodox Jews and their beliefs was still at its height. It would have been in no way apparent to anyone at the time that the early resistance of the Maccabee family was going to amount to anything, and the only hope available to Daniel was that the Day of the Lord should come.

Let us look at this final prophecy. First, Daniel forecasts that Antiochus will once again, for the third time, attack Egypt. Perhaps that was the expectation at the time, although that seems unlikely given that, as a result of the previous two forays into Egypt, Rome had exerted its own growing power and had forbidden any more such adventures south into what it regarded as its own sphere of influence. Certainly, at the end of his life in December 164 BC, Antiochus was up to his neck in troubles to the north and east – not south. The death of Antiochus seems to have been in Persia from a disease,⁵⁹ but it certainly was not at the hand of God as Daniel suggests:

> ... he shall be broken without hand.⁶⁰

and not, as Daniel would also have it, on:

> ... the glorious holy mountain ⁶¹

which is presumably the Mount of Olives. Daniel sees the death of Antiochus as a divine action 'at the time of the end'⁶² and it immediately ushers in what at first looks to be the usual Jewish apocalyptic events. First, there will be:

> ... a time of trouble, such as never was⁶³

or the Great Tribulation as we know it. This is followed by the Day of the Lord:

> ... and at that time thy people shall be delivered, every one that shall be found written in the book.⁶⁴

But then Daniel introduces a new thought that is not encountered in other Jewish apocalypse:

> And many of them that sleep in the dust of the Earth shall

---

59 Although ancient reports were variously that he drowned or fell from his chariot.
60 Daniel 8:25.
61 Daniel 11:45.
62 11:40.
63 12:1.
64 12:1.

awake, some to everlasting life, and some to shame and everlasting contempt.[65]

The second generation of prophets were focused on a material return to the Promised Land out of Babylon and the re-establishment of the Temple religion. Daniel is in a different position. The Jews are already in possession of their land but are under the heel of the Seleucid Empire. Daniel knows from the painful lesson of history that if God just kills Antiochus, there will be others like him. If not Seleucid, then some other Earthly empire. So, for the first time he introduces the idea that the Day of the Lord is not about physical salvation, but spiritual destiny. Scholars debate the detail: is this prophecy about the whole world, or just Jews, or just the Jews who resisted Hellenization? And Christian commentators love to picture this as not just the first biblical reference to Christian eschatology, but a genuinely inspired passage in which God foreshadows the glory that is to come through Jesus Christ.

Historicists and Futurists go further. They see in this scripture a genuine prophecy, not just of Christian salvation but of the eschatological characters that populate their End Time events. Historicists multiply Daniel's half a week/three-and-a-bit days, and multiply by 365 to arrive at a date 1,260 years in the future from the time of Antiochus. This brings them to about 1100, enabling them to equate Daniel's prophecy with the period of papal oppression that they regard as the true Historical interpretation of the Great Tribulation. Futurists on the other hand, reject those calculations and believe the Tribulation is still to come: in their *midrashic* interpretation, the references to Antiochus from Chapter 11 onwards (and for some, the references in the verses that

---

65 12:2.

precede this) refer allegorically to the future Antichrist or one of the Beasts from Revelation. We shall look more closely at Antiochus and his demonization in Jewish myth in the next section. But if, as I have argued and sane scholars believe, the writers of Daniel can be located to the time of Antiochus' sacrilegious persecutions, then we need look no further than that for the references here. And certainly what we do have here is a crucial passage, marking a sea change in the way some at least of the Jewish people were beginning to understand their destiny as God's chosen people; a shift from physical to spiritual salvation.

Daniel ends with yet another reference to the timing of the Day of the Lord. And again, the prophecy is broadly consistent with the others in the Book. There are three indications given. First, the persecution will last 'time, times, and an half' (12:7). Second, it will last 'a thousand two hundred and ninety days' (12:11). And third, a 'thousand three hundred and five and thirty days, (12:12). These are all around the three-and-a-bit years prophecy from elsewhere, but clearly differ slightly from each other. The second is slightly longer than the first, and the third is slightly longer than the second. Some have argued, and it is tempting to believe, that this is because some redactor(s) added the second and third forecasts in turn as each deadline passed without incident. No one really knows. What is certain is that the Book of Daniel sets the scene for the Book of Revelation. The references to Beasts, Horns, and Kings all re-emerge in Revelation and are reinterpreted there in terms of first century AD events rather than second century BC ones.

And this points to a fundamental issue: the Day of the Lord is the default escape clause for Judaeo-Christian belief down through the centuries. The first generation of prophets thought the Day would come in their time; the second generation awaited it in their time; the writers of Daniel expected it in their time. As we shall see, the writers of Revelation expected it in their time. And all the prophets and religious leaders over the ensuing two millennia, as we surveyed them briefly in Part Two of this book, all expected it in their time. And at each point along this long history of disappointed expectation, they have gone back to their predecessors for clues; each time, they have disinterred the same old scriptural passages and, by allegorical techniques, have reinterpreted them for their own times; and in that process, each has added his own ideas and beliefs to the growing theology, so that by the twenty-first century, the apocalypse has become so convoluted and disputed, it needs a book like this just to unravel the basics. What began as a simple idea – that things have got so bad, God just has to step in – has become a complicated series of Earthly and Heavenly events, spread out over 1,000 years, the order and timing of which is no clearer now than it ever was. And in that long chain of evolution, the Book of Daniel marks a major milestone.

APOCALYPTIC TOPIC NO. 11: THE ABOMINATION OF DESOLATION

Preterism: Either the desecration of Antiochus IV Epiphanes or the much later one of Titus.
Historicism: As Preterism.
Futurism: A future event associated with the Antichrist figure.

The course of Jewish history is marked by a few major events that define the Jewish race and its distinctive set of beliefs about Yahweh and their relationship with that divinity. The destruction of the Northern Kingdom and the subsequent Exile of the Southern Kingdom are two such. They are the key turning points of the Old Testament narrative, and the theme of all the prophets we find there. But at the time when Christianity came into being, they were ancient history. Much more recent and pertinent to the first-century believer were the events only just over a century before, when Antiochus IV Epiphanes, in pursuit of the Hellenization of the Jewish people and the eradication of their religion, desecrated the Holy of Holies in the Temple at Jerusalem. To the Jewish mind of the time, nothing could be worse in terms of their relationship with Yahweh; hence the description of the event as the 'abomination of desolation'. (The phrase means something like 'an appalling, detestable act of sacrilegious desecration'). The Maccabean Revolt had for a time reversed the Hellenizing trend and indeed, for a period, the Jews had lived in their own self-determining state again. But by the first century they were back in a Hellenistic empire again, under the thumb of Rome. When Pontius Pilate ordered the Roman eagle to be displayed in the Temple, he must have known what he was doing. Certainly, the Jewish people saw it as deliberate provocation, echoing the actions of Antiochus a century or so before. And thus, the term 'abomination of desolation' became not just a description of a crucial historical event, it became an apocalyptic topic of central importance. A sign of the Last Days would be when the Holy of Holies once again was violated, triggering the Day of the Lord.

Fundamentalists tie themselves in knots on this one because they have not understood what is really going on here. Daniel mentions the 'abomination of desolation' several times, and on each occasion there can be no doubt at all that he is referring to Antiochus. This is presented as a prophecy from the time of the Babylonian captivity but is of course a text written in the midst of the depredations of Antiochus, masquerading as ancient prophecy. Fundamentalists are tempted to see this as a prophecy about the first

The Dozen Jewish Apocalyptic Topics

century AD (or even later) because Jesus refers to it in the Olivet Discourse:

> When ye therefore shall see the abomination of desolation, spoken of by Daniel the prophet, stand in the holy place, (whoso readeth, let him understand:) Then let them which be in Judæa flee into the mountains:[66]

In its context, this seems to be an equally clear reference to the culmination of the Jewish War against Rome in the sixties AD. So, which is it? Well, it is both and more. The clue is in the phrase in brackets: 'whoso readeth, let him understand'. When this gets noticed at all by fundamentalist commentators, it is to debate whether Jesus actually spoke these words (given the reference to reading) or whether it is an addition by whoever recorded the words of Jesus here. If one accepts that the Gospel stories are a fiction based on *Midrash* from Old Testament sources, the truth falls into place. The writer of the Gospel introduces it here to indicate that this is a *Midrash* upon the Daniel text. The Book of Daniel is concerned with Antiochus. But as holy scripture, it also has hidden meaning for later generations: in this case, 'let the reader understand' that what we have here is an allegorical interpretation of Daniel applied to events current at the time the Gospel was written. Ironically, that is also exactly what Futurists are doing when they project this Olivet text into our own times and near future; their *Midrash* on this New Testament text is that God is secretly revealing to the initiated his plan for the future. Fundamentalist trainspotters, like the Pharisees of old, love nothing better than to tackle a juicy text like this and vie with each other to decode its hidden meanings, encrypted by God in His Holy scripture.

---

66 Matthew 24:15-16.

It really is an easy game to play. I have just at the time of writing reached across my desk for my Bible and opened it entirely at random (truly, but do try it yourself) and picked this verse out with my finger:

> They that dwell in the wilderness shall bow before him and his enemies shall lick the dust[67]

Preterists do not get to play this game. But for Futurists, this passage is *clearly* a hidden reference to the President of the United States' imminent invasion of a Middle Eastern country. Or for Historicists, it is *clearly* a reference to the War on Terror and has already been fulfilled by the invasion of Iraq (which if not an actual wilderness before, certainly is now). The point is that what we might regard as a game was deadly serious for first-century believers, using *Midrash* to ransack their scripture. The whole edifice of Christianity is based on nothing more or less than the allegorical correspondences they found there. We did not know this until we found the Dead Sea Scrolls and saw them in the process of doing it. Conspiracy theorists thought for years that something damaging to Christianity was being withheld by the scholars controlling the Scrolls. There was, but it was not an obscure text, it was the centrality of *Midrash* and *Pesher* to the way these people thought about religion.

APOCALYPTIC TOPIC NO. 12: THE ORIGINAL APOCALYPSE OF JOHN THE BAPTIST

Preterism: Fulfilled in the first century AD.
Historicism: Fulfilled in the seventh century AD.

---

[67] Psalm 72:9

The Dozen Jewish Apocalyptic Topics

Futurism: Yet to be fulfilled.

The writer of the First Apocalypse, John A, is quite clearly a prophet, speaking prophetic language and, as one would expect of the last prophet before the End of Days, authoritatively takes it upon himself to interpret the words and visions of the age of prophecy. Since the Baptist is clearly presented in the Gospels as a prophet, Ford regards him as the best candidate for authorship and I concur. He is dressed in traditional prophet garb; his hair and diet are traditional for prophets; the wilderness has strong eschatological associations; and not only do the Jewish populace regard him as a new 'Elijah', the hallmark of the last prophet, but *Jesus* himself is pictured as confirming that status. As we shall now see, Ford's instinct can be confirmed by the New Paradigm set out in Volume II of this trilogy.

Given the arguments behind that New Paradigm, we might ask the question: What would we expect to see as the key characteristics of the First Apocalypse if John A was in fact John the Baptist? I would suggest four things:

1. A strong influence of Zechariah generally, and specifically:
2. Clear reference to the twin Messiahs as described in Zechariah.
3. Clear reference to the Lamb of Isaiah Chapter 53 – that is, not as the Christian atoning Messiah figure, but as a symbol of the suffering nation of Israel.
4. A clear prophetic calling to the author in terms that recall the Baptist's own divine commission to 'prepare the way of the Lord'.

And that is exactly what we find. As noted already, the whole of Revelation is permeated with reference to the Jewish prophets and Jewish apocalypse, but one of the key influences is that of Zechariah, and the references to that prophet are to be found almost exclusively in the First Apocalypse. Marko Jauhiainen, in his book *The Use of Zechariah in Revelation*, says that 'Revelation alludes to more than three quarters of Zechariah'. He exhaustively identifies over fifty passages that commentators have identified over the years as possible allusions; around half of these he confirms as 'convincing', and **all** of these are to be found in the First Apocalypse.[68] Furthermore, the twin Messiahs can indeed be found there, described unmistakeably in terms that directly reference Zechariah's description of the two anointed ones:

> These are the two olive trees and the two lampstands which stand before the Lord of the earth.[69]

The suffering servant, symbolized as a Lamb, is introduced as the 'root of David' that alone is worthy to bring history to an end. And the author is directly commissioned by a 'mighty angel' to prophesy what he has seen, in a passage that immediately precedes the description of the two anointed Messiahs. Ford points out that certain key phrases and concepts appear only in Revelation *and* in the Gospel passages relating to the Baptist:

- 'the Lamb'; and
- 'He that cometh' in reference to *Jesus*; and
- 'baptism by fire'.

---

68 See Select Bibliography. This calculation is to be found in the Introduction, p. 2. The analysis in table form is to be found on page 100. Jauhiainen is a believing Christian so would (I believe) not subscribe to the arguments of this book. His book is based on his University of Cambridge doctoral thesis on the subject.

69 Revelation 11:4. Compare Zechariah 4:11: 'What are these two olive trees upon the right side of the candlestick and upon the left thereof?'.

The Dozen Jewish Apocalyptic Topics

Clearly, as the Christian story evolved, these phrases and concepts that had always been part of the Baptist's Jewish vision remained associated with his name, but took on new meanings in the context of the emerging Christian paradigm; meanings relating to a divine son of God that would have been entirely alien to him. In my view, it is inescapable (and exciting) that what we have here, as Ford has already suggested, is a written version of the original vision that set John the Baptist on the road to being the last prophet, and that led to the Jesus Movement and, over time, into Christianity itself.

It is worth pausing here to reflect on the likelihood of this claim. Of course, as with much else in this trilogy, I cannot prove it. But here are some interesting reflections. The Book of Zechariah is regarded by Christians and Jews alike as a 'minor' prophet. It is little read today, especially compared with other prophets like Ezekiel and Daniel, whose prophetic visions are favourites with fundamentalists. And even the originators of the Dead Sea Scrolls seem to have had little or no interest in Zechariah: it is a curious fact that although manuscripts of most Old Testament Books exist among the Scrolls, there is not a complete one of Zechariah. There are several fragments of Zechariah located in scrolls of the 'minor prophets', but they are comparatively scarce. If one were looking for evidence of connection between the Scrolls and 'Christianity', this would be a major stumbling block, because in the Gospel narratives of Christ's passion the most important single source is Zechariah. To quote Jauhiainen again:

> Zechariah's importance to the early Christian community is perhaps reflected in the fact that chapters 9-14 are the most quoted section of the prophets in the passion narratives of the Gospels' [Baldwin (1972)].[70] In addition to quotations,

---
70 See Bibliography.

there are also a number of allusions to Zechariah 9-14. [References to more than a dozen quotations and allusions follow] ... these are enough to indicate how Jesus was seen as the Zecharian righteous and humble king and as the struck and pierced shepherd closely associated or even identified with Yahweh but detested by the flock.'[71]

The Baptist's father is said to be one 'Zechariah' and the Baptist himself seems to know nothing of a suffering Messiah: his vision, as described in the Gospels, is of a Zecharian judge of mankind, winnowing the human wheat from the chaff. I believe there is only one inescapable conclusion: that the Baptist, heavily influenced by his reading of Zechariah, had his own visionary experiences that led him to believe he was the last prophet before the End of Days, commissioned by God to preach the coming Kingdom of God. His movement, through the historical events traced in Vol. II, eventually emerged in a garbled form as Christianity. The core of Revelation, the First Apocalypse, therefore preserves his original teachings as we shall now explore.

As noted under Topic No. 7, the problems with the First Apocalypse all arise in chapters 10 and 11, where the order of events serves to reduce the status of the twin Messianic figures of Zechariah, who should surely appear at the beginning of the Last Days, but who seem to have become relegated to impotent witnesses, active only when the Last Days events are virtually complete. In fact, these two chapters are strange and confused (beyond the strangeness and confusion normal for Revelation!) on a number of levels. Logically speaking, what is the point of the two Men of Oil prophesying at the *end* of the seven seals and the seven trumpets? This point is, of course, obscured because the Second Apocalypse

---

[71] Jauhiainen, pp.60-61.

rains even more destruction down on Earth, but this is a specious artefact caused by the conflation of two separate documents. Surely a just God would have sent His messengers *before* he began raining down 'curses' on the bare heads of mankind, not *after* destroying most of Creation. And if there was anyone left alive after all those 'curses', surely it would be obvious to them the need for recognition of the need to reconcile with such an angry God and that some sort of repentance was called for! This makes no logical sense at all, even by biblical standards. And indeed, that is surely what we are led to expect when we are first introduced to the two Men of Oil in Zechariah. Instead, we have a whole Christian theology arising from this absurdity, in which the two witnesses are sent to preach to the 'remnant' left on the Earth after God has vented his divine ire.

There are a number of clues that this is not what the writer intended. For example, the tenses in the crucial Chapter 11 are all over the place. Josephine Massyngberde Ford comments:

> Throughout this chapter, the tenses oscillate between present, future, and past. This may indicate the composite nature of the chapter.[72]

There is no 'may' about it; something has got snarled up here. Furthermore, there are evident problems of discontinuity. An angel announces that there will be three 'woes' inflicted on mankind: two are described but the third does not seem to materialize. On the other hand, the second woe appears to be two-fold – 2 million cavalry and a great earthquake that kills 7,000 – but these are separated by three unrelated passages including the one about the two witnesses. In

---

72 p.168.

my view, these three passages are out of their correct place as betrayed by the illogicality of the narrative, the missing third woe and the confusion of tenses. And I would argue that the reason this has happened is the phrase 'in the days of the voice of the seventh angel'. These passages have been moved to this point in order immediately to precede the blowing of the seventh trumpet, despite the fact that by doing so they interrupt the flow of the narrative, postpone the blowing, and create logical nonsense. The clue as to the correct position for these passages is given by the introduction to them at the start of Chapter 10: 'And I saw *another* mighty angel' (my italics). The only other 'mighty angel' appears back in Chapter 5, asking who is worthy to open the book with seven seals. Given that the second mighty angel holds a 'book' also, does it not seem likely that in the original version, the second mighty angel follows straight on from the first, and that the descriptions of the commission to prophesy and of the two witnesses also belong immediately after the description of the book with seven seals?

As currently structured, the first mighty angel introduces the seven-sealed book; the seven seals are opened and six trumpets are sounded; the Earth is bombarded with death and destruction time after time; then the Baptist is told to prophesy and the witnesses to witness to a beleaguered remnant; and then the Kingdom of God is established. But by the simple expedient of moving the disputed passages forward as I have suggested, we then have a structure that is logical and consonant with Zechariah and common sense:

Ch.5: the first mighty angel introduces the seven-sealed book;

Ch.10:1-10: the second mighty angel gives the Baptist a version of it to ingest;

Ch.10:11: on the basis of that ingestion, the Baptist is commissioned to prophesy the End Time events, preparing the way for:

Ch.11:1-12: the two Messiahs who provide mankind with its last chance of salvation, after which:

Ch.6:1–9:21: the End of Days begins. There are seven seals followed by seven trumpets, the last of which is;

Ch.11:13: the third 'woe' – a mighty earthquake; the kingdom of God then begins.

The consequences of this shift are twofold. First, the Baptist's commission to prophesy is emphasized right up front. This is entirely consonant with the traditional Jewish apocalyptic idea that the last prophet will appear at the beginning of End Time events to prophesy what is about to take place. It is also consonant with the role that the Baptist is traditionally assigned from the Gospels. He prepares the way. Second, the twin anointed ones of Zechariah also assume their rightful role as twin Messiahs, rather than inconsequential witnesses. Whether their relegation to a subsidiary role, apparently pointlessly preaching to an intransigent (and presumably therefore utterly stupid) 'remnant' was deliberate or just the result of well-meaning but erroneous editing, it is impossible to tell.

And when we look closely at the text above describing the two witnesses this becomes apparent, for these are not ordinary men. They may wear symbolic sackcloth, but God has given them powers of prophecy to speak on his behalf and they breathe fire on their enemies and rain down blood and plague. They appear after the Gentiles have been allowed by God to trample over Jerusalem for 42 months, or 3½ years. The period allotted for their prophecy is then also 1,260 days or 3½ years. At the end of that time, they will be killed by a Beast from Hell, lie reviled in a city street for 3½ days and then rise into Heaven. Clearly, all these references to periods of 3½ are based on half a week and we have, of course, come across them before, in the Book of Daniel from which John the Baptist has lifted them. They confirm again that the two witnesses of Revelation are much more important figures than the order of text here suggests: they are central Messianic figures involved in the Day of the Lord itself, not minor figures doing some kind of sweeping up after the fact. There is no doubt that if Christianity evolved out of the Baptist's visions, and those in turn were based upon his reading of Zechariah, then the twin witnesses of Revelation are the twin anointed ones or Messiahs – Priest Messiah of Aaron and King Messiah of David – prophesied by Zechariah. In which case, what are we to make of the Lamb figure in Revelation which is always understood by Christians to be their Messiah figure – the sacrificial Lamb of God?

This really is the crux of the issue. As I have already argued, the symbolic Lamb of Jewish apocalypse is primarily a symbol of the suffering Jewish nation. Over time, it becomes identified with the expected Jewish King Messiah. But for Jews, this has nothing to do with atonement. The two are separate and distinct in Jewish thought. It is only in later Christianity that the two become confused and identified together in the single saviour figure of Jesus Christ. That is how the Lamb appears in the Jewish document that is Revelation Chapter 5. He is a symbol of the Jewish people, whose suffering makes them worthy to open the book, bring about the Kingdom of God and become a 'priestly Kingdom' within it. It is only when read through the Christian paradigm that this becomes a Messianic figure.

Indeed, I would argue that it is this misunderstanding of the Lamb symbol that made possible the transformation of the Baptist's Jewish vision into Pauline Christianity. Once the twin witnesses/Messiahs are relegated to a minor role, this makes possible the conflation of messiahship with divine atonement that is the key characteristic of Pauline Christianity. It is then easy to see how, having arrived at that conception, Christians – seeking a name for their atoning Messiah – took the name of the original Jewish Priest Messiah and called him Jesus. We can see straight away how these Jewish apocalyptic ideas feed into Christianity. The rejection of the witnesses' prophecy by the Jewish people echoes the story of Jesus as the Gospels tell it, but for different reasons. The Jewish writer of these words is working in the long tradition of Jewish prophecy in which God's warnings to the Jews are unheeded and rejected until God punishes them and they repent. The Christian version, deriving from Gentiles, regards the Jews as the people that rejected Jesus and crucified him. The description of the people celebrating the death of the witnesses feeds into the Gospel descriptions of the masses choosing Barabbas over Jesus when Pilate offers them the choice. The reference to Sodom and Egypt is Jewish *Midrash* for unrepentant Jerusalem and in my view the phrase 'where also our Lord was crucified' is an obvious later Christian addition.[73]

The resurrection after 3½ days becomes Jesus' resurrection. The Anglican Apostle's Creed states that he rose on the third day, following the Apostle Paul:

For I delivered unto you first of all that which I also received, how that Christ died for our sins according to the scriptures; And that he was buried, and that he rose again the third day according to the scriptures;

but according to Matthew 12:40, Jesus says:

---

[73] The correct translation should be 'their Lord'.

> For as Jonas was three days and three nights in the whale's belly;[74] so shall the Son of man be three days and three nights in the heart of the Earth.

This would imply resurrection on the fourth day, consistent with 3½ days here. Which are we to believe? Interestingly, Paul says that he is quoting scripture. There are a number of Old Testament passages in which three days figures, but perhaps the most pertinent is Hosea 6:2:

> Come, and let us return unto the Lord: for he hath torn, and he will heal us; he hath smitten, and he will bind us up. After two days will he revive us: in the third day he will raise us up, and we shall live in his sight.

Obviously, in its original context, this is about God's punishment of the Israelites and His promise to restore them if they repent, but to the *Midrash* mentality, this can be applied to a crucified saviour or to a pair of murdered Messiahs. Three days or four days? What matters is the symbolic meaning not a precise period of time.

There are a number of specific prophecies within this First Apocalypse that have particular significance for different fundamentalist positions. The 144,000 souls (12,000 x 12 tribes) 'sealed' in Chapter 7 can be interpreted as those who survive the Great Tribulation: their identity, as we have seen, depending on your interpretation of the role of the Lost Tribes in the Last Days. Most are inclined to take an Idealist view of this, the numbers being obviously (one would think) symbolic; but Jehovah's Witnesses take a literal view and vie with one another to impress God and to secure their place in the 144,000. Futurists have a field day with Chapter 8 and

---

[74] Jonah 1:17.

regard most of the traumatic events described there as forthcoming nuclear holocaust. Verses 10-11 in particular describe a star called Wormwood falling to Earth and polluting no less than one-third of the planet's water sources. Apparently, Chernobyl means Wormwood.[75] The apocalyptic events described in Chapter 9 are ascribed by Historicists to the rise of Islam in the seventh century and its unbelievably rapid spread through Christendom. I could go on. The point is that this Apocalypse of John is pure, undiluted Jewish prophecy about the Day of the Lord. It has nothing to do with Christianity as it later evolved. It was written by John the Baptist in the early part of the first century and reflects Jewish expectation of salvation from Roman rule generally, and the actions of Pontius Pilate in particular. Like all such writings, it is symbolic and allegorical and as such is open to any and every interpretation. Its predictions never came about and never will.

---

[75] The key ingredient in absinthe – a more likely derivation one suspects.

3

The Dozen Christian Apocalyptic Topics

APOCALYPTIC TOPIC NO. 13: THE MOTHER AND CHILD AND DRAGON

Preterism: Fulfilled by the birth of Jesus and the subsequent Jewish War with Rome.
Historicism: Fulfilled by the birth of Jesus and the subsequent persecution of the early Christian Church.
Futurism: Partially fulfilled by the birth of Jesus and partially to be fulfilled by the Great Tribulation in the future.

This prophecy takes up the whole of Revelation Chapter 12 and therefore is the introduction to the Second Apocalypse of Revelation by John B. It comprises most of the rest of the Book and is usually dated to the period after the destruction of Jerusalem in AD 70. Because the two Jewish apocalypses of Revelation, written by different people and at different times in the first century, are run together, it comes as an abrupt surprise, straight after the description that ends

The Dozen Christian Apocalyptic Topics

Chapter 11 of the Temple of God in Heaven. Suddenly, we are told of a 'great wonder in Heaven':

> ... a woman clothed with the sun, and the moon under her feet, and upon her head a crown of twelve stars: And she being with child cried, travailing in birth, and pained to be delivered. And there appeared another wonder in Heaven; and behold a great red dragon, having seven heads and ten horns, and seven crowns upon his heads. . .and the dragon stood before the woman which was ready to be delivered, for to devour her child as soon as it was born. And she brought forth a man child, who was to rule all nations with a rod of iron: and her child was caught up unto God, and to his throne.[1]

Who are the woman and the child, and who or what is the dragon? Fundamentalists of all persuasions are pretty much agreed that the woman is the Virgin Mary, the child is Jesus, and the dragon is the forces of Rome. Except, surely we are told that it was not Rome that killed Jesus, it was those bad old Jews. Didn't Pontius Pilate himself try to save Jesus and finally washed his hands of the whole business? And why the emphasis on the woman's birth travails, and why no reference to either her virginity nor even the life and sacrifice of Jesus. Just a perfunctory 'her child was caught up'. The interpretation just does not fit, and I am not the only one to think that. Ford, for example concludes, having given the Mary/Jesus theory a good run, that she is 'not convinced', but fails to offer a coherent alternative.[2]

The chapter has the usual problems of showing evidence of additions and amendments: there are verses that seem to

---

[1] Revelation 11: 1-5.
[2] Ford, p. 207.

parallel each other,[3] and there are obvious later Christian additions.[4] But if we exclude these for simplicity, here is the rest of the chapter:

> And there was war in Heaven: Michael and his angels fought against the dragon; and the dragon fought and his angels, And prevailed not; neither was their place found any more in Heaven. And the great dragon was cast out, that old serpent, called the Devil, and Satan, which deceiveth the whole world: he was cast out into the Earth, and his angels were cast out with him. And I heard a loud voice saying in Heaven, Now is come salvation, and strength, and the kingdom of our God, and the power of his Christ: for the accuser of our brethren is cast down, which accused them before our God day and night. And they overcame him by the blood of the Lamb, and by the word of their testimony; and they loved not their lives unto the death. Therefore rejoice, ye Heavens, and ye that dwell in them. Woe to the inhabiters of the Earth and of the sea! for the devil is come down unto you, having great wrath, because he knoweth that he hath but a short time. And when the dragon saw that he was cast unto the Earth, he persecuted the woman which brought forth the man child. And to the woman were given two wings of a great eagle, that she might fly into the wilderness, into her place, where she is nourished for a time, and times, and half a time, from the face of the serpent. And the serpent cast out of his mouth water as a flood after the woman, that he might cause her to be carried away of the flood. And the Earth helped the woman, and the Earth opened her mouth, and swallowed up the flood which the dragon cast out of his mouth. And the dragon was wroth with the woman, and went to make war

---

[3] Verses 6 and 14.
[4] Verse 17.

with the remnant of her seed, which keep the commandments of God, . . . [5]

The first thing to notice here is that this is not a prophecy – apocalyptic or otherwise. It is not a vision or dream of the future: it is all in the past tense. Second, it is clearly religious myth, not history. It deals with supernatural events taking place in Heaven, and when the action transfers to Earth, it is clearly symbolic.[6] And third, whatever else it might be about, it concerns at the symbolic level the eternal struggle between the forces of Good and the forces of Evil. But is it more specific than that?

The writer has obviously been reading Daniel. He picks up on the 'time, and times, and half a time' prophecy,[7] and the dragon seems to be the fourth Beast from Daniel's prophecy, which also has ten horns. But he has also been reading Zechariah, and it is this that gives us the clue to what this is all about. Let us remind ourselves of the crucial passage upon which I have argued (in Volume II), the whole of Christianity is founded:

> And he shewed me Jesus the high priest standing before the angel of the Lord, and Satan standing at his right hand to resist him. And the Lord said unto Satan, The Lord rebuke thee, O Satan; even the Lord that hath chosen Jerusalem rebuke thee: is not this a brand plucked out of the fire? Now Jesus was clothed with filthy garments, and stood before the angel. And he answered and spake unto those that stood

---

[5] Revelation 11:7-17.

[6] Some Literalists suggest that the flood refers to Nero's attempt to build a Corinth canal; a connection that seems to me facetious at just about every level.

[7] And in a verse I have omitted because it parallels this, the woman is said to be fed for 'a thousand two hundred and threescore days' – the equivalent alternative from Daniel.

before him, saying, Take away the filthy garments from him. And unto him he said, Behold, I have caused thine iniquity to pass from thee, and I will clothe thee with change of raiment. And I said, Let them set a fair mitre upon his head. So they set a fair mitre upon his head, and clothed him with garments. And the angel of the Lord stood by. And the angel of the Lord protested unto Jesus, saying, Thus saith the Lord of hosts; If thou wilt walk in my ways, and if thou wilt keep my charge, then thou shalt also judge my house, and shalt also keep my courts, and I will give thee places to walk among these that stand by.[8]

Both the passage from Revelation and the one from Zechariah are set in Heaven and involve Satan. In Zechariah, Satan is depicted as resisting the elevation of Jesus and is rebuked for it. What is Satan doing in Heaven rather than Hell? In Jewish (and Christian) myth, Satan was originally an angel who rebelled and was cast out of Heaven. Prior to that, his role in Heaven was as a sort of prosecutor in the Heavenly court. When a soul came before God for judgement, his accuser was Satan and his defender was the angel Michael: Satan and Michael were archetypal symbols for Good and Evil. So, the scene in Zechariah occurs before Satan's fall. Now look at Revelation again: Satan is described there as 'the accuser of our brethren' and his conflict is with Michael. The connection between the two passages begins to emerge.

The mother in Revelation is not paralleled in Zechariah so who is she? Putting aside the absurd Virgin Mary interpretation, most rational scholars rightly see her as a symbol of the Jewish people. In fact, we can be more precise than that. Her crown and stars suggest a priestly figure and the sun and the

---

8 Zechariah 3: 1-7.

moon are the Priest Messiah and the King Messiah respectively; the latter under her feet because the Priest Messiah was always regarded as the superior. And she is in labour to give birth to the Priest Messiah. The vocabulary and syntax here combine to emphasize that this is no ordinary, human labour. It is prolonged and painful; her cries are not the ordinary cries of labour, but cries to God for deliverance, and her 'travails' express the anguish most often associated in contemporary texts with martyrdom. And her child is no ordinary child: he is the Priest Messiah, born to rule with a 'rod of iron'. The traditional identification with Jesus in this case is on the right track but it is not the fictional Jesus of the first century AD, but rather Jesus the High Priest of the sixth century BC, honoured in Zechariah. Note that Zechariah's Jesus is 'plucked up' to Heaven; in the same way, Revelation's child is 'caught up' to God: both terms are unusual and suggest a similar, involuntary removal from Earth.

I hope the meaning of Revelation 12 is now beginning to become apparent. It is based on Daniel and Zechariah and, putting the whole story together, can be paraphrased as follows:

> An iconic mother figure, symbolizing the Jewish nation and its faithful priesthood, gives birth to the child that is destined to become the Priest Messiah at the end of time. His name is Jesus. The labour is long and painful because the Jewish nation had waited long too for their salvation from continual tribulation. Satan the accuser wants to claim Jesus for Hell and is rebuked for resisting, and war breaks out in Heaven as a result, between Satan and his courtroom adversary, Michael. Satan and his angelic followers are expelled from Heaven and seek to persecute the Mother on Earth, symbolizing the continued persecution of the Jewish people. But he knows he has only a limited time to do this and the Mother

too is protected from him for a period.

The periods of time in question come from Daniel and are, therefore, symbolic too. But it will be recalled that Daniel spoke of a Messiah that would come at the end of the Babylonian Exile, and we also saw that the authors of the Anchor Bible identified that Messiah as Joshua/Jesus. So, the author of Revelation regards his Messiah figure, the war in Heaven and the subsequent persecution of the Jews (symbolized by the Mother) as all taking place at that time, because he was drawing on Daniel:

> Know therefore and understand, that from the going forth of the commandment to restore and to build Jerusalem unto the Messiah the Prince shall be seven weeks, and threescore and two weeks: the street shall be built again, and the wall, even in troublous times. And after threescore and two weeks shall Messiah be cut off, but not for himself: and the people of the prince that shall come shall destroy the city and the sanctuary; and the end thereof shall be with a flood, and unto the end of the war desolations are determined.[9]

The parallel here with the account in Revelation is irresistible; the Messiah figure, the symbolic time periods, the Messiah being 'cut off', and even the flood, which otherwise has no obvious explanation. The writer of Revelation is thus recounting Daniel's prophecy of Messiah and persecution at the time of the return from Exile in the sixth century. In this instance, he is not applying *Midrash* to the account, but simply recounting the myth as a preliminary to his own prophecy. He ends with a statement that has fundamentalists buzzing:

---

9 Daniel 9:25-26.

The Dozen Christian Apocalyptic Topics

And the dragon was wroth with the woman, and went to make war with the remnant of her seed . . .

Because the normal interpretation of this chapter is that the references are to Mary, Jesus and the Jewish War, fundamentalists need to explain this 'remnant'. There are various positions on this: the wider Jewish community outside Jerusalem; or the Christian community that fled the conflict to Pella as Jesus had advised in the Olivet Discourse; or the later Christian church; or the Futurist End Time battle with Satan. But once the parallels between Daniel, Zechariah and this passage are viewed in the light of the New Paradigm, all as usual falls neatly into place. The remnant are the first-century Jews of the time that Revelation was written, still fighting Satan, now in the guise of Rome, and awaiting the return of Jesus the Priest Messiah to usher in the End Time.

I cannot over-emphasize the importance of all this to my New Paradigm as set out in Volume II. I have argued that Christianity has its roots, not in a first-century fictional Jesus, but in a Jewish Priest Messiah figure of the sixth century. In this topic, we have begun to see the way in which Jewish myth evolved into Christian theology. If there was any doubt at all that the Jesus of Zechariah, whom God raises up from the clutches of Satan, was later regarded as a Messianic figure, the quotation from Daniel above surely clinches it. It seems inconceivable that the writer of Revelation Chapter 12 did not have Daniel Chapter 7 in mind when he described his own Messiah figure and Satan, even down to the detail of the persecution symbolized as flood. By putting these two passages together, with Zechariah that we know was a major source for Revelation, we begin to piece together how the original myth emerged that developed into Christianity. Whoever the writers of Revelation were, they were not Christians – they were Jews whose distinctive beliefs, put together originally by John the Baptist from the clues in these Old Testament Books, focused on the return of a Messianic figure waiting in Heaven, not an Earthly one on a cross. How Zechariah's Jesus got to Heaven is unclear. We have no record of his death, and the vocabulary here of snatching, being caught up or cut off seems to suggest that the writers knew nothing either. Zechariah just has a vision of Jesus in Heaven: did he die or did he somehow ascend there? The story of his crucifixion and death all comes from first-century *Midrash* on references in Books like Zechariah and the Psalms to a Messianic figure being 'pierced'. Whether the writers of Revelation knew of this development of the myth we do not know. If they did, then perhaps their writings could be characterized as 'proto-Christian'. My own view is that the piercing/crucifixion elements came later, via Paul and/or other Greek Gentile believers and these apocalypses in Revelation are what they have always been suspected of being once you strip out the odd obvious later Christian additions – undiluted Jewish apocalypse. The description in the Gospels of Jesus' Ascension into Heaven after his Death and Resurrection on the other hand is, I suspect, a reflection of the uncertainty about Jesus: did he die or did he ascend from life? To settle the matter, the Gospel writers depict Jesus as doing both.

The two key elements in all of this are the ideas that the Messiah would be 'pierced' and his life would in some way be cut off. In both of the major Old Testament sources of the Gospel account of Jesus, we find the same: in Isaiah 53, the Messiah is 'cut off'[10] and in Psalm 22, the Messiah says that 'they pierced my hands and my feet.[11]' A recent development in biblical scholarship has brought this issue into sharp

---

10 Verse 8.

11 Verse 16.

The Dozen Christian Apocalyptic Topics

relief. One of the Dead Sea Scrolls that only came to light when, after decades of struggle, all the Scrolls were made generally available,[12] makes reference to a Messiah figure called 'Prince of the Congregation', perhaps recalling Daniel's 'Messiah the Prince', who is either pierced by his enemies, or pierced his enemies. The difference in meaning is of course vast; the former sounds like a crucified Jesus, while the latter sounds more like a warlike Jewish Messiah. Unfortunately, the difference turns on a single vowel which, this being ancient Hebrew script, is not provided by the text. For those that would see the Scrolls as a whole, dating from the first century AD and therefore connected in some way with Christianity, the 'pierced Messiah' interpretation is attractive. For those who seek to defend the consensus view among the original Scrolls scholars that they all predate Christianity, the 'Messiah that pierces' is the correct interpretation. But once one understands that there was no Jesus the Messiah figure in the first century AD, but that the Jesus Movement (which may or may not be connected to the Scroll sect) awaited the return to Earth of their sixth century BC Messiah, who was in some way 'pierced' and 'cut off', all the heat comes out of the argument. In my view, in the context of this interpretation, there can be no doubt that the Scrolls manuscript refers to a 'pierced Messiah' and is further evidence of this expectation in the first century. Revelation itself uses the concept of a pierced Messiah:

> Behold, he cometh with clouds; and every eye shall see him, and they also which pierced him: and all kindreds of the Earth shall wail because of him.[13]

---

12 4Q285.
13 Revelation 1:7.

This belongs to the early part of Revelation that is almost certainly a later, proto-Christian addition and thus indicates perhaps the concept in transition from Jewish Messiah to Christian Saviour.

Revelation Chapter 12 ends with the Dragon standing on Earth, angry and ready for the final war. The next chapter starts these End Time events with the emergence of two more Beasts, agents of the dragon, and as we shall now see, these two Beasts do have contemporary historical parallels, as we move from ancient myth to the realities of the Jewish War against Rome. A word of warning here. Many fundamentalists, particularly Futurists, tend to lump all the dragons and Beasts of Revelation together and equate them with a single, apocalyptic Antichrist figure. This is an oversimplification. There are a number of different Beasts to be dealt with, and it is dangerous to start with an assumption that they are all the same. They are not.

APOCALYPTIC TOPIC NO. 14: THE BEAST FROM THE SEA

Preterism: Rome generally and Nero specifically.
Historicism: The Papacy.
Futurism: The empire of the Antichrist in the image of the Roman Empire.

The first of the Dragon's two Beasts emerges from the sea in Chapter 13 of Revelation and is based, again, on Daniel:

> And I stood upon the sand of the sea, and saw a beast rise up out of the sea, having seven heads and ten horns, and upon his horns ten crowns, and upon his heads the name of blasphemy. And the beast which I saw was like unto a leopard, and his feet were as the feet of a bear, and his mouth as the

mouth of a lion: and the dragon gave him his power, and his seat, and great authority. And I saw one of his heads as it were wounded to death; and his deadly wound was healed: and all the world wondered after the beast. And they worshipped the dragon which gave power unto the beast: and they worshipped the beast, saying, Who is like unto the beast? who is able to make war with him? And there was given unto him a mouth speaking great things and blasphemies; and power was given unto him to continue forty and two months. And he opened his mouth in blasphemy against God, to blaspheme his name, and his tabernacle, and them that dwell in heaven. And it was given unto him to make war with the saints, and to overcome them: and power was given him over all kindreds, and tongues, and nations. And all that dwell upon the earth shall worship him, whose names are not written in the book of life of the Lamb slain from the foundation of the world.[14]

Revelation says that this Sea Beast has ten horns and was like a leopard, but with the feet of a bear and the mouth of a lion. Daniel describes four Beasts also rising from the sea:[15] one like a lion, one like a bear, one like a leopard, and one with ten horns. So, the Sea Beast is an exact *combination* of Daniel's four. It will be recalled that Daniel's fourth Beast's ten horns were symbols of successive Hellenic rulers. The precise details were debatable, but it seemed clear that the tenth horn was Antiochus IV Epiphanes. Revelation's Dragon also has ten horns. I do not believe the writer of Revelation had any clearer an idea who the ten horns precisely represent than we do. He just adopts them and attributes them to his Satanic Dragon and the Sea Beast. He then adds his own

---

14 Revelation 13:1-8.

15 Daniel 7:3-7.

embellishments – he gives the Dragon seven heads and *seven* crowns, and he adorns the Sea Beast with seven heads and *ten* crowns. The different number of crowns indicates that the dragon and the beast symbolize different things, whatever their similarities.

Fundamentalist trainspotters have a lot of fun trying to match the various heads, horns and crowns of a whole range of monsters in Daniel and in Revelation with characters from the first millennium BC to the third millennium AD, depending on their Preterist, Historicist or Futurist inclination. I will offer in Topic 17 my own rationalist interpretation. Here it will be sufficient to assert that the Sea Beast is unmistakeably Rome, whose forces come from the sea and has power 'over all kindreds, and tongues, and nations'.[16] It bears 'the name of blasphemy'[17] because it imposed Emperor worship upon all nations. It is given its power by the Dragon/Satan, but Revelation prophesies that its power will be allowed to continue for only forty and two months'.[18] This of course comes from Daniel again: 42 months (3½ years) is Daniel's half a week of years – the symbolic time period for the Tribulation of the last days. If the Beast is Rome, then its heads must be the Roman emperors, but there is a raft of problems associated with identifying precisely which seven is envisaged here: it all depends on where you start and who you include.[19] If we could be sure of the seven, then we would have the earliest date from which this text could have been written. Unfortunately, a lot of the argument about this tends to be circular. If you assume from other evidence a certain date of composition, then you will interpret the emperors accordingly. Resolution of this must

---

16 Revelation 13:7.
17 13:1 and 6.
18 13:5.
19 For example, should Julius Caesar be counted as an emperor for this purpose?

wait until Topic 17. But there is one other piece of dating evidence here. The clue comes in verse 3 where, speaking of the Beast's seven heads, Revelation says:

> And I saw one of his heads as it were wounded to death; and his deadly wound was healed: and all the world wondered after the Beast.

The text does not say it was the last, seventh head that was wounded, but the writer clearly regards this as pertinent to his account, so perhaps we can conclude that it was a recent event or even contemporary. The favourite scholarly interpretation of this verse is that it refers to Nero, whose throat was cut on orders of the Roman Senate in June, AD 69. A persistent rumour arose, particularly in the eastern Empire, that Nero had survived and was planning a return to power. A more likely solution in my view (for reasons I shall outline in the next topic) is that it refers to the twelve months after Nero's death when three emperors – Galba, Otho and Vitellius – claimed the crown in rapid succession before Vespasian secured the throne for the next decade. The chaos this created could certainly be described as a dangerous wounding to the Empire, and the relief that met Vespasian's restoration of order and stability could be described as 'wonder'. The truth is that we do not know for certain. But it hardly matters: the important point is that both interpretations pin this passage to the period following Nero's death. Of course, the passage could have been written much later, but if so, why did John B choose to highlight this particular event in Roman Imperial history rather than any other? Surely he alluded to it because it was either current or fresh in memory. Equally, the passage could not have been written after the destruction of Jerusalem, the culmination of the Jewish/Roman War in AD 70, because it is prophesying the Day of the Lord that never happened. So, we have a putative date of composition between mid-AD 69 and AD 70. With this possibility in mind, let us move on to the next topic and the second of the Dragon's two Beasts.

APOCALYPTIC TOPIC NO. 15: THE BEAST FROM THE LAND

Preterism: Nero, or the Jewish rulers who acted for Rome.
Historicism: The United States of America.
Futurism: Future apostasy.

Interpreting the Beast from the Sea is relatively uncontentious. There may be unresolvable detail, but the essential identification with Rome is clear and unequivocal – to the rational mind that is. The second of the Dragon's two Beasts, that rises from the Land is, on the other hand, one of the most argued-over passages in Revelation, if not in the whole Bible. It is also, in my view, the single most misunderstood symbol too, and the interpretation I shall now outline is new and original. This is the Beast that we are told has the mystical number 666. I deal with this separately in the next topic, where I shall present more evidence in support of my interpretation. Here I shall confine the argument purely to the description of the Beast in the second half of Chapter 13:

> And I beheld another Beast coming up out of the Earth; and he had two horns like a lamb, and he spake as a dragon. And he exerciseth all the power of the first Beast before him, and causeth the Earth and them which dwell therein to worship the first Beast, whose deadly wound was healed. And he doeth great wonders, so that he maketh fire come down from Heaven on the Earth in the sight of men, And deceiveth them

The Dozen Christian Apocalyptic Topics

that dwell on the Earth by the means of those miracles which he had power to do in the sight of the Beast; saying to them that dwell on the Earth, that they should make an image to the Beast, which had the wound by a sword, and did live. And he had power to give life unto the image of the Beast, that the image of the Beast should both speak, and cause that as many as would not worship the image of the Beast should be killed. And he causeth all, both small and great, rich and poor, free and bond, to receive a mark in their right hand, or in their foreheads: And that no man might buy or sell, save he that had the mark, or the name of the Beast, or the number of his name.[20]

In the previous topic, I opined that I favour the interpretation of the 'head that was wounded' as referring to the Year of the Four Emperors, rather than the rumour regarding Nero's death. Here we find the reason for my choice. The Land Beast derives its power from the Sea Beast – Rome – and advocates worship of deified Roman emperors. But note that here the wound seems not to the head but to the body of the Beast: it is the Beast 'whose deadly wound was healed', not the head. This seems to me more in tune with the idea that Rome itself was damaged by the struggle for power after Nero's death, and the healing came when Vespasian took effective control; it does not fit so well with the idea that Nero had somehow survived.

This Beast has horns too, but only two 'like a lamb'. Clearly what is described here is some sort of Antichrist figure: this is a hellish version of the Holy Lamb of God, a caricature of the real Lamb. It suggests a human figure who in some way purports to be Messianic but in the view of the writer is the exact opposite: it may look like a lamb, but it

---

20 Revelation 13: 11-17.

speaks as a dragon because it is ultimately a creation of Satan. And as one might expect of a false Messiah, it seems to have magical powers demonstrated by great wonders and miracles. Specifically, it brings fire from Heaven and brings statues to life. We know from the Gospels and Josephus, that the Holy Land was awash with magicians and 'false prophets' of this sort. Could one of them be the reference here? Or at the end of the day, should we not take this literally? I think we must look for a literal interpretation in this case, otherwise, why introduce this new Beast at all? The previous two Beasts seem to have covered all the symbolic bases: the Dragon as Satan and the Sea Beast as Rome. Why introduce a third Beast unless it refers to someone specific? So, who? Ford, for example, suggests it is Josephus, but in my view really has to stretch the evidence to make it fit. I think there is a better alternative, and the clue comes in the rest of the description above.

The Beast has a 'mark'. In horror films, this is often equated with the 666 figure: in *The Omen* films, Damien Thorn, the son of Satan, has a 666 birthmark hidden under his hairline. But in the text, the two things are not specifically linked: the 'mark', whatever it is, is not said to be 666. What we *are* told is that the Beast 'causeth' everyone to have the mark on their hand or forehead and without it, they cannot 'buy or sell'. This really has fundamentalists busy. Futurists look for it in modern technology: bar codes, computer chips and the like, and some predict a time when these will indeed somehow be implanted in hand or forehead as a sort of cyborgian credit card. The European Community 'E' mark that is required to be on all consumer goods packaging to denote that the contents meet European standards is also a favourite, and some believers refuse to buy anything so marked. Preterists have a hard time of it, trying to identify evidence of any such mark in use in the Roman Empire at

The Dozen Christian Apocalyptic Topics

the time. Branding or stamping as a means of identification has been used throughout history, before during and after the Roman Empire, but no one has convincingly identified a contemporary practice of this sort that could be referred to here. So, if there is no Preterist explanation that works, maybe the Futurists have been right all along and this refers to an apocalyptic Antichrist figure who will arise in the future and through the creation of some all-powerful, totalitarian state will impose some sort of identity mark on people without which they will be consigned to an existence off the grid? Or, as another popular explanation has it, this is a Satanic travesty of the Orthodox Jewish requirement to wear phylacteries on the left hand and head,[21] in which case again, this must be interpreted idealistically rather than literally. None of this sounds very convincing to me and I think there is a better interpretation: the solution lies I believe in a simple misprint.

The Greek word for 'mark' used here, 'charagma', is highly unusual. Outside of its use in Revelation, it is only found in one other place in the Bible where it has a very specific meaning:

> . . . we ought not to think that the Godhead is like unto gold, or silver, or stone, graven ['charagma'] by art and man's device.[22]

In these words, from a sermon by St Paul, it is clear that 'charagma' means a graven image on metal or stone and, by extension, a pagan idol. Bible dictionaries will give it a broader meaning based on its use in Revelation, but this is another circular argument. In my view, the word 'charagma'

---

21 Small leather boxes containing scripture, fastened to the body with tapes.
22 Acts 17:29.

always means idol and never means just a physical mark. I think 'charagma' is a misprint or misreading for another word which is very similar indeed: 'charisma'. Change 'ag' for 'is' and you get something different. Charisma is a gift of God, or, in the Christian context, a gift of the Holy Spirit. In Part Two, we saw that the Charismatic movement in the modern church is characterized by divine gifts such as speaking in tongues, healing and prophecy. I believe that what is being described here is not a mark of some sort (charagma) but a Satanic perversion of the gift of the Holy Spirit (charisma), deployed by the Beast, who is himself a Satanic perversion of the Messiah.

Stated baldly like that it sounds possible, but why should it be plausible? The answer is in the twin references to hand and forehead and to buying and selling. The gift of the Holy Spirit was passed from one believer to another by the placing of the giver's hand on the forehead of the receiver. To this day, the 'laying on' of hands like this is used to initiate priests at every level of the church hierarchy up to and including the Pope, who is supposed to receive his gift in this way in a long line of hands all the way back to St Peter. Charismatic healing is done by the laying on of hands, often on the forehead, producing dramatic reaction. In Christianity this ritual is entirely free: both parties, in principle at least, enter into it purely for reasons of divine grace. A Satanic perversion of this would be to offer spiritual gifts through laying on of hands, but in return for money. The Church has a name for this: it is called Simony. And that is named after the first person in the history of the Church to want to do exactly that – a man called Simon. And his story is told in the Book of Acts:

> But there was a certain man, called Simon, which beforetime in the same city used sorcery, and bewitched the people of

Samaria, giving out that himself was some great one: To whom they all gave heed, from the least to the greatest, saying, This man is the great power of God. And to him they had regard, because that of long time he had bewitched them with sorceries. But when they believed Philip preaching the things concerning the kingdom of God, and the name of Jesus Christ, they were baptized, both men and women. Then Simon himself believed also: and when he was baptized, he continued with Philip, and wondered, beholding the miracles and signs which were done. Now when the Apostles which were at Jerusalem heard that Samaria had received the word of God, they sent unto them Peter and John: Who, when they were come down, prayed for them, that they might receive the Holy Ghost:(For as yet he was fallen upon none of them: only they were baptized in the name of the Lord Jesus.) Then laid they their hands on them, and they received the Holy Ghost. And when Simon saw that through laying on of the Apostles' hands the Holy Ghost was given, he offered them money, Saying, Give me also this power, that on whomsoever I lay hands, he may receive the Holy Ghost. But Peter said unto him, Thy money perish with thee, because thou hast thought that the gift of God may be purchased with money. Thou hast neither part nor lot in this matter: for thy heart is not right in the sight of God. Repent therefore of this thy wickedness, and pray God, if perhaps the thought of thine heart may be forgiven thee. For I perceive that thou art in the gall of bitterness, and in the bond of iniquity. Then answered Simon, and said, Pray ye to the Lord for me, that none of these things which ye have spoken come upon me.[23]

So, here we have an established magician, a sorcerer, holding himself out to be 'some great one' who demonstrates to have

---

[23] Acts 8: 9-24.

'the power of God'. Impressed by the preaching of Philip, he for a time becomes a follower of the nascent Christian religion until he sees the bestowal of the Holy Spirit through the ritual of the laying on of hands. Even more impressed, he wants this power for himself, presumably so he can make money from it, and offers money to acquire it. Peter is scandalized and threatens dire consequences which frighten Simon into begging for forgiveness. Surely the correspondences here are not coincidental. Revelation describes a magician with great powers and a ritual, involving not a 'mark', but a touching of hand and forehead, connected with buying and selling. Acts describes a magician with great powers who wants to acquire a ritual involving laying on of hands that he can then sell on for his own profit. Acts devotes half a chapter to Simon and clearly regards this as an important story in the progress of the early Church. Strange then, that we hear no more of it: we do not know from this if Simon genuinely repented and stayed with the Christians, or whether he went off again to pursue his own career as magician.

In fact, we know from other sources about this character. We met him in Volume II: he is almost certainly the Simon Magus who founded an important Gnostic sect. He appears in that guise in a set of narratives now known most commonly as the Pseudo-Clementines, because they claim to be written by a first-century Christian leader called Clement. We encountered a Clement earlier as a saint who was distinctly Gnostic in his views, but he came later. We can confidently assert that the Pseudo-Clementines are third-century forgeries. Like the Book of Acts which preceded them, the Pseudo-Clementines are largely fiction, but, also like Acts, they probably contain elements of tradition that have some basis in reality. The trick in both cases being to separate the wheat from the chaff.

The Dozen Christian Apocalyptic Topics

To cut a very long and implausible story short, these narratives relate a series of theological debates between Simon Peter and someone identified as Simon Magus, preceded by a violent incident in which Simon Magus physically attacks James, the leader of the Jerusalem Church. James is badly injured but not killed – evidence, if any were needed, that this attack is not to be identified with the stoning to death of James, son of Damneus in Josephus, discussed in Vol II. Nevertheless, the reason why some commentators have sought to make such an identification is that at places in the Pseudo-Clementines it seems as if Simon Magus and Paul are actually the same person. If you are confused by this, you are not alone; the confusion between Simon Magus and the Apostle Paul in the Pseudo-Clementines has been a huge puzzle for a very long time. One which I believe we can now solve.

Let us take a look first at what is known of this Simon Magus ('Magus' means sorcerer or magician). We know he is a historical character because he appears, or, more accurately, someone that sounds very like him appears, in Josephus:

> While Felix was procurator of Judæa, he saw this Drusilla [the sister of Agrippa II, married to 'Azizus, King of Emesa, upon his consent to be circumcised'] and fell in love with her; for she did exceed all other women in beauty, and he sent to her a person whose name was Simon, one of his friends; a Jew he was, and by birth a Cypriot, and one who pretended to be a magician; and endeavoured to persuade her to forsake her present husband, and marry him ... Accordingly she acted ill ... [and] was prevailed upon to transgress the laws of her forefathers, and to marry Felix; ... [24]

---

24 Antiquities 20:141-143.

Here we are in the years leading up to the Jewish War in the sixties AD and it will be recalled from Vol II that Felix and Drusilla appear prominently in the Acts (fictitious) narrative of Paul's imprisonment before being sent to Rome. This Simon was, it seems, a Jew from Cyprus and a magician. Josephus tells us nothing more, but the parallel with the character in Acts Chapter 8 is compelling. Acts is clear that Simon Magus operated in Samaria. Note that the text does not say that he was a Samaritan (i.e. born there) but just that he had been influential there for some time, so he may well have been identical with Simon the Magician, born in Cyprus. And indeed, Acts later relates a story about yet another magician or sorcerer in Cyprus itself.

This time it is Paul who confronts him, on his first missionary journey with Barnabas, and it is the occasion for the first actual miracle performed by Paul:

> And when they had gone through the isle unto Paphos, they found a certain sorcerer, a false prophet, a Jew, whose name was Bar-jesus: Which was with the deputy of the country, Sergius Paulus, a prudent man; who called for Barnabas and Saul, and desired to hear the word of God. But Elymas the sorcerer (for so is his name by interpretation) withstood them, seeking to turn away the deputy from the faith. Then Saul (who also is called Paul,) filled with the Holy Ghost, set his eyes on him, And said, O full of all subtilty and all mischief, thou child of the devil, thou enemy of all righteousness, wilt thou not cease to pervert the right ways of the Lord? And now, behold, the hand of the Lord is upon thee, and thou shalt be blind, not seeing the sun for a season. And immediately there fell on him a mist and a darkness; and he went about seeking some to lead him by the hand.[25]

---

25 Acts 13:6-11.

Several points need to be made here. First, note that this is a 'certain' sorcerer. Luke seems to refer to people as 'certain' when he does not know the true identity of a person.[26] Next, note that Paul calls him the 'enemy' of righteousness; the Simon Magus/Paul hybrid figure of the Pseudo-Clementines is also called the 'enemy'. Third, note the language that seems to suggest that this is an old and known 'enemy' – 'wilt thou not cease'. And finally, note that this sorcerer is blinded for a time as a punishment; remember that in Acts, though not in his own letters, the story is that Paul himself is also blinded for a time by God when he has his Damascus Road conversion.

So, what are to make of all this? Are we to conclude that Paul and Simon are really the same character; that he/they physically assaulted James; that perhaps they killed James; and that the Ebionites[27] were right in their demonization of Paul? Or can we make better sense of it all? I think we can. First, we need to restate the fact that in the New Paradigm proposed in Volume II, Paul was shipped to Rome under arrest in the mid-forties AD. We have no evidence from any source what happened after that. We know he wrote some letters from prison in Rome, but beyond that we have nothing. Surely that, in itself, is telling. If Paul had lived on, I think we would have heard something of his later activities, either by way of Church narratives, or by a further series of letters. My own view is that on the balance of probabilities, he died soon after arriving in Rome, either by execution or through the conditions of Roman imprisonment. Everything we know about the Roman Empire suggests that they would have had little or no patience with Paul; people in the service

---

26 Or perhaps is embarrassed in some way to identify them? In Volume II, we saw that interpreting 'certain men' was key to understanding the Council of Jerusalem.

27 See Volume II.

of that brutal empire did not enter into prolonged theological debate with troublemakers – they executed them. And whatever the truth of the matter, it seems hardly conceivable that Paul would have made his way back to Jerusalem in time to get involved in the murder of someone called James in the sixties AD – whoever he was.

On the other hand, it does seem as if there was someone who was active in the fifties and sixties AD who has somehow got muddled up with Paul, and that is the character known as Simon Magus. This character seems to have been a Jew, born in Cyprus, but later becoming active in Samaria.[28] Perhaps, as related in Acts, he fastened onto the early Church as a way to increase his powers as a magician but having fallen out with the Apostles (even to the extent of physical confrontation with James the Great) he gravitated towards powerful Romans like Sergius Paulus and Felix, who might be influenced by a Jewish Magus. Of course, Paul himself also eventually split from the Jerusalem Church and operated in a Roman/Gentile milieu, but those parallels hardly seem sufficient to account for the confusion in the later Church about these two characters. In simple terms, how did stories about Paul and stories about Simon Magus get so mixed up? Was there some other parallel between them that was responsible for all the later confusion? I think there is, and I think the stories in Acts about the two sorcerers provide the clue that unlocks the puzzle. I believe that, as Occam's Razor might suggest in this case, the two sorcerers are in fact one and the same: Simon Magus. And that the two stories of temporary blindness, that of Simon Magus and of Paul himself, are the vital key.

The blindness of Paul is tantalizing because there are

---

28 Or perhaps he was a Samaritan, and Cyprus is a mistake, either for the Judæan fortress of the same name; or for the Kittim, which, as many have argued, stands for the Romans and Western powers generally.

vague clues in the New Testament that he suffered a bodily affliction. In 2 Corinthians, having spoken of his visions, he refers to what he calls his 'thorn in the flesh':

> ... yet of myself I will not glory, but in mine infirmities. For though I would desire to glory, I shall not be a fool; for I will say the truth: but now I forbear, lest any man should think of me above that which he seeth me to be, or that he heareth of me. And lest I should be exalted above measure through the abundance of the revelations, there was given to me a thorn in the flesh, the messenger of Satan to buffet me, lest I should be exalted above measure. For this thing I besought the Lord thrice, that it might depart from me. And he said unto me, My grace is sufficient for thee: for my strength is made perfect in weakness. Most gladly therefore will I rather glory in my infirmities, that the power of Christ may rest upon me. Therefore I take pleasure in infirmities, in reproaches, in necessities, in persecutions, in distresses for Christ's sake: for when I am weak, then am I strong.[29]

Commentators have had a field day for years with various explanations for this, and many, both believers and sceptics alike, have concluded that this is a reference to blindness, either from birth, or since his conversion. In the Acts narrative of the stoning of Stephen, Paul is pictured as looking after the clothes of Stephen's stoners who have stripped for their task, and he personally only 'consents' to the stoning, rather than taking an active part. And in 1 Corinthians, referring to his disability, he says in tribute to the Galatians' loyalty to himself:

Ye know how through infirmity of the flesh I preached the Gospel unto you at the first. And my temptation which was

---

29 2 Corinthians 12:5-10.

in my flesh ye despised not, nor rejected; but received me as an angel of God, even as Christ Jesus. Where is then the blessedness ye spake of? for I bear you record, that, if it had been possible, ye would have plucked out your own eyes, and have given them to me.[30]

Perhaps the blindness on the road to Damascus reflects a folk memory of something more permanent. Perhaps this is the explanation for Paul's failure to recognize the High Priest at his Sanhedrin trial; perhaps that is why he always travelled with one or more companions; perhaps that is why so much of his travelling was by sea; and perhaps that was why he wrote letters so often, in large letters,[31] and dictated them to an amanuensis.[32] Many commentators over the years have speculated that Paul was blind, but the argument has always been that if he had been, Acts would have said so. But what if Luke deliberately avoided saying so? What if he was embarrassed about Paul's blindness, not *per se*, but because there was someone else at the time that was also a Jew operating among influential Romans; someone who was the 'enemy' of the Church in a way that Paul had never been? What if Simon Magus too was blind?

Acts says that Paul blinded the Paphos sorcerer. What better way to separate the two and prove Paul's superiority? But I think Simon Magus was already blind. We are told that the sorcerer was called Elymas. This name has always been a puzzle. Some have sought to argue that it has an Arabic root meaning 'wise', but most scholars, rightly in my view, reject this because the spoken language of the region was Aramiac. But all attempts to find a root for the name in Aramaic, or

---

[30] Galatians 4:15.
[31] Galatians 6:11.
[32] Romans 16:22.

even in Hebrew or Greek, have failed. Most scholars accept that the 'El' root is the Aramaic name for God, which appears countless times in the Old Testament. But the 'ymas' root has eluded them. But if Luke was embarrassed by this whole matter, perhaps he took a simple step to disguise what he was doing. Aramaic, like Hebrew, is written in consonants only and is read from right to left, rather than left to right as you are doing now. So, in Aramaic, the name Elymas would be written thus:

S M Y L

And this has an obvious meaning in Aramaic if read as a Greek like Luke would read it – from left to right. The S-M-Y root has a straightforward meaning: it is Aramaic for 'blind'! Indeed, it is used exactly like that a few lines further on in the text of Acts. And as already noted, the L stands for eL, the Aramaic for God. So, a simple translation would be 'blinded by God'. Remember, the text says that this was the sorcerer's name before Paul is said to have blinded him. There can be only one conclusion if the text is to be trusted: Simon Magus, like Paul, was blind – if not from birth, then certainly before any encounters with Paul or Peter. They were both blind seers, in a long tradition in the classical world, epitomized by the blind hermaphrodite seer Tiresias. Their blindness was a gift from God, who in recompense gave them holy visions of truths hidden from sighted people. This is the reason that writers in the second, third, and fourth centuries AD got Paul and Simon Magus so confused. Stories of their blindness were preserved in the Acts narratives of Paul's temporary blindness on the road to Damascus and the temporary blinding of Elymas.

Paul's blind visions led him to a view of Jesus that, while rooted in Zechariah, embraced other prophetic texts and classical philosophical thought, to free Christianity from the shackles of Mosaic Law. Christianity ever since has been built on those Pauline visions. But Simon's blind visions went far beyond anything that Paul or the early Church could sanction. Again, his two names in the Acts story of his blinding give the game away. It will be remembered that Elymas was supposed to be a translation of the name Bar-jesus. This literally means 'Son of the Saviour'. By calling himself this, Simon was in some sense doing what no one in the Jesus Movement would have dreamt of doing; he was claiming divinity for himself. And in fact, that is what his other name really means. A reasonable translation of the S-M-Y-L root would be 'blinded by God' as suggested above. But if we put in the vowels from Elymas, we get:

SaMYeL

And this has a different meaning of course; we have met it before in Volume II as one of the names for the Gnostic Demiurge. It means not 'blinded by God' but 'the blind God'. Samyel was one of the fallen angels in Jewish mythology. This then transmuted into one of the names that the Gnostics used for Yahweh – and it is precisely eLYMaS in reverse! Simon Magus was one of the earliest Gnostic cultists and here is portrayed calling himself by the name of the Gnostic God, and claiming some sort of divinity for himself.

If the overall paradigm presented in this trilogy is accepted, then it seems inescapable to me that Paul and Simon Magus were different people that somehow got confused. Christians writing in the second century and later, separated from the key events by a century or more and the annihilation of the Jewish nation through two disastrous wars, were confronted by a paradox. The traditional chronology that placed the death of Jesus in around AD 30 had Paul active throughout

The Dozen Christian Apocalyptic Topics

the thirties, forties and fifties. But (because in reality he was off the scene by mid-forties) they found no narrative to substantiate that. Instead they had narrative about someone who sounded rather like Paul, in his early career at least, who was called Simon and seemed to have been involved in some way with the early Church. From this arose all the genuine confusion in the Pseudo-Clementines and other related literature.[33] I would argue on the above evidence that there is a strong case to be made that Simon/Elymas and Paul were both blind and this explains how easy it was for them to become confused. All these sorcerer characters have come down to us in history as Simon Magus or Simon the Sorcerer.[34] He appears on a number of occasions in the Bible and in Josephus; he became very well connected and influential in the Roman administration; and he was regarded in the early Church as the 'enemy'. I believe that his role as an antichrist figure in the first century has never been properly recognized and, more to the point here, that he is indeed the historical figure who is being mysteriously symbolized as the Beast from the Land.

When all the references are put together, a picture emerges of an important and influential character. The Pseudo-Clementines assert that he was born in Samaria and studied in Alexandria, where he learned his magic. He began his career as a leading follower of John the Baptist but became convinced that he was a God incarnate – a Samaritan rival to the Jewish Christ – and founded his own sect of Simonians. He had a consort, Helen, who he claimed was *the* Helen of Troy. Thus, the Pseudo-Clementines are broadly in accord

---

33 It may also help explain how, in the Book of Acts, it was a 'Simon' rather than Paul, who first came to understand the inclusion of Gentiles in the Jesus Movement. If Simon Magus could get confused with Paul, it is not hard to see how he could also have got confused with Simon Peter.

34 Not the computer game character of that name!

with the Acts account above: the delusions of divinity, the sorcery, the Samaritan background, and the association at some point with the Jesus Movement. The last is borne out again by Hippolytus in the third century, who claims that Simon was reduced to despair by Peter's curse on him in Acts and broke away to pursue his own career. Similarly, the Samaritan connection is borne out by Justin Martyr in the second century who, coming from Samaria himself, claims that nearly all Samaritans of his own time were adherents of a 'Simon of Gitta' in Samaria; this must be the same Simon, and the sect described here must be the Simonians.

The Simonians were a Gnostic sect, believing like all Gnostics that the principle of salvation by faith and divine grace means that the saved are not bound to follow any moral laws at all. This principle, known as antinomianism, takes St Paul's theology to its logical conclusion and can result in behaviour, particularly sexual behaviour, that for orthodox Christians is sinful and reprobate. Like all Gnostics, Simonians also believed in a female divine principle, known as Sophia or Wisdom. What marks out the Simonians, however, is that they regarded Simon and his consort Helen, as the human incarnations of God and Sophia respectively. And Hippolytus tells us that, presumably following the example of Simon and Helen, the Simonians practised what we now call 'free love'. The Simonians seem to have survived in Samaria and Asia Minor as a Gnostic sect into the fourth century, although by then they were virtually extinct.

There are various apocryphal accounts of Simon's magic, including resurrection of the dead, calling fire down from Heaven, and in the *Acts of Peter* and the *Acts of Peter and Paul*, he is depicted in Rome, presumably at some time after the sixties, levitating in the air above the Forum, an act which leads to his stoning as a sorcerer and his eventual death. But of most interest here is that he was known for bringing statues to life: he makes this claim for himself in the Pseudo-Clementines:

> I am the first power, who am always, and without beginning. But having entered the womb of Rachel [his mother], I was born of her as a man, that I might be visible to men. I have flown through the air; I have been mixed with fire, and been made one body with it; I have made statues to move; I have animated lifeless things; I have made stones bread; I have flown from mountain to mountain; I have moved from place to place, upheld by angels' hands, and have lighted on the Earth. Not only have I done these things; but even now I am able to do them, that by facts I may prove to all, that I am the Son of God, enduring to eternity, and that I can make those who believe on me endure in like manner for ever.[35]

This of course was one of the characteristics of the Beast from the Land. Given the parallels, it amazes me that my identification of this Beast with Simon Magus has not been made before. Partly to blame, I suspect, is that he has always been seen as a peripheral figure. But if all the above testimony from the Church Fathers and the apocryphal writings is insufficient to convince that we have here a major figure in first-century religious belief, we have the testimony of the Jewish Historian Josephus as well. And as we now turn to examine the topic of 666, we shall see how this, in fact, unlocks the identification.

APOCALYPTIC TOPIC NO. 16: 666

Preterism: The Emperor Nero.
Historicism: The USA.

---

35 3:47

Futurism: The Antichrist.

The famous passage referring to 666 runs thus:

> Here is wisdom. Let him that hath understanding count the number of the Beast: for it is the number of a man; and his number is Six hundred threescore and six.[36]

The reference to 'wisdom' here could well be an oblique nod to Simon's consort, Helen, who presented herself as the human incarnation of Sophia/Wisdom. And note that we are told unequivocally that the Beast is a man; presumably with just the one head (although it has a couple of devilish horns). The wisdom in question here is, by I think universal consent, that required to deal with the Jewish word code that is known as 'gematria'. Gematria originated as an Assyrian system of alphanumeric code or cipher later adopted into Jewish culture via the Babylonians and Greeks. It assigns numerical value to a word, name, or phrase in the belief that they bear some relation to the number itself. An example often quoted is the word 'chai' ('alive'), which is composed of two letters that add up to eighteen. This has made eighteen a 'lucky number' among Jewish people, with whom gifts of money in multiples of eighteen are popular to this day. The assumption is that the writer of Revelation is using gematria here to refer archly to the identity of the Beast. Every student of eschatology down the ages, from the early Church Fathers to modern day Futurists, seeks to manipulate the numbers to come up with their favourite candidate. If any consensus at all emerges from all this mathematical effort, it is that 666 refers to Nero, reinforcing the Preterist view of the Beast. The argument runs that this was why the

---

36 Revelation 13:18.

The Dozen Christian Apocalyptic Topics

writer used code, because to characterize the divine Roman emperor as a Beast would not be the most prudent thing to do, especially in the explosive environment of the sixties AD.

To arrive at 666 from Nero, it is necessary to add the word Caesar to Nero. Revelation was written in Greek and the Greek form of this is Neron Caesar. Written in Hebrew characters, this becomes NRWN QSR which does indeed produce 666. But the Latin form of the same name is NRW QSR and this reduces the number to 616. Strangely, this does not rule it out of court, because it now seems that the text should read 616 not 666. Iranaeus, writing in the second century, was aware of manuscripts existing at his time that had 616, but he dismissed them because, like fundamentalists of today, he preferred the mysticism of all three characters being identical. Most surviving manuscripts do have 666, but this majority reflects the consensus opinion that dates back to Iranaeus, and the minority that have 616 do seem to be among the oldest. Scholars have debated the issue ever since Iranaeus right up until the end of the twentieth century, when the sensational discovery of the earliest manuscript ever[37] – around 100 years earlier than any other – confirmed 616 as the correct number. So, is the Latin form of Nero Caesar, which equals 616, the solution to the puzzle? Only if you accept that the writer of Revelation took a *Latin* phrase, translated it into *Hebrew*, did the calculation, and then inserted it into his *Greek* text. Is this likely? I think there is a much more straightforward solution.

As we have seen, Simon Magus went under a few different pseudonyms. In Acts he is called Elymas, but in Josephus some manuscripts call him not Simon, but Atomus. And in some manuscripts of Acts, Elymas is called Etoimas or

---

37 Papyrus 115 (P. Oxy. 4499), dated to *c.* AD 225-275. Now in the Ashmolean Museum.

Etomas. In the Pseudo-Clementines, he claims that he is 'the first power': it seems that Simon, thinking of himself as God incarnate, liked to represent himself as a primal force or 'atom'. The theory that matter is made up of indivisible atoms was first formally put forward (as far as we know) by the Greek philosopher Democritus in the fifth century BC. It was not the prevailing theory in the first century (and indeed, not until modern times) but it was in the aether and would have been attractive to those of a mystical bent. The Hebrew for atom is מוטא and subjected to gematria, amazingly it yields 616.[38] On its own this piece of evidence would perhaps not convince. But linking as it does the Josephus account of Simon/Atomus with the other references to Simon Magus, it is part of an overall argument for the identification of Simon with the Beast from the Land. Certainly, Nero was a Beast of the worst kind, but that is not the monster being described here. The Dragon's first Beast is clearly Rome, in which case, what does the second Beast add to the Apocalypse if it is just a Roman emperor? And the description just does not fit with an emperor. This text is clearly describing a sorcerer/magician: Nero did many ghastly things, but ventriloquism is not one of them, as far as we know. The man described here, throwing his voice to make statues speak, drawing down fire from Heaven like Elijah before the prophets of Baal, and deceiving the multitude with miracles, is no emperor: he is a Satanic Christ, caricaturing the Jewish prophets and Messiah, and outraging the writer of Revelation as someone complicit with

---

38 There are, in fact, myriad versions of gematria. Two are the most authoritative. The first is a simple version (the basic or Ragil method) that assigns numbers to letters in a straightforward way. But it ignores the fact that five Hebrew letters – known as sofits – are written differently at the end of words. The Great Number Method (or Mispar Gadol) assigns different numbers to these five letters. This is the method used to derive 18 from the Hebrew for 'alive' noted above and is the method I have used here.

the highest levels of the Roman regime and in league with Rome and Satan himself: Simon Magus.

APOCALYPTIC TOPIC NO. 17: THE SEVEN, EIGHT AND TEN KINGS

Preterism: Ancient history.
Historicism: Ancient and modern history.
Futurism: Rulers yet to come.

This topic is yet another that gives fundamentalist trainspotters glorious opportunity for speculation. It starts with the fourth Beast of Daniel, which has ten horns (plus a little one). This then feeds into the Satanic figure of the Dragon in Revelation, which also has ten horns because it is based on Daniel, but also has seven heads with seven crowns. The Beast from the Sea is the same except, for some reason, it has ten crowns, not seven. Now, in Chapter 17, we are told about yet another Beast:

> a scarlet coloured Beast, full of names of blasphemy, having seven heads and ten horns.[39]

This sounds like the Dragon and the Beast from the Sea: all three have the same number of heads and horns, and many interpretations of this passage accept that they are the same symbol. I think this is wrong for reasons that will become clear. But even at this stage, I would argue that if they were all the same symbol, why would the writer keep repeating himself in this way. We have become accustomed in Revelation to endless repetition, but as I have stressed, much if not

---

39 Revelation 17:3.

all of this derives from the composite nature of the Book: two different apocalypses covering similar ground, jammed together with only perfunctory regard to consistency. In these days of word processing, it is hard to envisage the difficulties faced by these writers in the first century. They did not even have books to work with, just parchment scrolls. Everything had to be done with handwriting on unwieldy scrolls. No wonder mistakes creep in and the editorial process is rudimentary. If the writer of this text introduces a third Beast it must be because he wants to make another point, not simply repeat himself.

Perhaps the writer began to worry himself that all these Beasts, horns and crowns were getting a bit confusing, because later in Chapter 17, he has an angel explain it all:

> The Beast that thou sawest was, and is not; and shall ascend out of the bottomless pit, and go into perdition: and they that dwell on the Earth shall wonder, whose names were not written in the book of life from the foundation of the world, when they behold the Beast that was, and is not, and yet is. And here is the mind which hath wisdom. The seven heads are seven mountains, . . . And there are seven kings: five are fallen, and one is, and the other is not yet come; and when he cometh, he must continue a short space. And the Beast that was, and is not, even he is the eighth, and is of the seven, and goeth into perdition.[40]

Unfortunately, this explanation has served only to confuse fundamentalists even more. The identity of these kings and this Beast depend crucially on when this was written. Thus far in this book, we have begun to suggest that the Second Apocalypse of Revelation was written at some point during

---

40 Revelation 17:8-11.

the Jewish War with Rome in the late sixties AD when Simon Magus was flourishing. And that makes a lot of sense. We have seen how previous generations of Jewish prophets flourished at similar times of upheaval – the destruction of the Northern Kingdom, the Exile of the Southern Kingdom, and the repressions of Antiochus leading to the Maccabean Revolt. Then the First Apocalypse of Revelation was written by John the Baptist at the time of Pontius Pilate's repressions early in the first century. If we had to guess when the Second Apocalypse of Revelation was written, surely our first port of call would be the Jewish War of the sixties. The question we must then answer is whether the prophecy about 'kings' in Chapter 17 can be fitted sensibly into that time period. Many commentators look for a later time period – usually the later reign of Domitian – for the fit, because they cannot see how the fit can be managed in the sixties AD. But as usual, these commentators have not looked closely enough at what the text is telling us. Let me now demonstrate.

We are told that this particular Beast 'was, and is not . . . and yet is'. Then we are told that the Beast represents a king of some kind, the eighth of seven. So, to identify the Beast, we must first identify the seven kings. It is the eighth king that confuses the issue for many commentators, so for the moment, let us put it to one side. If the text simply said that there are seven kings, the interpretation would be absolutely straightforward. We are told that the figure seven is a symbol not only of seven kings but of seven mountains also. This can only mean Rome – famously built on seven hills and known for that throughout antiquity, before the city geography became obscured by modern construction. It will be recalled that the Dragon also had seven heads with seven crowns. So, the seven kings are seven emperors of Rome. The first five are easy. They comprise the Julio-Claudian Dynasty: Augustus, Tiberius, Caligula, Claudius and Nero. The list does not start with Julius Caesar because he was never crowned emperor. And we are told that five emperors have fallen, which takes us to the death of Nero in June AD 68, right in the middle of the Jewish War. But now it gets tricky. As referred to earlier, Nero's death precipitated a power struggle that saw three emperors come and go in a few short months: Galba seized power and held it for seven months, then he was murdered in January AD 69 in a coup that put Otho on the throne, Otho was challenged by Vitellius, who defeated him in battle and took the crown in December AD 69. However, in the background to all this was Vespasian, who had been despatched to Judæa by Nero when the Jewish War broke out and who now left the province to wrest the crown from Vitellius in the December of AD 69. He stabilized the situation and ruled successfully until his death a decade later. His son Titus, who finished off the War in Judæa in his father's place, succeeded his father to the crown in AD 79.

So, who was the sixth emperor who 'is', and the seventh who 'is not yet come; and when he cometh, he must continue a short space'? In my view we can discount Galba and Otho. The power struggle in which they were engaged lasted only ten months in all and was conducted entirely in the Western Empire, far from the concerns of a small province like Judæa in the east. I suspect that if the writer of Revelation were writing at around this time, he would have heard of them only when the struggle was all over. Vitellius on the other hand, was a more substantial figure and would be known to the writer and considered of real significance, because it was to defeat Vitellius with the support of the Eastern Empire and claim the crown, that Vespasian abandoned the Judæan campaign, leaving command to his son. Vitellius was supported in his imperial ambitions by the forces of the Western Empire in Germany and France, which proclaimed him Emperor in the West in early AD 69, and this was formally sanctioned a little later by the Roman Senate. But the Eastern Empire was unhappy with this and proclaimed Vespasian as their choice of emperor. Vitellius had no stomach for a fight and by the middle of the year AD 69 agreed terms to hand over the crown to Vespasian: indeed, he was halfway to the Temple of Concord in Rome to hand over his insignia of office when the Praetorian Guard stopped him. When Vespasian's forces arrived in Rome, Vitellius was taken and killed. Vespasian was finally proclaimed emperor by the Senate in December. So, there was a period of a few months in early/mid AD 69 when Vitellius was the reigning emperor but had agreed to hand over to Vespasian. In my view, therefore, the sixth king who 'is' was Vitellius, and the seventh king who 'is not yet come' was Vespasian. This confirms that the Second Apocalypse of Revelation was written during the first half of AD 69. Vespasian is prophesied to 'continue a short space', not because the writer is writing with hindsight in the Eighties. John B, like the writer of Daniel before him, is confident that he is living in the Last Days, that this really is at last the moment that the Jews have waited so long for, and the Day of the Lord is imminent in which the power of Rome under Vespasian will be smashed and God's Kingdom established on Earth.

We can now go back to the complication of the eighth king who is 'of the seven, and goeth into perdition'. Vespasian held the throne for a decade, died peacefully in his bed in June 79, and was succeeded in an orderly fashion by Titus his son. Titus only reigned for a couple of years, dying in September AD 81. He was certainly 'of' Vespasian, being his son, but if he is the eighth king, and unless you believe the writer of Revelation really could see into the future, this pushes the date of composition of this text into the Eighties. Luckily, there is a simpler solution. The text says:

And here is the mind which hath wisdom...And the Beast that was, and is not, even he is the eighth, and is of the seven, and goeth into perdition.

The writer is being arch here, but I think to any reader of this passage living in Judæa in the first century would have understood what is going on. The eighth king is of the seven, not because he is the son of the seventh king but because he is a different kind of king altogether and he owes his allegiance to the seventh king. There were eight kings in the region as well as the Roman emperors: the Herodian client kings of the Roman Empire. And there were eight of them in all:

1. Herod the Great – the King Herod of the Christian nativity stories, who ruled over Judæa and the surrounding Semitic lands as a client king of the Roman Empire. Died *c.* 4 BC. After his death, his kingdom was divided at various times and in various ways among his descendants.
2. Herod Archelaus – a son of Herod the Great: Died *c.* AD 18.
3. Herod Philip the Tetrarch – another son of Herod the Great. Died AD 34.
4. Herod Antipas – the third son of Herod the Great. Died *c.* AD 39.
5. Herod Agrippa I – grandson of Herod the Great. Died AD 44.
6. Herod of Chalcis – another grandson of Herod the Great. Died *c.* AD 49.
7. Aristobulus of Chalcis – grandson of Herod the Great. Died AD 92.
8. Herod Agrippa II – great-grandson of Herod the Great. Died *c.* AD 92.

The Dozen Christian Apocalyptic Topics

All these Herodian kings were client rulers of Rome: they owed their position and allegiance to Rome and were regarded by nationalistic Jews as traitors to their nation. Herod Agrippa II as the third generation after Herod the Great, was the eighth and last ruler of this Herodian dynasty. He is, in my view, far and away the best candidate for the eighth king of Revelation 17 and, indeed, for the identity of the Beast there described.

Agrippa II was the son of Agrippa I. He had three sisters: Berenice,[41] Mariamne, and Drusilla.[42] He was educated at the court in Rome and was King in Jerusalem from AD 48 onwards. He was not unsympathetic to the grievances of his countrymen but knew at first hand the power of the Roman State and in the final analysis, that was where his loyalties, if not his sympathies, lay. His power waxed and waned over the decades leading up to the War, but by the sixties he seems to have ruled over all the original territories of his great grandfather except for the province of Judæa itself, which was ruled by a series of Roman Procurators. Agrippa nevertheless had considerable influence in Jerusalem (as is depicted in Acts) – generally because he inherited the title 'King of the Jews' and specifically as he had supervision of the Jerusalem Temple. As relationships between the Jews and Rome deteriorated into the sixties, he tried to avert the coming war by urging the Jews in Jerusalem to resign themselves to the inevitability of Roman rule, but to no avail. In AD 66, when the revolt broke out finally, he and his sister Berenice were expelled from Jerusalem by the populace. The die now being cast, he sided unequivocally with Rome, not only sending his loyal troops to support Vespasian in suppressing the revolt but campaigning person-

---

41 We shall return to Berenice in the next topic where we shall find her in symbolic guise.

42 Drusilla was married to the Roman Procurator Felix: it was this marriage that resulted from the intervention of Simon Magus.

ally alongside Titus. So, when Revelation describes the eighth king as being 'of' the seventh', it refers to Agrippa's status as client to Rome. And when it describes the Beast as the king 'that was, and is not, . . . and goeth into perdition', it refers directly to Agrippa's status in mid AD 69 when the text was written. King Agrippa had ruled for nearly two decades with the connivance of his Roman masters, but as far as the Jews were concerned he had been thrown out and was no longer king; and for his traitorous siding with the Roman forces, he would surely 'go into perdition' when the great Day of judgement came. One final piece of evidence seems to me to clinch the identification. All the Herodian dynasty, including Agrippa, descended from Herod the Great, were of Idumean descent. As we saw in Vol II, Idumea was originally the land of Edom, and 'edom' meant 'red' - the colour of the scarlet beast!

Finally, we must deal with the most perplexing element of all in this Chapter of Revelation: who or what are the ten horns that characterize the Dragon, the Beast from the Sea and the Harlot's Beast. Daniel's fourth Beast also had ten horns, and as we saw, these are easily identified as the Greek rulers up to and including Antiochus IV Epiphanes. It is tempting to argue that the writer of Revelation had no idea who they were so just carries them into his own Beasts. But the ten horns in Revelation do seem to be something else:

> And the ten horns which thou sawest are ten kings, which have received no kingdom as yet; but receive power as kings one hour with the Beast. These have one mind, and shall give their power and strength unto the Beast. These shall make war with the Lamb, and the Lamb shall overcome them: for he is Lord of lords, and King of kings: and they that are with him are called, and chosen, and faithful.[43]

---

43 Revelation 17:12-14.

So, these horns also represent kings, but presumably not the ones identified so far. For Futurists, this presents no problem at all; they are happy to accept everything literally and since it is in our future, the identity of the ten kings can be whoever they fancy. But Preterists really struggle with this one. None of the explanations they come up with seem very convincing in meeting all the requirements of fit:

- they have not yet received their sovereignty;
- they will come into power for a short space of time ('one hour');
- they will side with the Beast against the Jewish Messiah ('the Lamb');
- the Messiah will triumph.

The first thing to understand about all this is that the writer is making a prophecy about the imminent Day of the Lord when the Messiah will come and triumph over Rome and her allies. That is why the kings have yet to come to their power – this is an apocryphal event in the writer's future. Beyond this it is important to establish, as I have stressed before, that it is a mistake to lump all these monsters together: just because two Beasts have a similar number of horns, heads or whatever, doesn't mean they symbolize precisely the same thing; otherwise, what is the point of them all? Let us take each in turn:

Daniel's fourth Beast: has ten horns symbolizing ten Greek kings.

The Dragon/Satan: has ten horns because he is based on Daniel's Beast. But it also has seven heads and seven crowns in addition, thus bringing Daniel's prophecy up to date to include the seven Roman emperors from Augustus to Vespasian (omitting Galba and Otho).

The Beast from the Sea: has seven heads, ten horns and ten crowns. If the Beast is Rome, then the seven heads are the seven emperors ending with Vespasian. Ford suggests, and I agree, that the ten horns represent the ten provinces of the Roman Empire: Italy, Achaea, Asia, Syria, Egypt, Africa, Spain, Gaul, Britain and Germany. The ten crowns in this case sit on the ten horns. The word for crown here is better translated as 'diadem' and refers to the local rulers over each of the ten provinces.

The Scarlet Beast: has seven heads, which we know again to be the seven emperors. But in this case, the ten horns cannot be the rulers of the ten provinces because this would not fit the requirements.

In my view, given that this Beast is Agrippa II, then these are *his* territories. The first Herod the Great controlled eleven territories: the province of Judæa, plus ten surrounding Semitic areas: Iturea, Batanea, Gaulanitis, Trachontis, Aurantis, Gaulea, Perea, Samaria, Idumea and Chalcis. Following his death, all these were ruled by the Herodian dynasty, the detail of who ruled what at any particular time depending on the relationship between each Herodian and each emperor. But by the sixties AD, the third-generation Agrippa II, the last of the Herodian rulers and the last to hold the title King of the Jews, once again like his great-grandfather, ruled over them all except Judæa which, as a separate province, was ruled by a Procurator. So, we can now interpret the text referring to these ten kings. At the time of writing they do not exist – the ten kingdoms are all ruled by Agrippa. But the writer has just told us that Agrippa will on the Day of the Lord go to perdition – that is, he will be killed by the Messiah. In the war that then ensues, the future rulers of these ten territories will side with Rome as Agrippa had done. But the story of these ten kings does not end there:

> ... And the ten horns which thou sawest upon the Beast, these shall hate the whore, and shall make her desolate and naked, and shall eat her flesh, and burn her with fire. For God hath put in their hearts to fulfil his will, and to agree, and give their kingdom unto the Beast, until the words of God shall be fulfilled.[44]

The whore referred to here is the Great Harlot and the subject of our next topic.

APOCALYPTIC TOPIC NO. 18: THE GREAT HARLOT

Preterism: Rome or Jerusalem.
Historicism: Roman Catholic Church.
Futurism: A future figure like the Antichrist.

The third Beast, unlike the others, has a rider and she is known as the Great Harlot or Whore and is also described in Chapter 17:

> And there came one of the seven angels which had the seven vials, and talked with me, saying unto me, Come hither; I will shew unto thee the judgement of the great whore that sitteth upon many waters: With whom the kings of the Earth have committed fornication, and the inhabitants of the Earth have been made drunk with the wine of her fornication. So he carried me away in the spirit into the wilderness: and I saw a woman sit upon a scarlet coloured Beast, full of names of

---

44 Revelation 17:16-17.

blasphemy, having seven heads and ten horns. And the woman was arrayed in purple and scarlet colour, and decked with gold and precious stones and pearls, having a golden cup in her hand full of abominations and filthiness of her fornication: And upon her forehead was a name written, Mystery, Babylon The Great, The Mother Of Harlots And Abominations Of The Earth. And I saw the woman drunken with the blood of the saints, *and with the blood of the martyrs of Jesus*: and when I saw her, I wondered with great admiration.[45]

The italicized phrase in the penultimate line is clearly a later Christian addition to what is otherwise a quintessentially Jewish text. From the way she is dressed and adorned, and from her location in the wilderness, this whore figure is clearly the Satanic antithesis of the Mother in Chapter 12. A little later we are told what she represents:

And the woman which thou sawest is that great city, which reigneth over the kings of the Earth.

So, yet another reference to Rome. Harlotry in the Bible is usually a symbol of idolatry: the idea that the Jews betray their 'marriage' to God by whoring after other false gods. All that makes sense. But I think, as with the Beasts, the reference is more specific than that. Again, why introduce a new symbolic figure unless to add new detail. If the Beast she rides is Agrippa II, does that give us a clue? It will be recalled that Agrippa had a sister, Berenice, who was ejected from Jerusalem with him at the start of the war. She was still with him when the war ended, and Agrippa went to Rome to receive plaudits and rewards from Vespasian. And if the

---

45 Revelation 17:1-6.

terms 'whore' and 'harlot' can be applied to anyone at this time, Berenice would be the front runner.

Berenice and Agrippa her brother appear in the Bible. Paul is brought before them some time after his arrest and recounts to them his life story and conversion to Christianity. Agrippa famously responds: 'Almost thou persuadest me to be a Christian'.[46] Whatever the historicity or otherwise of this, we do know a good deal about Berenice, and she was certainly a study. In the early forties AD, she married a minor local prince, the son of the Alabarch of Alexandria. On his early death in 44 AD, she was then married to her uncle, the brother of her father, and one of the eight Herodian kings, Herod of Chalcis. After *he* died in 48 AD, she lived with her brother Agrippa for several years and then married Polemon II, King of Cilicia. And here we get to the juicy part: Berenice seems to have requested this marriage to dispel rumours that she and her brother were carrying on an incestuous relationship. These rumours were renewed when she soon abandoned her third husband and returned to the court of her brother. We know that the rumours of incest were widespread; Josephus tells the story, as does Juvenal, the Roman satirist. Certainly, Agrippa never married, Berenice spent much of her life at the court of Agrippa, and accounts like that in Acts link them together in such a way that it seems they shared almost equal power. Whatever the truth of the matter, such rumours would be more than enough to reduce Berenice in the eyes of the Jewish populace to a harlot or whore. And her harlotry did not end there. When Vespasian arrived in Judæa to put down the revolt, he was accompanied by his son Titus who, although eleven years her junior, soon became her lover. Bad enough that she should have had three marriages, worse still that one of them should have

---

46 Acts 26:28. For an account of this, see Volume II.

been to her uncle – a practice acceptable to Rome, but anathema to Orthodox Jews, and unforgivable to flaunt an incestuous relationship with her brother in the holy city itself. But to take as lover the very man who, on Vespasian's departure to take up the crown, was leading the forces attacking Jerusalem, was the very last straw.

Surely Berenice is the Great Whore, drunk on the blood of the Jewish martyrs she had a hand in slaying along with her two lovers, Agrippa and Titus. She is an Idumean and like him, she is clothed in scarlet (and purple, the colour of royalty). I think it is not going too far to point out that she is depicted 'riding' the Beast who is her brother. The sexual disgust that charges this text with its emotional power is not just an abstract depiction of Rome: it is the depiction of a lascivious, traitorous and incestuous couple who betrayed their own people and sided with the enemy in wartime. And as we saw at the end of the previous topic, when the Messiah triumphs on the Day of the Lord, the ten rulers of the Semitic states that surround Judæa will turn upon the Great Harlot and tear her to shreds. Except of course, yet again, it did not happen. The Messiah did not come, Jerusalem was destroyed, and Agrippa and Berenice not only survived the war but retired to Rome where they received rewards for their loyalty to the Empire.

APOCALYPTIC TOPIC NO. 19: THE MILLENNIUM

Preterism: The period of Christ's reign, from his Ascension until his Second Coming.
Historicism: As Preterism.
Futurism: A future period following the Last Days.

The Christian (as opposed to the Jewish) concept of the Millennium really stems from just one reference in Revelation:

> And I saw an angel come down from Heaven, having the key of the bottomless pit and a great chain in his hand. And he laid hold on the dragon, that old serpent, which is the Devil, and Satan, and bound him a thousand years, And cast him into the bottomless pit, and shut him up, and set a seal upon him, that he should deceive the nations no more, till the thousand years should be fulfilled: and after that he must be loosed a little season. And I saw thrones, and they sat upon them, and judgement was given unto them: and I saw the souls of them that were beheaded for the witness of Jesus, and for the word of God, and which had not worshipped the Beast, neither his image, neither had received his mark upon their foreheads, or in their hands; and they lived and reigned with Christ a thousand years. But the rest of the dead lived not again until the thousand years were finished. This is the first resurrection. Blessed and holy is he that hath part in the first resurrection: on such the second death hath no power, but they shall be priests of God and of Christ, and shall reign with him a thousand years. And when the thousand years are expired, Satan shall be loosed out of his prison, And shall go out to deceive the nations which are in the four quarters of the Earth, Gog, and Magog, to gather them together to battle: the number of whom is as the sand of the sea.[47]

As we have seen, this topic was a crucial one for early apocalyptic belief and has re-emerged in the current era as a key bone of contention between different fundamentalist positions. The literal view is today known as **Premillennialism** (Christ returns *before* the Millennium). The Augustinian symbolic view is known as **Amillennialism** (there is no literal Millennium, just the period of Church victory). In the nineteenth century a third alternative became popular – **Postmillennialism**,

---

[47] Revelation 20:1-8

which parallels Amillennialism but asserts that there will indeed be a thousand-year Millennium, but that it begins *after* the period of the Church's ascendancy; in other words, the Church itself, empowered by the Holy Spirit and equipped with the Gospel, will over a long and unspecified period of time, inaugurate a Millennium by its own efforts, and Jesus will not return until that has taken place.

As I have stressed, all these theological controversies that surround this topic arise because an essentially Jewish concept is being forced into an uncongenial Christian framework. John B here is trying to square the circle. No other writer in the New Testament seems to understand that there is a circle to be squared, except perhaps the writer of 2 Peter:

> . . . there shall come in the last days scoffers, walking after their own lusts, And saying, Where is the promise of his coming? for since the fathers fell asleep, all things continue as they were from the beginning of the creation. . . But, beloved, be not ignorant of this one thing, that one day is with the Lord as a thousand years, and a thousand years as one day. The Lord is not slack concerning his promise, as some men count slackness; but is longsuffering to us-ward, not willing that any should perish, but that all should come to repentance. But the day of the Lord will come as a thief in the night; in the which the heavens shall pass away with a great noise, and the elements shall melt with fervent heat, the earth also and the works that are therein shall be burned up. . . Nevertheless we, according to his promise, look for new heavens and a new earth, wherein dwelleth righteousness.[48]

In many ways this parallels 2 Thessalonians where the writer, almost certainly not Paul it will be recalled, also seeks to

---

48 2 Peter 3:3-13.

reassure believers about the delay in Christ's return. There the line taken was that the delay gave more time for sin to abound; here, the line is more consonant with Christianity as we would like to understand it – that God is giving us all more time to repent. Clearly though, Christ's imminent return was the teaching of the early Apostles and the expectation of early converts. This is largely ignored by the Church today, which wants to believe either that history has a long way to run yet, or that Christ's return is imminent now. So much of the teaching of early Christianity should be viewed in the light of this expectation: the way one behaves if one thinks the world is about to end is different from the way one would conduct one's life if one expected three score years and ten. Injunctions to abandon family and exclude unbelievers (teachings which sects like the Exclusive Brethren and the Jehovah's Witnesses apply to today with disastrous consequences for so many people's lives) were never intended to be long-term rules for life. Were the Apostles alive today, they would not only be astounded that we are still waiting for the Second Coming 2,000 years on, they would think we were crazy to be still following their short-term guidance on matters such as these.

The writer of 2 Peter seems to envisage Christ's return coming 'like a thief in the night' – so, when you least expect it. But it will be accompanied by the destruction of the old Earth and the creation of a new Heaven and Earth. We are not told sufficient detail to determine exactly how Heaven and Earth will relate to each other or where humans will live, so in terms of Millennial theology he either is unaware that there is an issue, or he just fudges it. I do not believe that any of these New Testament writers or their contemporaries ever really thought these matters through. It was enough for them that Jesus was returning any day and that, as the old Jewish prophets had promised, the Day of the

Lord would introduce a new era of 'righteousness'. When this text talks about 1,000 years, it is only in the context of explaining the delay in Jesus' return: God's sense of time is different from our own. We sense postponement; He probably has not even had breakfast yet. John B knows that 2,000 years of Jewish prophecy talk about an Earthly paradise that will be re-established after the Day of the Lord. But he is also influenced to some degree by the belief that the true destiny of mankind is not Earthly at all; it is to spend eternity in Heaven. He solves the problem to his own satisfaction here by limiting the Earthly paradise to just 1,000 years, but in doing so, of course, just creates the chronological conundrums that so test the ingenuity of fundamentalists to explain.

It could be argued that the belief in eternal life enters Revelation here because John B at least, if not John A, was an early Christian. But this is not necessarily so. Although it is true that the concept of eternal life is almost totally absent from Jewish scripture, that is because the Old Testament ends half a millennium before the Christian era begins. During the Intertestamental Period, the concept of eternal life after death spent in a Heaven after a limited earthly paradise did begin to emerge and survives in the non-canonical texts that proliferated in the last century or so before Christ. In 1 Enoch, there is reference to an Earthly Messianic Kingdom before the New Creation. And in Jubilees 23:26-31, where there is a description of the Messianic Kingdom when man 'will draw nigh to one thousand years' and 'no satan or evil destroyer will be in the land'. The Jewish thought behind this seems to be the allegory of the seven days of creation: each day equates to 1,000 years; the world will last for 6,000 years and then there will be a seventh 'day' – effectively a thousand-year sabbath – after which the world will be brought to an end. In my view, John B is expressing this kind of eschatology in the above passage, still based firmly in Jewish tradition. If Christianity wants to claim him as their own, it can do so. But only at the expense of revealing the true Jewish roots of his apocalyptic ideas and the theological compromise that the Christian Millennium represents.

From a rational point of view, the whole Millennial debate is unfathomable. An Earthly paradise is one of those ideas that sounds wonderful in theory, but when you look at the detail, evaporates. Put at its crudest: if the lion lays down with the lamb, what is it going to eat? And at the human level, what would life be without goals to aim for and the satisfaction of overcoming obstacles to get there? Every enquiry into what constitutes human happiness reaches the same conclusion: happiness comes from the striving to achieve, not the achievement itself. When we attain our goals, whatever they may be, we enjoy them for a limited period before we start looking around for new ones. And if we do not find new goals, we go into a decline. That is why retirement from work is such a challenge and why early death in retirement happens so often. The Christian, of course, will answer that the goal of human existence is oneness with God. But in that case, what is the point of Earthly existence at all? In what possible sense can a puny seventy years or so of Earthly existence be a 'preparation' for eternity – whether one imagines that as aeons of years, or as timelessness. Some sects regard the Millennium itself as an extended period to prepare, but again, even 1,000 years is quite literally nothing compared to eternity. I do not get the logic. And perhaps my limited human understanding is incapable of grasping the joy of an eternity spent praising the Lord in Heaven, but nonetheless I persist in wondering just at what point I might tire of an existence spent telling God just how jolly wonderful he is. Satan certainly felt that way and Milton, when telling his story, could not help but be unconsciously on his side.[49] 'Sympathy for the Devil' isn't just a Rolling Stones song.

Meanwhile, the reference to Jesus coming like a thief in the night leads us on to our next topic: the Rapture.

APOCALYPTIC TOPIC NO. 20: THE RAPTURE

Preterism: The Second Coming.
Historicism: The Second Coming.
Futurism: One of three or four 'Comings'.

The Rapture, as it is nowadays conceived by fundamentalists, is a relatively modern phenomenon. Up until Darby invented Dispensationalism, the Rapture was regarded as a synonym for the Second Coming: biblical references to both were talking about the same, single event. Darby separated the two in order to deal with the twin problems of the Millennium and the role of Jews in the End Times. But as we have seen, this just created a set of new problems, solved in different ways by different sects, depending on the precise ordering of events in the Last Days. The Rapture becomes a critical piece of eschatology because, depending on when it occurs in relation to the Great Tribulation and the Millennium, believers will either escape the trauma altogether, or experience some or all of it with the rest of us. It will be recalled that Premillennial Dispensationalists are the smug ones who get away scot-free. I have no intention here of going through all the various positions on this again since all of it is just trying to make sense of the senseless. At the risk of repeating myself all these problems arise from one source:

---

49 William Blake said 'he was a true Poet and of the Devils' party without knowing it'.

The Dozen Christian Apocalyptic Topics

the conflation of inimical Jewish and Christian world views. Keep to a high level of abstraction, as I am certain early Christians did, and there is no problem: the Day of the Lord will usher in a new era of righteousness. Full stop. But as soon as you start to ask questions at the next level of detail, the problems start. In particular, where does man's destiny lie after the Day of the Lord – in the new Heaven or the new Earth? As soon as you try and put the opposing concepts of a New Earth and a New Heaven together, you end up with the Millennium. Then you must decide whether that comes before or after the Great Tribulation, which is also an established element of Old Testament prophecy. At which point, for very many fundamentalists, especially in the USA, the Rapture comes along as a very welcome 'get out of jail free' card.

The concept of being somehow bodily taken up to Heaven without having to go through all the unpleasantness of dying first goes all the way back to Genesis. There we are told that Enoch, an early descendent of Adam, 'walked with God: and he *was* not; for God took him'. The Intertestamental Books of Enoch relate his various visits to Heaven in the form of travels, visions and dreams, but there seems to be a tradition that at the end of it all, he did not die either but was mystically translated to Heaven. The Messiah figure from Zechariah (the original Jesus) may have been regarded in a similar way. Certainly, the Messianic child of Revelation 12 seems not to have died but to have been 'caught up unto God'. And of course, Jesus Christ of the Gospels, after his resurrection appearances, ascends to Heaven before the eyes of his disciples. It is not difficult to see therefore where the concept of the Rapture has its roots. And for that reason, we do not question it as a concept: it feels right. But of course, it isn't. It requires a primitive belief that God is a great spirit *up* in the sky, sitting among the clouds, perhaps, looking *down* on his Creation. Heaven is up there. Hell is down below. All nonsense of course – wherever Heaven and Hell are located, they are not in this universe and, therefore, like the Grand Old Duke of York, they are neither up nor down. Levitation into the Heavens to meet Jesus is a fairy tale.

Unfortunately, the Rapture as a concept comes loaded with immense emotional baggage. The idea that one second you can be holding a loved one's hand, and the next second that loved one is floating into space, leaving you behind, has all the power of a horror movie. The only explicit mention of the Rapture in the New Testament comes not in Revelation at all, but in 1 Thessalonians:

> For the Lord himself shall descend from heaven with a shout, with the voice of the archangel, and with the trump of God: and the dead in Christ shall rise first: Then we which are alive and remain shall be caught up together with them in the clouds, to meet the Lord in the air: and so shall we ever be with the Lord.[50]

But the emotional impact is best expressed in this passage from the Olivet Discourse where Jesus seems to be talking about the same thing:

> Then shall two be in the field; the one shall be taken, and the other left. Two women shall be grinding at the mill; the one shall be taken, and the other left. Watch therefore: for ye know not what hour your Lord doth come.[51]

Of course, I will be told by fundamentalists that the 'levitation model' for the Rapture is not to be taken literally, although they seem to take most else literally so why should this be any

---

[50] 1 Thessalonians 4: 16-17.
[51] Matthew 24:40-42.

different? But in that case, how are the chosen ones to be 'taken'? Are we to assume that our loved one just vanishes before our eyes? Or perhaps, just fades away? Or angels swoop down and pick up the Elect in their arms, sticking two allegorical fingers in the air to the rest of us poor losers who did not have the sense to believe, leaving us to deal with the now driverless car, pilotless plane, and motherless baby in its pram, hurtling towards the driverless truck heading out of control in her direction. However it happens, it is a devastating idea with considerable evangelical power. If it is true, no one in their right mind would want to be 'left behind'. Irrespective of the Great Tribulation to be endured, just the sense of loss would be bad enough. A recent successful HBO TV series, *The Leftovers,* explores just this. Based on a book by Tom Perrotta, it is set in a world where 140 million people, 2% of the world's population, just disappear. Unlike the *Left Behind* novels and TV series, this is apparently not the Rapture, but a seemingly random disappearance. The show explores the feelings of loss, betrayal, bereavement, anger and despair that the people left behind feel and how they cope with it. At the end of the series, we learn that perhaps in some parallel world, the 2% are living with similar feelings. It was powerful television that explored, in a purely secular way, the extraordinary emotional impact of a concept like this. One can only wonder at the continuing ability of Christianity to find new ways to saddle its audience with fearful acquiescence in what are, reviewed sanely and rationally, utter inanities.

APOCALYPTIC TOPIC NO. 21: THE GREAT APOSTASY

Preterism: The falling away of many early Christians under persecution and disappointment at the apparent delay in Christ's return.

Historicism: The teachings of the Catholic Church which deviate from the 'original' Church of Christ and His Apostles.

Futurism: The Apostasy – a rejection of religious belief – will be one of the characteristics of the future reign of the Antichrist.

This is yet another concept that appears only fleetingly in the Bible. One passage that is often taken to refer to the Great Apostasy is this:

> Now the Spirit speaketh expressly, that in the latter times some shall depart from the faith, giving heed to seducing spirits, and doctrines of devils; Speaking lies in hypocrisy; having their conscience seared with a hot iron; Forbidding to marry, and commanding to abstain from meats, which God hath created to be received with thanksgiving of them which believe and know the truth. For every creature of God is good, and nothing to be refused, if it be received with thanksgiving: For it is sanctified by the word of God and prayer.[52]

But a closer examination of the text shows that this is nothing to do with apostasy. The letter purports to be by Paul, but most scholars are agreed that it dates to the end of the first century or even the first half of the second century and it refers to a growing trend in some parts of the Church towards asceticism. That tendency has been inherent in Christianity from the start, and certainly by the second century there were sects like the Encratites who not only abstained from eating meat but anticipated later Church dogma by forbidding marriage.

---

[52] 1 Timothy 4:1-5.

The Dozen Christian Apocalyptic Topics

The core text for the concept of a Great Apostasy occurs in the passage in 2 Thessalonians in which 'Paul' seeks to explain the delay in the Second Coming:

> Let no man deceive you by any means: for that day shall not come, except there come a falling away first, and that man of sin be revealed, the son of perdition . . .[53]

Here he links the Apostasy directly with what sounds to be the Antichrist. This passage is often linked to the purported words of Jesus to his disciples in the Olivet Discourse:

> Then shall they deliver you up to be afflicted, and shall kill you: and ye shall be hated of all nations for my name's sake. And then shall many be offended, and shall betray one another, and shall hate one another. And many false prophets shall rise, and shall deceive many. And because iniquity shall abound, the love of many shall wax cold.[54]

The last sentence is taken to refer to the Great Apostasy. The sense is that there will be a falling away among the faithful and the rising of an antichrist figure before Jesus returns. In the Olivet Discourse, we are also told about the other things that must take place too: false messiahs, the preaching of the Gospel to all nations, wars, famines, pestilences, earthquakes, persecution, betrayal, the abomination of desolation, the sun and moon will darken, and the stars will fall from the sky. In the context of all this, a few Christians losing their faith – and who could blame them? – seems a minor matter.

---

53 2 Thessalonians 2:3.
54 Matthew 24: 9-12. Last sentence omitted in Mark and Luke's versions of the same Discourse.

I intend to show over the remaining topics in this book, that the Great Apostasy, as currently conceived among fundamentalists, is a completely artificial construct. There was never, and there never will be, a Great Apostasy. As I showed above, the passage from 1 Timothy was written later and deals with second-century sectarian squabbles. The passage from the Olivet Discourse does indeed refer to apostasy, but it is not some great apocalyptic event, it is just the inevitable weakening of faith in the face of persecution. The whole story of Jesus is focused around persecution, denial and rejection: of Jesus himself, and of his disciples. This passage is just one among very many in the Gospels that warn that the Christian life is one of hardship and challenge to faith. The passage from 2 Thessalonians, however, is the crux of the matter. The way we interpret that will determine the issue because, on the face of it, it does describe a major apocalyptic event. But I think there has been a mistranslation here that completely throws the interpretation. This needs to be understood in the context of the remaining topics, all of which also stem from the same source – 2 Thessalonians. I shall draw all the threads of this together when we have dealt with all the relevant topics.

But there are reasons why the Great Apostasy has become a major apocalyptic topic, and they are more to do with disputes among fundamentalists than the prominence or otherwise of the concept in scripture. If these texts refer to anything at all, it is to the reality of life for early Christians. It is evident from these and other texts that people were drifting away from the new faith, back to mainstream Judaism if they were Jews, or the paganism of their choice for Gentiles. The unfortunate fact of Christ's non re-appearance de-motivated many as we have seen. But for the rest, persecution by the Roman authorities was a daily occurrence. It is hard to maintain your faith when, on the one hand, the major promise of your faith fails you, and on the other, you could be imprisoned, tortured or lose your life, for a set of unsubstantiated beliefs. In Volume II, I dealt with a parallel issue: the concept of Judaizers: Christians who never really 'got' the Christian message and drifted back to their old ways. I showed that this is a fiction, based on the idea that the disciples were stupid and never really understood what Jesus was saying to them. In my view, there was no Jesus to say such things and the split in the early Church was not between Judaizers and Christians, but between two wings of the Jesus Movement: those that were content to await the Day of the Lord passively (wrongly interpreted as Judaizers) and those who were *gung-ho* for war (the early 'Christians'). No doubt the writers of the passages about apostasy were referring to all these people. Preterist interpretation of the Great Apostasy would run along these sorts of lines (without, of course, accepting the fictionality of their Jesus).

However, historically, the temptation to give it a different interpretation was too great. It will be recalled that the Protestant Reformers were keen to take a Historicist approach to matters like this, because that allowed them to interpret the Antichrist as any one of a series of popes or the papacy in general. Because the Great Apostasy is linked in the Bible to antichrist figures, they chose to regard the Great Apostasy as referring to the Catholic Church's doctrines. Specifically, they argued that the original Christianity, as taught by Jesus and as promulgated by the Apostles, had become perverted by the Roman Church. It had become adulterated ever since Constantine with pagan ideas, symbols and rituals, and it had invented a range of doctrines for its own convenience that had no biblical sanction and were therefore departures from true Christianity. They saw Protestant Reform as putting an end to the Great Apostasy and getting Christianity back on a righteous and biblical path. Some centuries later, some modern fundamentalist thinkers, regarding the Antichrist as a future bogeyman, also regard the Great Apostasy as a future event – one the roots of which can be discerned today in the rise of atheism and secularism generally, and the decline in traditional church attendance. Such Futurists are of course reluctant to give up the identification of the Antichrist with the Roman Catholic Church, compelling as that identification seems to the extreme Protestant mind, but the wider gains of the Futurist position – particularly in its Dispensational guise – more than make up for it.

APOCALYPTIC TOPIC NO. 22: THE MAN OF SIN

Preterism: Antichrist.
Historicism: Antichrist.
Futurism: Antichrist.

This is another character originating in 2 Thessalonians, following on immediately from the reference to the Great Apostasy – 'the man of sin' or the 'son of perdition' will be 'revealed' at that time and before the Second Coming.[55] Most commentators assume that this is another name for the Antichrist and thus, whatever interpretation they support for the latter figure, they apply to the former. I am not so sure. Almost all modern translations prefer 'the man of lawlessness' and the respected New International Version renders the 'son of perdition' as 'the man doomed to destruction'. The 'man of lawlessness' seems to me to point to something else. Lawlessness is not just sin in this context; it is the belief

---

55 2 Thessalonians 2:3.

known as Antinomianism. As described already, this takes the Pauline doctrine of Christian freedom from the Jewish Law, and taken to its logical conclusion, argues that any behaviour by the Christian is permissible, even if it transgresses common morality. The Gnostics had antinomian tendencies, so perhaps the individual here is not some future Antichrist, but someone contemporary with the early Church with Gnostic connections. There is one person in Revelation who also will 'go to perdition' or be 'doomed to destruction' – the Beast that the Great Harlot rides. We have identified him as Agrippa II, who was certainly not a Gnostic. But his lackey, the Beast from the Land, does have real Gnostic connections – Simon Magus.

I do think that there is evidence to suggest that Simon Magus really was a much more important figure in early Christianity than has until now been understood. Indeed, I would go so far as to suggest here not only that he is the man of sin/lawlessness, doomed to destruction, but that from early on in the Christian story he was the 'enemy' who not only opposed the Apostles and sucked up to the Romans, but who actually created his own rival movement to Christianity that is responsible for provoking many of the New Testament references to 'seducing spirits, and doctrines of devils'.[56] I think what we have here is a tantalizing glimpse of an early alternative Christianity. In a passage in 2 Thessalonians 2, a few verses on, we are told that 'the mystery of iniquity doth already work'.[57] We know from the story in Acts that Simon came from Samaria and was revered throughout that region. Samaria for centuries had its own alternative version of Judaism, including its own holy mountain and its own Temple to the north of Judaea. So one

---

56 1 Timothy 4:1.
57 Verse 7.

might suppose it likely that, if a new sect of Judaism emerged, then a rival to it might come out of Samaria too. Certainly there was something coming out of that region and infecting the nascent Christian communities to the north, because in the third part of Revelation, written by an unknown but Christian hand (John C), we are given plenty of evidence of it. Until now we have ignored the first few chapters of Revelation because they do not contain apocalypse, but they certainly are germane to this topic. The writer is divinely instructed to write seven letters to seven churches all in modern-day Turkey, on the main route north from Judaea into Asia Minor.[58] Let us look at them in turn:

Letter One: to the church in Ephesus. They are reprimanded for a loss of enthusiasm but are commended for hating 'the deeds of the Nicolaitans'. No one can be certain what this means, but based on the Church Father's interpretations, this seems to be a reference to antinomianism. The 'deeds' of these people are presumably behaviours – probably sexual – that offend traditional Jewish morality but are now regarded as permissible through Christian freedom from the Law.

Letter Two: to the church in Smyrna (now Izmir). This speaks of the 'blasphemy of them which say they are Jews, and are not, but are the synagogue of Satan'. The last phrase is an unfortunate translation that has been misappropriated by anti-Semites of one kind or another for years. The word 'synagogue' just means assembly (as in the Christian charismatic sect known as 'Assemblies of God'). But what it does seem to suggest is that an alternative Christian group has set up their own assembly or church in rivalry. They claim to be

---

58 To be precise, to the 'angels' of the seven churches: there seemed to be an idea that each church had its own guardian angel to protect it.

Jews but are not, so perhaps they are Samaritans: I wonder if Gentiles in Smyrna would have understood the difference.

Letter Three: to the church in Pergamos (Pergamon). This apparently is 'Satan's seat' where 'Satan dwelleth' and where there are also the 'Nicolaitans' and those who teach that it is permissible 'to eat things sacrificed unto idols and to commit fornication'. This again sounds like antinomianism.

Letter Four: to the church in Thyatira (now Akhisar). These too seem to have been seduced into 'fornication, and to eat things sacrificed unto idols', but in this case by a false 'prophetess' – 'that woman Jezebel'. This was not her real name but a reference to the Old Testament queen who persuaded King Ahab to abandon Yahweh for false idols: her name became a symbol for false prophets, harlots and worshippers of idols. But the implication here is that she sleeps around and preaches 'doctrine' from 'the depths of Satan'. God says he has given her a chance to repent which she refused.

Letter Five: to the church in Sardis (now ruins, close to the highway from Izmir to Ankara). The sins of this church are not specified.

Letter Six: to the church in Philadelphia (now Alaşehir). They seem to have been behaving themselves so God says he will make the 'synagogue of Satan' fall down at their feet.

Letter Seven: to the church in Laodicea (near modern Denizli). These are chastized for being lukewarm in their faith and worldly.

So, the last three seem to holding to the faith, but the first four have all been infected with antinomianism by some kind of alternative group of believers, one of the leaders of whom is a Jezebel figure. Simon Magus of course went around with a woman called Helen, the famous Greek 'Jezebel' who was also guilty of adultery if not harlotry. Is this a clue?

Let us look back at the core passage in Acts where we first

meet Simon.[59] There are several things here to notice. First, the story was clearly an important one: Acts is very selective in its coverage of events in the early Church, particularly if they do not involve Paul as is the case here. Second, we are not told the end of the story. It is as if we do not need to be told what happened next because readers of Acts would know. Did Simon go on to become famous? And third, Simon was looking for something more than just buying spiritual gifts; Peter says:

> Thou hast neither part nor *lot* in this matter: for thy heart is not right in the sight of God.[60] [Author's emphasis].

The Apostles were all directly appointed by Jesus except for one: Matthias, who replaced Judas Iscariot and was chosen by *lot*. Is the suggestion here that Simon wanted to become an Apostle himself? This would certainly be the implication of my interpretation above about the laying on of hands in the context of the mark of the Beast. It will be remembered that we know from sources outside the Bible, that Simon seemed to represent himself as an alternative Messiah and, indeed, as God incarnate like Jesus. Certainly, if he had the sort of reputation and stature that I am suggesting here, it makes more credible the idea that he would have had entrée into the palace circles that Josephus would suggest.

Now let us look at the way the Man of Lawlessness is described in 2 Thessalonians:

> Who opposeth and exalteth himself above all that is called God, or that is worshipped; so that he as God sitteth in the temple of God, shewing himself that he is God.[61]

---

[59] Acts 8:9–24.
[60] Acts 8:21.
[61] 2 Thess. 2:4.

The Dozen Christian Apocalyptic Topics

And:

> And then shall that Wicked be revealed, whom the Lord shall consume with the spirit of his mouth, and shall destroy with the brightness of his coming: Even him, whose coming is after the working of Satan with all power and signs and lying wonders[62]

I can think of no contemporary figure who meets these descriptions other than Simon Magus. We know that he called himself God incarnate and that he demonstrated signs and wonders of Satanic sorcery. The identification is not conclusive, but perhaps persuasive? Let us try to piece together the story as it might have happened:

> Simon was a magician/sorcerer who had built a reputation as such in Samaria. He was grounded in the Samarian form of alternative Judaism but was attracted by the early Jesus Movement, which he assumed was as phony as himself but which seemed to have real possibilities. He approached the Movement on those terms but was vigorously rebuffed. Not put off by this, he went on to develop his own version of Christianity, combining Samaritan religion with an antinomian interpretation of Pauline Christianity. On this basis, he became prominent among all the other sorcerer figures that (according to Josephus) roamed the Holy Land at this time and wormed his way into the confidence of Agrippa, Berenice and the Roman administration. Perhaps from these contacts, he picked up a good sprinkling of pagan ideas about atoms among other things, and further developed his theology to embrace the sort of paganism that would appeal to Rome. He gradually took his new religion northwards towards

---

62 2 Thess. 2:8.

Rome, evangelizing as he went and establishing alternative Churches along the way, that vied with the already existing Pauline Churches and which were viewed by them as 'synagogues of Satan'. For a time, he based himself in Pergamon ('Satan's Seat') – a major land and sea hub – from which he evangelized nearby Cyprus, where he met Paul. On arrival in Rome, he associated himself with the trendy ideas of Gnosticism, with which his doctrines had a natural fit, and put them at a more comfortable remove from Christianity, thus avoiding the persecutions of that faith that were by then underway. He is depicted in early Christian texts, both within and without the Bible, as the Enemy of Christianity, a Servant of Satan, a false Prophet and a false Messiah.

We shall now move on to examine the third apocalyptic topic that arises from this passage in 2 Thessalonians, and at last pull all the threads together in a definitive interpretation.

APOCALYPTIC TOPIC NO. 23: THE RESTRAINER.

Preterism: Nero, the Roman Empire or God.
Historicism: The Church and its Gospel.
Futurism: A future figure associated with the Antichrist.

Topics 21, 22 and this one, 23, all derive from one source in 2 Thessalonians, so it would be as well to quote the passage in its entirety, leaving in the King James verse numbers for ease of reference:

> 1. Now we beseech you, brethren, by the coming of our Lord Jesus Christ, and by our gathering together unto him,

2. That ye be not soon shaken in mind, or be troubled, neither by spirit, nor by word, nor by letter as from us, as that the day of Christ is at hand.
3. Let no man deceive you by any means: for that day shall not come, except there come a falling away first, and that man of sin be revealed, the son of perdition;
4. Who opposeth and exalteth himself above all that is called God, or that is worshipped; so that he as God sitteth in the temple of God, shewing himself that he is God.
5. Remember ye not, that, when I was yet with you, I told you these things?
6. And now ye know what withholdeth that he might be revealed in his time.
7. For the mystery of iniquity doth already work: only he who now letteth will let, until he be taken out of the way.
8. And then shall that Wicked be revealed, whom the Lord shall consume with the spirit of his mouth, and shall destroy with the brightness of his coming:
9. Even him, whose coming is after the working of Satan with all power and signs and lying wonders,
10. And with all deceivableness of unrighteousness in them that perish; because they received not the love of the truth, that they might be saved.
11. And for this cause God shall send them strong delusion, that they should believe a lie:
12. That they all might be damned who believed not the truth, but had pleasure in unrighteousness.[63]

I cannot emphasize enough how crucial this passage is to fundamentalist eschatology. The Great Apostasy, the Man of Sin, and the Restrainer all come from these twelve verses, with little or no corroborating support from elsewhere in the

---

[63] 2 Thessalonians 2:1-12.

New Testament. I suspect that if one were to ask the average fundamentalist believer where these apocalyptic concepts are to be found in the Bible, most would wrongly point to the Book of Revelation. All three topics are interwoven here and reinforce the importance of each other. I shall now offer a new, rationalist interpretation, based on careful reading of the text before us, resisting the temptation to read into the text what is not there. And the way into this mare's nest is through the topic of this section: the Restrainer.

According to verses 6 and 7, the influence of the Man of Lawlessness is being retarded, hindered or held back by someone or something that is now known as the Restrainer. This really has everyone puzzled, because there are no other relevant references to this topic in the Bible and this is all we have to go on. Preterists search in vain for a contemporary individual and failing that quest, fall back either on the Roman Empire if they are Literalists, or the Holy Spirit, or God, or the Archangel Michael if they are Idealists. Historicists tend to plump for the Gospel or the Church. But as ever, it is the Futurists who get obsessed with this one because if they can identify the Restrainer with contemporary individuals, institutions or movements, they can use this as further evidence that the Day of the Lord is just around the corner. I can think of no other topic that has fundamentalists scratching their heads quite so much as this one. There is absolutely no definitive interpretation, even within the ranks of the main interpretive schools of thought. Virtually every interpretation I have seen lists a range of possibilities, shrugs its shoulders, and plumps without any great sense of conviction for one or another of them. Surely this points to something important: perhaps there has been a fundamental misinterpretation somewhere along the line.

The first misinterpretation comes in verse 3 and stems from the translation of 'falling away' itself. I said in my comments

The Dozen Christian Apocalyptic Topics

on the Great Apostasy that, in my view, this does not refer to any such concept. The Greek here is 'apostasia', which of course looks like the English 'apostasy' and can indeed have that meaning. For anyone reading or translating this text coming from the traditional Christian paradigm, that translation comes easily, seems natural, and is consonant with the other passages we saw that speak of Christians falling away from the faith from persecution or disappointment. But the Greek has other possible meanings – notably 'rebellion' or 'revolt', and indeed, some modern translations render it thus. If this is right, then of course the whole idea of the Great Apostasy dissolves before our eyes. What rebellion could the writer be referring to? For Futurists, the issue is minor: indeed, if the future Antichrist brings some cataclysmic revolt rather than a less dramatic Great Apostasy, this only plays into their melodramatic imaginings. But for those seeking rational interpretation in history it makes all the difference in the world and interpretation is reliant on dating the text.

2 Thessalonians is one of those Epistles of Paul that has divided scholars regarding authenticity. It purports to be written by Paul to his companion Timothy, soon after the First Epistle to the Thessalonians, which all are agreed is genuine. Many scholars, ancient and modern, accept this and provide powerful arguments for the case. Others demur on two grounds: technical issues of structure, syntax, vocabulary, tone etc., which are difficult for the layman to judge; and issues to do with the eschatology itself in relation to the rest of the canon. The latter argument tends, as so often, to be circular. However, among those who dispute Pauline authorship, very many believe that it was written by someone close to Paul, and for those reasons it is usually judged to be the best candidate for elevation to the ranks of accepted Pauline texts, if one was looking to do so. In my view, whoever wrote it, we can date it to the lifetime of Paul, or very

soon after, and whether you accept my own revised chronology for events in the first century or not, this places it in the period of rising unrest and revolt, leading to the great rebellion of the Jewish War against Rome in the sixties AD. In which case, of course, the rebellion anticipated by the Greek 'apostasia' would be that very same event.

The next misinterpretation comes in verse 4 This contains two clauses, linked by a semicolon. The usual understanding of the sense here is that the Man of Lawlessness is 'already' not only claiming to be God but sitting 'in the temple' as such. This gives fundamentalist Preterists problems that they solve by interpreting this idealistically rather than literally. In my view there is no need for this: the literal interpretation is right, but the meaning is that while the Man of Lawlessness claims now to be God, it is when he 'reveals' himself in the Last Days, that he will physically enthrone himself as such in the Temple. Futurists like this interpretation because they see in this the coming Antichrist doing just that. But if this text was written before the Jewish War in anticipation of that rebellion, then they might well envisage the Man of Lawlessness desecrating the Temple in this way. And now at last we can come to the Restrainer himself, described in verses 6 and 7. There is no Restrainer. The text is saying that God will allow the Man of Lawlessness to reveal himself and seat himself in the Temple, and it will be this 'abomination of desolation' that will trigger the Day of the Lord, at which point the Man of Sin along with all the forces of Satan will be swept aside. To make the point clear, here is a paraphrase of the whole text, as it would be interpreted by fundamentalists:

> The Day of the Lord will not arrive until there is a Great Apostasy and the Antichrist is revealed. This Man opposes (or will oppose) everything God stands for and even puts (or will put) himself above God, enthroning (or will enthrone) himself

in the Temple itself. As I have already told you, this Man of Sin is active right now, but is being restrained by someone, until Jesus returns and destroys him along with all unrighteousness.

My interpretation is totally different:

The Day of the Lord will not arrive until there is a rebellion and the Man of Lawlessness is revealed to the world. This Man is already active, claiming to be God incarnate, and when he is revealed, he will desecrate the Temple, as Antiochus once did. But as I have already told you, God will allow all this to take place as the necessary Tribulation before He finally intervenes. On that great Day of the Lord, he will sweep away the Man of Lawlessness and establish His Kingdom.

Read like this, the text is consonant with Revelation and the development of Christian eschatology as we have traced it through this book. There is no need to invent a Great Apostasy or a Restrainer: they are found nowhere else in scripture and are just an artificial construct of fundamental misreading of this text. What is emphatically not a construct is the Man of Lawlessness. The text suggests that he is a magician of some sort, he is active already and he will be exposed to the world only when the Day of the Lord dawns. And that will only take place when the great rebellion starts and God is prompted to step in. In Volume II, I showed that the Jesus Movement believed that God would not act unless and until the Jews themselves took action against their oppressors. That is what the Restrainer concept is about: the delay in the Second Coming is the need for the rebellion to start. When it did start, of course, it indeed ended with the desecration of the Temple – but by the Roman General Titus, son of Vespasian, not the Man of Lawlessness. Prophecy got it wrong again.

APOCALYPTIC TOPIC NO. 24: THE ANTICHRIST

Preterism: Nero.
Historicism: Popes.
Futurism: Bogeyman.

And so, at last, we arrive at the final topic, the Antichrist – the central figure in Futurist imaginings and the papal bogeyman of Historicists. As noted already, like the Restrainer and the Man of Lawlessness, he is nowhere to be found in Revelation, contrary to common belief. Revelation has all its Beasts and its Dragon and these, like the Antichrist, are tools of Satan. But the simplistic belief that these are all one and the same – a single apocalyptic figure who will arise in the Last Days and institute a worldwide regime of evil – is just not borne out by the texts. The term *antikhristos* is found solely in the First Epistle of John and Second Epistle of John. There it is mentioned five times – once in plural form and four times in the singular – in just four passages:

> Little children, it is the last time: and as ye have heard that Antichrist shall come, even now are there many antichrists; whereby we know that it is the last time. [64]

> For many deceivers are entered into the world, who confess not that Jesus Christ is come in the flesh. This is a deceiver and an Antichrist. [65]

> Who is a liar but he that denieth that Jesus is the Christ? He is Antichrist, that denieth the Father and the Son. [66]

---

[64] 1 John 2:18.
[65] 2 John 1:7.
[66] 1 John 2:22.

> Hereby know ye the Spirit of God: Every spirit that confesseth that Jesus Christ is come in the flesh is of God: And every spirit that confesseth not that Jesus Christ is come in the flesh is not of God: and this is that spirit of Antichrist, whereof ye have heard that it should come; and even now already is it in the world. [67]

From all this we gather that, Jesus and his disciples were living in the 'last time'; Antichrists (plural) are already at work in the world; and the characteristics of an Antichrist are deception and lies, both of which are defined as denying that Jesus was the Messiah. It is quite clear from this, contrary to all Futurist belief, that there is no coming bogeyman called Antichrist, just several people active at the time of Jesus (and note, *this* was the 'last time', not some future period) who denied Jesus' divinity. What a surprise!

For this reason, people who want to argue for a single Antichrist figure like to focus on the references we have been discussing, in 2 Thessalonians, to the Man of Lawlessness. From this perspective they may have a point. There is a reference to a similar term – *pseudokhristos* – in the Gospels of Matthew and Mark, where the case is again plural and the meaning again is quite clearly 'false messiahs':

> For there shall arise false Christs, and false prophets, and shall shew great signs and wonders; insomuch that, if it were possible, they shall deceive the very elect. [68]

The reference here to 'signs and wonders' does take us back again to the world of first-century magicians and sorcerers – and, of course, to Simon Magus. From this perspective, it

---

[67] 1 John 4:2–3.
[68] Matthew 24:24.

is interesting to examine again the first reference to the Antichrist above, but this time in its full context:

> Little children, it is the last time: and as ye have heard that Antichrist shall come, even now are there many antichrists; whereby we know that it is the last time. They went out from us, but they were not of us; for if they had been of us, they would no doubt have continued with us: but they went out, that they might be made manifest that they were not all of us. But ye have an unction from the Holy One, and ye know all things. I have not written unto you because ye know not the truth, but because ye know it, and that no lie is of the truth. Who is a liar but he that denieth that Jesus is the Christ? He is Antichrist, that denieth the Father and the Son ... These things have I written unto you concerning them that seduce you. But the anointing which ye have received of him abideth in you, and ye need not that any man teach you: but as the same anointing teacheth you of all things, and is truth, and is no lie, and even as it hath taught you, ye shall abide in him.[69]

For me this is quite startling. We learn from it that:

- the many antichrists were originally part of the Christian community but left.
- they are now trying to seduce the remaining believers into their sect.
- the Christian's protection from seduction is his 'unction' or 'anointing'.

The last is clearly important: it is mentioned three times. It refers to the Jewish practice of anointing with oil. Christians

---

69 1 John 2:18-27.

The Dozen Christian Apocalyptic Topics

replaced this with another ritual – the Gift of the Holy Spirit, passed to the true believer by the laying on of hands. This is what Simon Magus wanted from Simon Peter and what he went on to offer his disciples through his own Satanic 'mark'. For me, the case is strong; each particular piece of evidence alone would not convince, but taken all together, I believe there can be little doubt that among all the conflicting sects of the first century there were a number that, in one way or another, had their roots in the Jesus Movement founded by John the Baptist. I have traced two of these: the activists of Judas the Galilean and the passivists of John, who in turn spawned the followers of Paul. I then disentangled Paul from Simon Magus so that we could view them both more clearly. Now we can at last see Simon Magus' true stature in his times – not 'the Antichrist' singular, but certainly a prominent alternative Messiah figure who, having split from the Jesus Movement, became its arch enemy and almost certainly is the key figure lying behind all the references to antichrists, pseudochrists, deceivers, liars and beasts.

AFTERWORD

I have tried to show that the apocalyptic prophesies of the Bible are fictions written after the event, and where the events they describe cannot be located in past history they are just imaginative fictions reflecting the prejudices, hopes and expectations of historical religious zealots. For present-day religious zealots who choose to opt for supernatural explanations rather than rational ones, I doubt if this or any other book will convince them to change their minds. But irrationality is irrationality, in the first or the twenty-first century. It is impervious to the sorts of rational enquiry conducted by this book. This is a cause for major concern for the rest of us, because many of them not only look forward to the fulfilment of bloodthirsty apocalypse, they seek actively to influence contemporary events to bring it about. In doing so, they of course follow in the footsteps of Judas the Galilean, the first-century religious zealot who believed that his God would not intervene to redeem the Jewish nation and the world unless believers like him took up arms against the Roman Empire and thus precipitated the End Time events. Other fundamentalist Christians today reflect the more passive views of John the Baptist, but these too are

Afterword

dangerous. For example, some[1] would argue that we need not worry about global pollution, species extinction, the depletion of the ozone layer, the choking of the oceans with microplastics or climate change – all this and more will be put right when Jesus returns and the world is made anew. The American religious right is infected with ideas like this and American politicians, in need of their votes, are thus able to avoid signing up to international environmental agreements that have unpleasant and unpopular economic consequences.

The subjects of biblical apocalypse are now more than ever part of the popular fictional imagination. Until the twentieth century, these fictions were illustrated vividly enough: in stained glass windows; in the paintings of Hieronymus Bosch; and in the vivid descriptions of woe and torment hurled at frightened congregations by Catholic and Protestant preachers alike, as they for centuries kept their flocks under control with fear, trembling and threat. But with the invention of the popular, sensational novel, and then the arrival of cinema and TV, the opportunities to use these fictions scarily to entertain as well as to terrify believers, have become legion. The Antichrist, the Beast with the number 666, the End of Days, the Rapture and the Guilty Remnant have all become the stock in trade of horror genres in cinema, books and television. I enjoy these as much as anyone, but I am always uncomfortably aware that for many – particularly Catholics and fundamentalist Protestants – the scariness does not end with the end of the fiction; the belief that these things are real and that the world could be plunged into events of this sort at any moment creates, for many, a life of living hell, and for many more becomes the justification for a sanctimonious smugness: 'You laugh at my beliefs right now, but just wait and you will be sorry then.' My hope is that this book will be of comfort for the vast numbers

---

[1] Exclusive Brethren for example.

of people who are sceptical of the supernatural but nevertheless left with an uneasy feeling that perhaps there might be some truth in it all.

Much the same could be said for the utterances of modern prophets – the fortune tellers, psychics and spiritualists who claim to connect with the dead and the future. They are not the subject of this book, but if the prophets of old, enshrined in the Bible, can be shown to be charlatan, then I think we can safely assume the same for the Derek Acorahs of our own civilization. As the Bible itself came under attack from the nineteenth century onwards, and Christianity began its corresponding long-term decline, so can be traced the rise of new 'spiritual' beliefs to replace it. Other rationalists more qualified than me have dedicated their time and energies, and even their reputations and fortunes, on exposing all this nonsense, and it is fitting that I pay tribute to them here. People like the Great Randi, whose longstanding offer to pay a million dollars to anyone that can prove the existence of either the supernatural or extrasensory powers has never been claimed. Or in Britain, the superb Derren Brown, who continually entertains audiences with feats of clairvoyance, séance and other miraculous powers and, while avoiding giving his game away, overtly states that there is absolutely nothing supernatural about what he does and is scathing about performers like Uri Geller who suggest otherwise. Unfortunately, these debunkers were not around when the likes of Isaiah, Jeremiah, Zechariah and John the Revelator were peddling their dismal prophecies of gloom, despair and destruction. But the texts they wrote betray the truth at every turn if you know how to look for it, and this is what this book sets out to do.

The belief that somehow God will call an end to time, and in the Last Days bring about His Kingdom on Earth and judge everyone that has ever lived, consigning to Heaven or

Hell as appropriate, is to my mind the most pernicious of all Christianity's absurd claims. For 2,000 years people have lived their lives under its shadow, fearing death for its consequences and, at certain times, living in panic and despair that the End of Days is imminent. But even more appalling is that some people have lived their lives in smug confidence that they are of the Elect; that they would be raised to Glory at the end of time, and consequently, they have both awaited God's intervention with pleasure, and also actively worked through history to bring about the conditions for that event. Revelation, in their view, provides the context for this. Its 'prophecies' set out the conditions for God's return. And since those conditions are bloodthirsty and vengeful, so too are their actions. As I review this text for publication in November 2022, the Russian war in Ukraine persists. Predictably, the televangelist Pat Robertson has dragged himself out of retirement, where he is living a life of luxury on his ill-gotten millions, to pronounce that this is the beginning of the End Times, that Putin is God's puppet in this, and the invasion of Israel will be next. If this book does anything at all to cut the prophetic ground from under these people, then it will have served a noble purpose.

Finally, I mentioned earlier the predictions of one 'David Meade' about the end of the world, made as I was beginning to write this book. Finishing the book now, in the late summer of 2018, I thought I would check to see how he had handled subsequent events (or rather, non-events), since. This is what I found on Wikipedia:

> Meade predicted that planet Nibiru would collide with Earth on September 23, 2017, destroying it. After his prediction failed, he revised the apocalypse to October, where he stated that the seven-year tribulation would possibly start followed by a millennium of peace. In 2018, Meade again made several

predictions for that year, for instance, North Korea becoming a superpower in March 2018 and that Nibiru would destroy the Earth in spring. Meade announced that the apocalypse would begin in March 2018, but he didn't predict the exact date. After March 2018 passed, he moved the apocalypse to April 23, 2018, in which he also predicted the Sun, Moon, Jupiter, and Virgo will signal the rapture, and that Nibiru would destroy the Earth that day. However, before that date he said that reports that he predicted the end on 23 April were 'fake news', but that the rapture – but not the end of the world – would take place on an unspecified date between May and December 2018.

So, his latest prediction is still in my future but not yours, but again I confidently predict that as you read this, the 'Rapture' will not have taken place – unless of course it was a 'secret Rapture' as some expect, in which case, who the hell knows?
David Meade is actually the pen name of an American writer for fundamentalists and he keeps his real identity secret. He makes several claims about himself and his academic credentials, none of which can be verified. How much truer must that be of all the apocalyptic writers of the Bible. We know nothing for certain about any of them – who they were, when they lived, or what experiences and motives led them to write as they did. Good scholarship can retrieve much but, at the end of the day, if you want to believe the 'David Meades' of this world, no amount of rational explanation can prove you wrong. As I also pointed out earlier, we are not in the realm of proof here but of likelihood. All I can say in conclusion is that Paul McGrane is not a pseudonym. You can check me out on my website, and you can verify my academic credentials with the institutions concerned. Those are facts. The rest is surmise. But how many times can the

Afterword

likes of 'Meade' shift their prophetic ground without at some point the whole house of cards collapsing. How many times can we read in the Bible about the imminent Day of the Lord that never comes without at least beginning to wonder whether it is not, after all, a human fiction. And wonder also whether texts that claim to be divinely inspired and therefore inerrant, but that make predictions that seem forever postponed, are not, after all, humanly inspired. Corporal Fraser amid the Blitz had every reason to believe that we were all doomed. And looking at the world around us today, we too might conclude that humanity is making a pretty bad fist of things. But doomed or not, our future is in our own hands – not in some fictional spirit in the sky who, if he exists at all, seems on all the evidence presented in this book, remarkably unwilling to show himself.

Select Bibliography

PRIMARY SOURCES

The Bible, The Authorised King James Version, www.kingjamesbibleonline. org.
Whiston, William (Trans.) *Josephus: The Complete Works* (Nashville, TN: Thomas Nelson, 1998).
The Loeb Classical Library translations into English of:
Philo.
Pliny.
Tacitus.
Cassius Dio.
Suetonius.
Paulus Orosius.
Charlesworth, James H., (ed.), *The Apocrypha and Pseudepigrapha of the Old Testament, 2 vols.* (Oxford: Oxford University Press, 1913).
Elliott, J. K., *The Apocryphal New Testament* (Oxford: Clarendon Press, 1993).
Vermes, Geza, *The Complete Dead Sea Scrolls in English* (London: Allen Lane, Penguin, 1997).
Eisenman, Robert and Wise, Michael, *The Dead Sea Scrolls Uncovered* (Shaftesbury: Element Books, 1992).
Robinson, J.M. (ed.), *The Nag Hammadi Library in English: Revised Edition* (San Francisco: Harper & Row, 1988).

SECONDARY SOURCES

Albanese, Catherine L., *A Republic of Mind and Spirit: A Cultural History of American Metaphysical Religion* (New Haven, CT: Yale University Press, 2007).
Allegro, John M., *The Dead Sea Scrolls* (London: Penguin, 1956).
Allen, Don Cameron, *The Star Crossed Renaissance: The Quarrel About Astrology and Its Influence in England* (New York: Routledge, 1967).
Aveni, Anthony, *The End of Time: The Maya Mystery of 2012* (Boulder, CO: Colorado University Press, 2009).
Baldwin, Joyce G., *Haggai, Zechariah, Malachi* (London: Tyndale, 1972).
Barkun, Michael, *A Culture of Conspiracy: Apocalyptic Visions in Contemporary America* (Berkeley, CA: University of California Press, 2003).
Barnes, Robin Bruce, *Prophecy and Gnosis: Apocalypticism in the Wake of the Lutheran Reformation* (Redwood City, CA: Stanford University Press, 1988).
Barrett, C. K., *The New Testament Background: Selected Documents* (New York: Harper & Row, 1961).
Baur, F.C., *Church History of the First Three Centuries* (London: Williams & Norgate, 1878). [Translation by Allan Menzies of the original *Kirchengeschichte* (Tübingen, 1853)].
Baylor, Michael G., (ed.), *The Radical Reformation* (Cambridge: Cambridge University Press, 2000).
Boyer, Paul S., *When Time Shall Be No More: Prophecy Belief in Modern American Culture* (Cambridge: Harvard University Press, 1992).
Brandon, S.G.F., *Religion in Ancient History* (London: George Allen & Unwin, 1969).
Boardman, J., Griffin, J., Murray, O., *The Oxford History of the Classical World* (Oxford: Oxford University Press, 1986).
Burtchaell, J. T., *From Synagogue to Church* (Cambridge: Cambridge University Press, 1992).
Cameron, Euan, *The European Reformation* (Oxford: Oxford University Press, 2012).
Capp, Bernard S., *Fifth Monarchy Men: A Study in Seventeenth Century Millenarianism* (London: Faber, 1972).
Carroll, R. P., *The Bible as a Problem for Christianity* (Philadelphia, PA: Trinity, 1991).

Select Bibliography

Charles, Robert Henry, (ed.), *The Book of Enoch* (London: SPCK, 1952).
Charlesworth, J., (ed.), *The Messiah: Developments in Earliest Judaism and Christianity* (Minneapolis, MN: Fortress Press, 1992).
Clark, Victoria, *Allies for Armageddon: The Rise of Christian Zionism* (New Haven, CT: Yale University Press, 2007).
Cohn, Norman, *Cosmos, Chaos, and the World to Come: The Ancient Roots of Apocalyptic Faith* (New Haven, CT: Yale University Press, 1993).
Cohn, Norman, *The Pursuit of the Millennium* (Oxford: Oxford University Press, 1970).
Collins, J. J., *The Apocalyptic Imagination* (New York: Crossroad, 1984).
Collins, J.J., *The Scepter and the Star* (New York: Doubleday, 1995).
Delaney, Carol, *Columbus and the Quest for Jerusalem: How Religion Drove the Voyages that Led to America* (New York: Simon and Schuster, 2011).
Dunn, J. D. G., *The Parting of the Ways Between Christianity and Judaism* (London: SCM Press, 1991).
Ehrman, B. D., *The Orthodox Corruption of Scripture* (Oxford: Oxford University Press, 1993).
Faulkner, Neil, *Apocalypse: The Great Jewish Revolt Against Rome, AD 66–73* (Stroud: Tempus, 2002).
Feldman, L. H., *Jew and Gentile in the Ancient World* (Princeton, NJ: Princeton University Press, 1993).
Finegan, J., *Handbook of Biblical Chronology* (Princeton, NJ: Princeton University Press, 1964).
Fishbane, M., Biblical *Interpretation in Ancient Israel* (Oxford: Oxford University Press, 1988).
Fitzmyer, J.A., *Essays on the Semitic Background of the New Testament* (London: Chapman, 1971).
Friedrich, Otto, *The End of the World: A History* (New York: Coward, McCann and Geoghegan, 1882).
Fuller, Robert C., *Naming the Antichrist: The History of an American Obsession* (Oxford: Oxford University Press, 1996).
Glasson, T. Francis, *Jesus and the End of the World* (Edinburgh: St. Andrew Press, 1980).
Harrison, John Fletcher Clews, *The Second Coming: Popular Millenarianism 1780–1850* (London: Routledge, 1979).
Hartman, Louis F. and Di Lella, Alexander A., *The Book of Daniel in The Anchor Bible* (New York: Doubleday, 1978).
Hill, Christopher, *A Nation of Change and Novelty: Radical Politics,*

Religion and Literature in the Seventeenth Century (London: Routledge, 1990).

Hoekama, Anthony A., *The Four Major Cults: Christian Science, Jehovah's Witnesses, Mormonism, Seventh Day Adventism* (Grand Rapids, MI: Eerdman, 1963).

Horsley, R. & Hanson, J. S., *Bandits, Prophets, and Messiahs: Popular Movements in the Time of Jesus* (Minneapolis, MN: Winston Press, 1985).

Jauhiainen, Marko, *The Use of Zechariah in Revelation* (Tübingen: Mohr Siebeck, 2005).

Kersten, Holger, *Jesus Lived in India* (Shaftesbury: Element Books, 1994).

Kidd, Thomas S., *The Great Awakening: The Roots of Evangelical Christianity in Colonial America* (New Haven, CT: Yale University Press, 2007).

Kingsley, P., *Ancient Philosophy, Mystery and Magic* (Oxford: Oxford University Press, 1995).

Kinane, Karolyn and Ryan, Michael A., (eds.), *End of Days: Essays on the Apocalypse from Antiquity to Modernity* (Jefferson, NC: McFarland, 2009).

Landes, Richard, Gow, Andrew, and Van Meter, David C., (eds.), *The Apocalyptic Year 1000: Religious Expectation and Social Change, 950–1050* (Oxford: Oxford University Press, 2003).

Leaney, A.R.C., *The Jewish and Christian World: 200 BC to 200 AD* (Cambridge: Cambridge University Press, 1984).

Massyngberde Ford, J., *Revelation* in *the Anchor Yale Bible* (New Haven, CT: Yale University Press, 1975).

McGregor, J. F., and Reay, Barry, *Radical Religion in the English Revolution* (Oxford: Oxford University Press, 1984).

Meeks, W. A., *The First Urban Christians: The Social World of the Apostle Paul* (New Haven, CT: Yale University Press, 1983).

Metzger, Bruce M., *The Canon of the New Testament* (Oxford: Oxford University Press, 1987).

Metzger, Bruce M. and Coogan, Michael D., (eds.), *The Oxford Companion to the Bible* (Oxford: Oxford University Press, 1993).

Negru, Catalin, *History of the Apocalypse*, (lulu.com: ebook, 2015).

Neusner, J., Green, W.S. and Fredrichs, E., *Judaisms and their Messiahs at the Turn of the Christian Era* (Cambridge: Cambridge University Press, 1987).

Pagels, Elaine, *The Gnostic Gospels* (London: Weidenfeld & Nicolson, 1979).

Select Bibliography

Parfitt, Tudor, *The Lost Tribes of Israel: History of a Myth* (London: Phoenix, 2003).

Pritchard, James B. (ed.), *The Times Concise Atlas of the Bible* (London: Times Books, 1991).

Reeves, Marjorie, *The Influence of Prophecy in the Later Middle Ages: A Study in Joachimism* (Oxford: Oxford University Press, 2000).

Rowland, Christopher, *The Open Heaven: A Study of Apocalyptic in Judaism and Early Christianity* (London: SPCK, 1982).

Rubinsky, Yuri, and Wiseman, Ian, *A History of the End of the World* (New York: Morrow, 1982).

Ryrie, Charles C., *Dispensationalism* (Chicago, IL: Moody, 2007).

Safrai, S. and Stern, M., *The Jewish People in the First Century*, 2 vols. (Philadelphia, PA: Van Gorcum, 1974).

Smith, Morton, *Jesus the Magician* (New York: Harper & Row, 1978).

Stone, Jon R., (ed.), *Expecting Armageddon: Essential Readings in Failed Prophecy* (London: Routledge, 2000).

Stone, Michael E., *Scriptures, Sects, and Visions: A Profile of Judaism from Ezra to the Jewish Revolts* (Philadelphia, PA: Fortress Press, 1980).

Synan, Vinson, *The Holiness-Pentecostal Tradition: Charismatic Movements in the Twentieth century* (Grand Rapids, MI: Eerdmans, 1997).

Tenney, Merrill C., *Interpreting Revelation* (Grand Rapids, MI: Eerdmans, 1988).

Upton, Charles, *Legends of the End: Prophecies of the End Times, Antichrist, Apocalypse, and Messiah from Eight Religious Traditions* (Hillsdale, NY: Sophia Perennis, 2004).

Vaganay, L. and Amphoux, CB., *An Introduction to New Testament Textual Criticism* (Cambridge: Cambridge University Press, 1991).

Webb, Robert, *John the Baptizer and Prophet: A Socio-Historical Study* (Sheffield: JSOT, 1991).

Wink, W., *John the Baptist in the Gospel Tradition* (Cambridge: Cambridge University Press, 1968).

www.ingramcontent.com/pod-product-compliance
Lightning Source LLC
Chambersburg PA
CBHW052130070526
44585CB00017B/1772